S0-AHD-267

American
Drama Criticism

Supplement IV
to the
Second Edition

COMPILED BY

LaNELLE DANIEL

The Shoe String Press, Inc.
North Haven, Connecticut
1996

First edition 1967
Supplement I published 1970
Supplement II published 1976
Second Edition published 1979
Supplement I to the Second Edition published 1984
Supplement II to the Second Edition published 1989
Supplement III to the Second Edition published 1992
Supplement IV to the Second Edition published 1996

Library of Congress Cataloging-in-Publication Data

American drama criticism:
supplement IV to the second edition
compiled by LaNelle Daniel.
p.   cm. — (Drama explication series)
Includes bibliographical references and index.
ISBN 0-208-02393-3 (alk. paper)
1. American drama — History and criticism—
Bibliography.   2. Theater — United States —
Reviews — Bibliography.   3. Dramatic criticism —
United States — Bibliography.
I. Daniel, LaNelle.   II. Series.
Z1231.D7P3   1996 Suppl. 4
PS332
016.813009 — dc 20   95-26277

The paper used in this publication meets the minimum
requirements of American National Standard for Information Sciences—
Permanence of Paper for Printed Library Materials, ANSI Z39.48-1984. ∞

For Claude and Elaine

CONTENTS

PREFACE

This Fourth Supplement to the Second Edition of *American Drama Criticism* lists references to American plays published in books, periodicals, monographs, and various audiovisual materials through 1993. Interest in early American plays as well as in Canadian drama continues. Feminist criticism is proliferating; female playwrights and performance artists continue to influence the drama genre strongly. Interest remains intense concerning plays by or about African Americans, Chinese Americans, and Hispanic Americans. Special studies deal with the exploding field of gay and lesbian drama, particularly plays involving AIDS and related issues. Other studies look at Jews, Native Americans, immigrants, and women in American drama.

The quality of the articles cited here was not considered, and inclusion does not imply recommendation. The only criterion was that a particular play was mentioned in a particular piece of writing and was not listed in a previous volume of this series. An exhaustive search cannot be claimed, but in addition to books and periodicals not listed in indexes, these indexes were examined: *UNCOVER, Expanded Academic, Magazine Index, WorldCat, Dramatic Index, Essay and General Literature Index, Humanities Index, Internationale Bibliographie der Zeitschriftenliteratur, MLA International Bibliography,* and *Reader's Guide to Periodical Literature.*

To avoid duplication and to conserve space, the full names of authors of books and the subtitles of books are provided only in the *List of Books Indexed,* and the full names of critics are provided only in the *Index of Critics.* Subtitles of journals appear in the *List of Journals Indexed.* The same system is followed in dealing with audiovisual materials.

Articles of a general nature are listed immediately below the playwright's name, followed by those on specific works. The general works include items by or about the playwright as well as articles about the playwright's work in general.

The arrangement is like that of the preceding supplements—alphabetical by playwright, with the plays alphabetized under the playwright's name. In this volume, however, the playwright's name is presented in traditional bibliographic form—last name first, followed by the first name. If known, dates of premieres, often not in New York City, have been included. Occasionally, a date of publication is used. References from books, journals, and periodicals (or other publications) are then alphabetized by author, or, if anonymous, by title. References to periodicals include volume number (issue number when available), page or pages, and date. A standard format has been followed.

One index is new to this supplement. Due to the current growth of electronic media, references to publications are now given in that format. This section will expand greatly as material (interviews, previews, critiques) is more and more frequently put out on videocassette, audiocassette, CD, or internet.

Every effort has been made to prevent and/or to correct errors and omissions. If some mistakes have escaped detection, both the compiler and the publisher will be grateful to have them pointed out.

I wish to express my thanks to the members of the staff of the Hinckley Library of Northwest College: to Dr. Jerome Halpin, Director, for his knowledgeable guidance and support as well as his friendship; to Diane Martin, Reference Librarian, for her incredible ability to find corners to look in as well as her unending good nature; and to Elfriede Milburn for her astute working of the interlibrary loan system.

LaNelle Daniel
Northwest College
Powell, Wyoming

ABBOTT, GEORGE

Grode, E. "Happy 106th, George Abbott," *TheaterWeek* 6(47):19, 28 Jun. 1993
Leiter, S. L. *From Belasco to Brook: Representative Directors of the English-Speaking Stage*

ABBOTT, GEORGE, DOUGLAS WALLOP, RICHARD ADLER, and JERRY ROSS

Damn Yankees (adapted from the novel *The Year the Yankees Lost the Pennant* by D. Wallop), 1955
    Braunagel, D. *Variety* 352(11):85, 25 Oct. 1993
    Henry, W. A., III. "Forward to the Past," *Time* 142(22):64, 22 Nov. 1993

ABDOH, REZA

"Reza Abdoh," *Mime Journal* 91/92:10, 1991
Sagal, P. "Walking Nightmares," *TheaterWeek* 4(23):24–28, 14 Jan. 1991
Stayton, R. "Hellraiser: Reza Abdoh's Shocking Plays," *American Theatre* 8(11):26–33, 1 Feb. 1992

Bogeyman, 1991
    Hornby, R. *Hudson Review* 44:634–5, Wntr. 1992
    Lochte, D. *Los Angeles Magazine* 36(10):214, Oct. 1991
    Marowitz, C. *TheaterWeek* 5(10):34–5, 14 Oct. 1991
    Roman, D. *Theatre Journal* 44(3):395–7, Oct. 1992

The Law of Remains, 1992
    Bell, J. *TheaterWeek* 5(33):15–16, 23 Mar. 1992
    Harris, J. E. "PWA's—Playwrights with AIDS," *Christopher Street* 14(20):5–7, 13 Apr. 1992

Tight Right White, 1993
    Bell, J. *TheaterWeek* 6(28):16, 15 Feb. 1993
    ———. *TheaterWeek* 6(38):14–16, 26 Apr. 1993
    Wehle, P. *American Theatre* 10(4):13, Apr. 1993

ABELL, JEFF

The Best Revenge, 1992
    Meyer, M. *Theatre Journal* 44:394–5, Oct. 1992

ABRAMS, MARILYN, and BRUCE JORDAN

Shear Madness (adaptation of the Swiss play *Scherenschnitt*), 1980
    Fanton, B. "Theatrical Madness," *Nation's Business* 81(7):12, Jul. 1993
    Lochte, D. *Los Angeles Magazine* 38(12):174, Dec. 1993

ABUBA, ERNEST

Cambodia Agonistes, 1992
    Horwitz, S. "The Killing Fields," *TheaterWeek* 6(16):22–26, 23 Nov. 1992

ACKAMOOR, IDRIS, and ED BULLINS

An American Griot, 1991
    Bell, J. *TheaterWeek* 4(29):35, 25 Feb. 1991

ACKERLY, J. R. (JOE RANDOLPH)

Clum, J. M. " 'Myself of Course': J. R. Ackerly and Self-Dramatization," *Theater*
    24(2):76, Sprg. 1993
McCourt, J. "Ackerly," *Yale Review* 79:729–44, Summ. 1990

The Prisoners of War, 1925
    Spender, S. *TLS* (4690):19, 19 Feb. 1993

ADAMS, JOHN. *SEE* GOODMAN, ALICE, and JOHN ADAMS

ADAMS, LEE, MITCH LEIGH, and THOMAS MEEHAN

Ain't Broadway Grand, 1993
    Gerard, J. *Variety* 350(12):52, 19 Apr. 1993
    Gussow, M. *New York Times* 142:B1, 19 Apr. 1993
    Kanfer, S. *New Leader* 76(6):23, 3 May 1993
    Mandelbaum, K. *TheaterWeek* 6(40):28–29, 10 May 1993
    Richards, D. *New York Times* 142:H21, 2 May 1993
    Simon, J. *New York* 26(18):82, 3 May 1993

ADAMS, LEE, CHARLES STROUSE, and MICHAEL STEWART

Bye Bye Birdie
    Adilman, S. "Triple-Play Fouls Toronto *Birdie*," *Variety* 343(11):53, 24 Jun.
        1991
    Alleman, R. *Vogue* 181(8):166, Aug. 1991
    Filichia, P. "How *Let's Go Steady* Became *Bye Bye Birdie*," *TheaterWeek*
        4(51):17–22, 29 Jul. 1991
    Gerard, J. "Weisslers Settle in *Birdie* Suit," *Variety* 347(12):47, 13 Jul. 1992
    Variety 343(6):46, 20 May 1991
    Weales, G. *Commonweal* 118(15):516, 13 Sep. 1991

ADLER, RICHARD. *SEE* ABBOTT, GEORGE, DOUGLAS WALLOP,
RICHARD ADLER, and JERRY ROSS

AHRENS, LYNN, STEPHEN FLAHERTY, and JOSEPH DOUGHERTY

Witchel, A. "They Aren't Rodgers and Hammerstein Yet," *Vogue* 180(9):428, Sep. 1990

My Favorite Year
    Anderson, P. "Movie/Musical," *TheaterWeek* 6(19):14–17, 14 Dec. 1992
    Disch, T. M. *Nation* 256(4):135, 1 Feb. 1993
    Evans, G. "All Dressed Up But . . . Party Bookers Ponder Autumn's Slim Pickings," *Variety* 348(3):61, 10 Aug. 1992
    Gerard, J. *Variety* 349(8):50, 14 Dec. 1992
    Gillen, M. A. *Billboard* 104(52):49, 26 Dec. 1992
    Harris, J. *Christopher Street* (196):7, 18 Jan. 1993
    Heilpern, J. *Vogue* 182(12):122, Dec. 1992
    Kallen, L. "A Comedy Writer Remembers Her Favorite Years," *New York Times* 142:H5, 29 Nov. 1992
    Kanfer, S. *New Leader* 76(1):21, 11 Jan. 1993
    Lahr, J. *New Yorker* 68(45):192, 28 Dec. 1992
    Mandelbaum, K. "Season Preview: The Musicals," *TheaterWeek* 5(1):12 Aug. 1991
    ———. *TheaterWeek* 6(21):25–26, 28 Dec. 1992
    Rich, F. *New York Times* 142:B1, 11 Dec. 1992
    Richards, D. *New York Times* 142:H5, 20 Dec. 1992
    Rosen, R. "The Anatomy of a Smile," *New York Times* 142:H6, 29 Nov. 1992
    Sandla, R. *TCI* 26(4):135, 1 Feb. 1993
    ———. *TCI* 27(3):30, Mar. 1993
    Simon, J. *New York* 26(1):50, 4 Jan. 1993
    Time 140(25):79, 21 Dec. 1992
    Wilson, E. *Wall Street Journal* A8, 23 Dec. 1992

Once on This Island, 1990
    Dalva, N. *Dance Magazine* 65(1):70, Jan. 1991
    Lazare, L. *Variety* 346(13):72, 13 Apr. 1992

AICHER, SARAH

Heaven, 1991
    Sanz, C. *People Weekly* 35:49, 18 Mar. 1991

AIKEN, GEORGE L.

Uncle Tom's Cabin (dramatization of novel by H. B. Stowe), 1852
    McConachie, B. A. *Melodramatic Formations*, 178, 253

AKALAITIS, JO ANNE

Brustein, R. "On Theater: Akalaitis Axed," *New Republic* 208(17):29, 26 Apr. 1993

————. "On Theater: Opinions," *New Republic* 206(19):31, 11 May 1992
Charlotte, S. *Creativity: Conversations with 28 Who Excel*
Gerard, J. "Visions of Jo Anne," *Variety* 350(8):55, 22 Mar. 1993
Haff, S. "Wovzeck's Erratic Pulse," *American Theatre* 9(10):12, Feb. 1993
Harris, J. "Mama Will Provide," *TheaterWeek* 5(17):12, 2 Dec. 1991
Hoban, P. "Going Public," *New York* 24(42):42–7, 28 Oct. 1991
Horwitz, S. "Jo Anne Akalaitis," *TheaterWeek* 4(32):17–25, 18 Mar. 1991
————. "The Post-Papp Public," *TheaterWeek* 5(37):16–22, 20 Apr. 1992
Kauffmann, S. "Akalaitis Axed," *New Republic* 208(17):29, 26 Apr. 1993
Kroll, J. "Fireworks Behind the Scene," *Newsweek* 121(13):63, 19 Mar. 1993
Meyers, D. L. *Three Women Directors of Broadway, Off-Broadway, and Regional Theatres: Susan Schulman, Jo Anne Akalaitis, and Zelda Fichandler.* M.A. Thesis; Texas Tech U, 1993
O'Quinn, J. "Change of Will," *American Theatre* 10(5–6):43, May–Jun. 1993
Pearce, M. "Don't Tell Mother," *American Theatre* 10(9):11, Sep. 1993
Rich, F. "Opening a Window at a Theatre Gone Stale," *New York Times* 42:H1, 21 Mar. 1993
Riedel, M. "Papp Chooses Successor," *TheaterWeek* 5(4):6, 2 Sep. 1991
Simon, J. "Theater: Akalaitis Dethrones Henry . . . ," *New York* 24(10):90, 11 Mar. 1991
Weber, B. "Papp Theater's Changes Are Debated," *New York Times* 142:B4, 16 Mar. 1993
————. "Shakespeare Festival Dismisses Papp's Heir," *New York Times* 142:1(N), 13 Mar. 1993

ALASA, MICHAEL

Born to Rumba!, 1992
Wontorek, P. "And the World Goes Rumba," *TheaterWeek* 5(24):27–28, 20 Jan. 1992

ALBEE, EDWARD

Albee, E. "Finding the Sun," *Antaeus* (66):15, Sprg. 1991
————. "Exclusive: The Hamlet Machine from the Unpublished Play Fragments," *American Drama* 2(2):100, Sprg. 1993
————. "On Alan Schneider and Playwriting," *American Drama* 1(2):77, Sprg. 1992
————. "You Take the Trouble," in R. McKnight and R. Tauber, eds. *An Inaugural Commemorative Keepsake: The Thurber Center Opening, December 1992*
Allen, R. C. *Horrible Prettiness: Burlesque and American Culture.* 184–91
Berkowitz, G. M. *American Drama of the Twentieth Century.* 127, 148, 177
Bigsby, C. W. E. *Modern American Drama, 1945–1990*
Blum, D. "What's It All About, Albee?" *New York* 26(45):70, 15 Nov. 1993
Ditsky, J. "Steinbeck and Albee: Affection, Admiration, and Affinity," *Steinbeck Quarterly* 26(1–2):13, Sprg. 1993
Egri, P. "Dramatic Exposition and Resolution in O'Neill, Williams, Miller, and Albee," *Neohelicon: Acta Comparationis Litterarum Universarum* 19(1):175–84, 1992

Geis, D. R. "Staging Hypereloquence: Edward Albee and the Monologic Voice," *American Drama* 2(2):1–11, Sprg. 1993

Goldman, J. "An Interview with Edward Albee," *Studies in American Drama, 1945–Present* 6(1):59–69, 1991

Goyeau, C. S. *The Decline of Edward Albee.* M.A. Thesis; San Diego State U, 1991

Gspann, V. *Edward Albee Dramai*

Gussow, M. "Edward Albee, Elder Statesman, Is in a State of Professional Reprise," *New York Times* 143:C17, 1 Dec. 1993

Harris, A. B. "All Over: Defeating the Expectations of the 'Well-Made' Play," *American Drama* 2(2):12–31, Sprg. 1993

Hilldale Art Museum Collection. *Edward Albee's Other Eye: Sculptural Objects from the Edward Albee and Edward F. Albee Foundation Collections.* (Includes essay by Albee)

Israel, L. "Step into a Theatrical Time Machine," *TheaterWeek* 4(26):22–24, 4 Feb. 1991

Jones, C. "An Unlikely Haven for New Plays," *American Theatre* 10(10):103, Oct. 1993

Klaver, E. T. "Postmodernism and Metatextual Space in the Plays of Beckett, Ionesco, Albee, and Mamet," (#DA9034598; U of California, Riverside) *DAI* 51(7):2377A, Jan. 1991

Kolin, P. C. "The Ending of Edward Albee's *A Delicate Balance* and *Agamemnon*," *Notes on Contemporary Literature* 2(3):3–5, May 1991

Konkle, L. E. "Errand into the Theatrical Wilderness: The Puritan Narrative Tradition in the Plays of Wilder, Williams, and Albee," (#DA9134329; U of Wisconsin, Madison) *DAI* 52(10):3611A, Apr. 1992

Lewis, A. "Who's Afraid of Edward Albee?" *OUT-LOOK* (14):16, Fall 1991

Luere, J. "Terror and Violence in Edward Albee: From *Who's Afraid of Virginia Woolf?* to *Marriage Play*," *South Central Review* 7(1):50, Sprg. 1990

McKnight, L. A. *Isolation: Loneliness in Three of the Plays of Edward Albee.* M.A. Thesis; U of Maryland, College Park, 1993

O'Loughlin, M. "Edward Albee Sucks," *High Performance* 14(2):11, Summ. 1991

Post, R. M. "Salvation or Damnation? Death in the Plays of Edward Albee," *American Drama* 2(2):32–49, Sprg. 1993

Schwendenwien, J. "Edward Albee, 'Accumulator,' " *Art & Auction* 13(11):112, 1 Jun. 1991

Shewey, D. "The Persistence of Edward Albee." *American Theatre* 9(1):14–21, 1 Apr. 1992

Solomon, R. H. "Crafting Script into Performance: Edward Albee in Rehearsal," *American Drama* 2(2):76–99, Sprg. 1993

Wang, Q. "Who Troubled the Waters: A Study of the Motif of Intrusion in Five Modern Dramatists: John Millington Synge, Eugene O'Neill, Edward Albee, Tennessee Williams, and Harold Pinter," (#DA9209537; Indiana U, Pennsylvania) *DAI* 52(12):4325A, Jun. 1992

Wang, Qun. "On the Dramatization of the Illusory World in Tennessee Williams, Arthur Miller, and Edward Albee's Major Plays," (#DA9101987; U of Oregon) *DAI* 51(8):2569A, Feb. 1991

Yoffe, E. "Act II," *Texas Monthly* 21(5):98, May 1993

Ziobro, L. J. "A Tour of the Zoo, Guidebook in Hand," *Journal of Evolutionary Psychology* 12(1–2):83–88, Mar. 1991

A Delicate Balance, 1966
> Bowman, C. A. "*A Delicate Balance* by Edward Albee: Commentary," *Academic Medicine* 67(6):378–79, Jun. 1992
> Smith, L. N. *A Delicate Balance by Edward Albee: A Creative Thesis in Directing*. M.A. Thesis; Miami U, 1991

Lolita, a Forbidden Oasis of Love (dramatization of novel by V. Nabokov), 1981
> Markus, T. *Theatre Journal* 44:249–51, May 1992

Marriage Play, 1987
> Hampton, W. *New York Times* 142:C19(L), 20 Oct. 1993
> Leydon, J. *Variety* 346(1):146, 20 Jan. 1992
> Marowitz, C."Letter from Miami," *TheaterWeek* 6(22):31, 4 Jan. 1993
> Richards, D. *New York Times* 141:H5, 23 Feb. 1992
> Scasserra, M. P. "Edward Albee's *Marriage Play*: The Playwright Directs His New Play in New Jersey," *TheaterWeek* 5(31):22–28, 9 Mar. 1992
> Weales, G. *Commonweal* 119(7):18–19, 10 Apr. 1992

Three Tall Women, 1992
> Luere, J. *Theatre Journal* 44:251–2, May 1992

Who's Afraid of Virginia Woolf?, 1962
> Bede, K. F. *Speech Act Research in the American Drama: Textual Subtleties in Albee*. M.A. Thesis; Central Missouri State U, 1992
> Collins, J., and R. J. Wilson, III. "Albee's *Who's Afraid of Virginia Woolf?* The Issue of Originality," *American Drama* 2(2):50–75, Sprg. 1993
> Kelly, K. E. *Theatre Journal* 42:372–3, Oct. 1990
> Sisko, N. J. "Comic Strategies in *The Tempest* and *Who's Afraid of Virginia Woolf?*" *English Language Notes* 28(4):63–7, Jun. 1991
> Solomon, R. H. "Text, Subtext, and Performance: Edward Albee on Directing *Who's Afraid of Virginia Woolf?*" *Theatre Survey* 34(2):95–110, 1 Nov. 1993
> Spector, S. "Telling the Story of Albee's *Who's Afraid of Virginia Woolf?*" *Theatre Survey* 31:177–99, Nov. 1990
> Taylor, M. *Variety* 346(1):147, 20 Jan. 1992

The Zoo Story, 1959
> Arnold, L. *The Drama of Alienation: An Interpersonal Examination of Edward Albee's The Zoo Story and Sam Shepard's Buried Child*. M.A. Thesis; U of North Dakota, 1991
> Harvey, S. "O'Neill's *Hughie* and Albee's *Zoo Story*: Two Tributes to the Teller and His Tale," *Journal of American Drama and Theatre* 3(2):14–26, 1992

ALLEN, BROOKE

Lustiger, J. C.. "From Despair to Hope. Translated by Brooke Allen," *Common Knowledge* 1(2):110, Fall 1992

SEE ALSO ALLEN, JAY PRESSON, and BROOKE ALLEN

ALLEN, JAY PRESSON

Tru (about Truman Capote), 1989
  Lochte, D. *Los Angeles Magazine* 36(3):134, Mar. 1991

ALLEN, JAY PRESSON, and BROOKE ALLEN

The Big Love (based on a book by F. Aadland and T. Thomey), 1988
  Kanfer, S. *New Leader* 74(4):22, 11 Mar. 1991
  Kaplan, J. *Vanity Fair* 54:84, Mar. 1991
  Kramer, M. *New Yorker* 67:83–4, 18 Mar. 1991
  Simon, J. *New York* 24(11):76–7, 18 Mar. 1991
  Sneerwell, R. *TheaterWeek* 4(32):37, 18 Mar. 1991
  Variety 342(8):60, 4 Mar. 1991

ALLEN, PETER

Goodman, M. S. "Obituary," *People Weekly* 38:49–51, 6 Jul. 1992
Kellogg, M. A. "Caught Between the Moon and New York City," *Gentlemen's Quarterly* 61:75, Apr. 1991
"Tribute," *People Weekly* 38(1):49, 6 Jul. 1992

ALLEN, RALPH, JIMMY McHUGH, and MICHAEL VALENTI

Sugar Babies II, 1991
  Mandelbaum, K. "Season Preview: The Musicals," *TheaterWeek* 5(1):18, 12 Aug. 1991

ALVAREZ, LYNNE

Alvarez, L. "On Sundays," *Antaeus* (66):44–52, Sprg. 1991

ANDERSON, JANE

Watt, I., and J. Alverson. "Notes on Jane Anderson: 1955–1990," *Conradiana* 23(1):59–88, 1991
———. "An Additional Jane Anderson Item," *Conradiana* 24(3):232, Fall 1992

The Baby Dance, 1989
  Anderson, J. *The Baby Dance: A Drama in Two Acts*
  Flatow, S. *Playbill* 10(2):56, 30 Nov. 1991
  Gerard, J. *Variety* 345(2):78, 21 Oct. 1991
  Greene, A. "Linda's Choice," *TheaterWeek* 5(12):22–27, 28 Oct. 1991
  Gussow, M. *New York Times* 140: B3, 1 Apr. 1991
  Holbrook, C. *TheaterWeek* 5(16):39, 25 Nov. 1991

Morrison, M. K. *Theatre Journal* 43(1):121–2, Mar. 1991
Oliver, E. *New Yorker* 67(36):85, 28 Oct. 1991
Simon, J. *New York* 24(43):121, 4 Nov. 1991

Food and Shelter, 1991
Anderson, J. *Food and Shelter: A Drama in Two Acts*
Gussow, M. *New York Times* 140:26, 2 Jun. 1991
Simon, J. *New York* 24(23):58, 10 Jun. 1993
Ungaro, J. *TheaterWeek* 4(47):41, 1 Jul. 1991
Variety 343(8):58, 3 Jun. 1991

Lynette at 3 AM, 1992
Osborn, M. E. "Letter from Louisville," *TheaterWeek* 5(38):32, 27 Apr. 1992

The Pink Studio, 1990
Erstein, H. *Insight* 6(18):54, 30 Apr. 1990

ANDERSON, LAURIE

Auslander, P. "Intellectual Property Meets the Cyborg: Performance and the Cultural Politics of Technology," *Performing Arts Journal* 14:30–42, Jan. 1992
Brustein, R. "Laurie Anderson," *New Republic* 206(15):28, 13 Apr. 1992
———. "What Do Women Playwrights Want?" *New Republic* 206:28, 13 Apr. 1992
Carr, C. "Media Kids: On Replicants," *Artforum* 29:19–21, Mar. 1991
Dery, M. "Signposts on the Road to Nowhere: Laurie Anderson's Crisis of Meaning," *South Atlantic Quarterly* 90(94):785–801, Fall 1991
Gordon, M. "Performance Artist/Art Performer: Laurie Anderson," 195–204 in B. King, ed. *Contemporary American Theatre*
Howell, J. *Laurie Anderson*
Phillips, L. "Laurie Anderson Politicizing Her Voices," *Iris* 26:20, Fall 1991

ANDERSON, MAXWELL

Adam, J. *Versions of Heroism in Modern American Drama: Redefinitions by Miller, Williams, O'Neill and Anderson*
Adler, T. P. "The Messianic Figure in American Political Drama: Anderson and After," 41–57 in N. J. D. Hazelton and K. Krauss, eds. *Maxwell Anderson and the New York Stage*
Bloch, B. "American Drama Comes of Age in the New York Stage: 1924–25," 9–25 in N. J. D. Hazelton and K. Krauss, eds. *Maxwell Anderson and the New York Stage*
Buchanan, R. J. "Maxwell Anderson's Rules of Playwriting and Their Use in His Plays," 59–79 in N. J. D. Hazelton and K. Krauss, eds. *Maxwell Anderson and the New York Stage*
Cantor, H. "Anderson and Odets and the Group Theater," 27–39 in N. J. D. Hazelton and K. Krauss, eds. *Maxwell Anderson and the New York Stage*
Engle, R. "The Critical Reception of Maxwell Anderson's Plays in Foreign Lan-

guage Translations on the European Stage," 113–148 in N. J. D. Hazelton and K. Krauss, eds. *Maxwell Anderson and the New York Stage*

Friedman, A. B. "Interview with Georg Schaefer, Chair of the Department of Theater, Film, and Television, UCLA," 149–56 in N. J. D. Hazelton, and K. Krauss, eds. *Maxwell Anderson and the New York Stage*

Jones, J. B. "Maxwell Anderson, Lyricist," 97–111 in N. J. D. Hazelton and K. Krauss, eds. *Maxwell Anderson and the New York Stage*

Klink, W. R. "Maxwell Anderson in the 1980's: An Annotated Bibliography," 157–70 in N. J. D. Hazelton and K. Krauss, eds. *Maxwell Anderson and the New York Stage*

Luckett, P. D. "Maxwell Anderson's Skepticism and the Making of His Plays," 81–95 in N. J. D. Hazelton and K. Krauss, eds. *Maxwell Anderson and the New York Stage*

Miller, J. Y., and W. L. Frazer. *American Drama Between the Wars: A Critical History*, 122–33

Oliver, J. M. "From Image to Identity: The Search for Authenticity in the Early Modernist Drama of Maxwell Anderson, John Millington Synge, Federico Garcia Lorca, and D. H. Lawrence," (#DA9200079; Louisiana State U) *DAI* 52(7):2548A 1992

"Springtime for Hitler: New York Public Library Surveys the Artistic Outcry against Facism," *American Theatre* 10(4):35, Apr. 1993

Both Your Houses, 1933
Scharine, R. G. *From Class to Caste in American Drama.* 4–9

ANDERSSON, BENNY. *SEE* NELSON, RICHARD, TIM RICE, BENNY ANDERSSON, and BJÖRN ULVAEUS

AOKI, BRENDA WONG

Obake! Tales of Spirits Past and Present
Moy, J. S. *Theatre Journal* 45(3):378–79, Oct. 1993

APRILL, ARNOLD. *SEE* HOLLANDER, NICOLE, ARNOLD APRILL, TOM MULA, STEVE RASHID, and CHERI COONS

ARCADE, PENNY

Sandla, R. "Not Dead Yet," *Dance Magazine* 65(3):70–71, Mar. 1991

Bitch! Dyke! Faghag! Whore!, 1992
Bell, J. *TheaterWeek* 6(31):25–30, 8 Mar. 1993

The Penny Arcade Sex and Censorship Show, 1992
Holden, S. *New York Times* 141:C13(L), 28 Jul. 1992

ARCHIBALD, WILLIAM

The Innocents (dramatization of *The Turn of the Screw* by H. James), 1950
Armstrong, I. *TLS* (4631):16, 3 Jan. 1992

ARRICK, LARRY. *SEE* ROMAN, FREDDY, and LARRY ARRICK

ASCH, SHOLOM

God of Vengeance, 1923
Backalenick, I. "Manhattan Transfer: Ran Avni Moves Jewish Rep Uptown and Directs the Controversial *God of Vengeance*," *TheaterWeek* 6(14):28–29, 2 Nov. 1992
Bruckner, D. J. R. *New York Times/NYTIA* 142:C22(L), 4 Nov. 1992
Chansky, D. *TheaterWeek* 6(27):30, 8 Feb. 1993
Evans, G. *Variety* 349(3):70–71, 9 Nov. 1992
Schiff, E. "A Play with a History, Both Dramatic and Legal," *New York Times* 142:H6(N), 18 Oct. 1992
Simon, J. *New York* 25(45):98, 16 Nov. 1992

AUSTIN, GAYLE

Austin, G. "Creating a Feminist Theatre Environment: The Feminist Theory Play," *Studies in the Literary Imagination* 24(2):49–56, 1991

AUSTIN, MARK

The White Rose, 1988
Gerard, J. *Variety* 345(4):66, 4 Nov. 1991
Simon, J. *New York* 24(44):120, 11 Nov. 1991

BABB, ROGER

Green Eyes Are Fine, 1991
Bell, J. *TheaterWeek* 4(30):39–40, 4 Mar. 1991

Simpatico, 1993
Bell, J. *TheaterWeek* 6(28):14, 15 Feb. 1993

BABILLA, ASSURBANIPAL

Dialectica Diabolico or A Dog Spelled Backward, 1992
Bell, J. *TheaterWeek* 5(27):12, 10 Feb. 1992

Slam, Bang, & Poof, 1992
Bell, J. *TheaterWeek* 6(14):14, 9 Nov. 1992

BAITZ, JON ROBIN

Anderson, P. "The Substance of Jon Robin Baitz," *TheaterWeek* 5(38):20–24, 27 Apr. 1992
Baitz, J. R. "Coq au Vin," *TheaterWeek* 5(26):30–31, 3 Feb. 1992

"A Conversation with Jon Robin Baitz," *American Theatre* 10(3):66, Mar. 1993
Grimes, W. "Playwright-Moralist for the Modern Day," *New York Times* 141:B1, 7 May 1992
"Hot Playwright: Jon Robin Baitz," *Rolling Stone* (630):91, 14 May 1992
"NEA Grant Winner Donates Award," *Facts on File* 52(2690):429, 11 Jun. 1992
"A Playwright Decides the Shows Must Go On," *New York Times* 141:E2, 7 Jun. 1992
Witchel, A. "Arts Grant Winner Donates to Losers," *New York Times* 141:B1, 2 Jun. 1992

The End of the Day, 1992
   Kramer, M. *New Yorker* 68(9):79, 20 Apr. 1992
   Rich, F. *New York Times* 141:B1(N), 8 Apr. 1992
   Simon, J. *New York* 25(16):101–02, 20 Apr. 1992
   Stevens, A. "In Search of an Authentic Hero," *New York Times* 141:H6, 5 Apr. 1992
   Stuart, O. "No Ordinary Tormented Playwright," *Advocate* (601):77, 21 Apr. 1992

The Substance of Fire, 1991 (written 1989–90)
   Brustein, R. *New Republic* 204(23):27–9, 10 Jun. 1991
   Disch, T. M. *Nation* 254(15):534–535, 20 Apr. 1992
   Marowitz, C. *TheaterWeek* 6(36):32, 12 Apr. 1993
   Oliver, E. *New Yorker* 67:75, 1 Apr. 1991
   Raymond, G. *TheaterWeek* 4(43):36, 3 Jun. 1991
   Resnikova, E. *National Review* 43:55, 12 Aug. 1991
   Simon, J. *New York* 24(13):65–6, 1 Apr. 1991
   Torrens, J. S. *America* 164:576, 25 May 1991
   Ungaro, J. *TheaterWeek* 4(36):38, 15 Apr. 1991

Three Hotels, 1993
   Baitz, J. R. "Three Hotels," *American Theatre* 10(9):33–42, Sep. 1993
   Greene, A. *TheaterWeek* 6(38):27, 26 Apr. 1993
   Hornby, R. *Hudson Review* 46:535–6, Autm. 1993

BAKER, EDWARD ALLAN

Dolores, 1992
   Moran, T. *TheaterWeek* 6(17):33, 30 Nov. 1992

BALDERSTON, JOHN

Homan, R. L. "Freud's 'Seduction Theory' on Stage: Deane's and Balderston's *Dracula*," *Literature and Psychology* 38(1/2):57–70, 1992

BALDWIN, JAMES

Blues for Mr. Charlie, 1964
   Campbell, J. *TLS* (4674):17, 30 Oct. 1992

BALL, ALAN

Five Women Wearing the Same Dress, 1993
    Gerard, J. *Variety* 350(3):90, 15 Feb. 1993
    Greene, A. *TheaterWeek* 6(29):23, 22 Feb. 1993
    Gussow, M. *New York Times* 142:C22(L), 18 Feb. 1993
    Simon, J. *New York* 26(9):116, 1 Mar. 1993

BARAKA, IMAMU AMIRI

Angelou, M., moderator. *Amiri Baraka*. Videocassette.
Bernotas, B. *Amiri Baraka*
Lee, M. A. *Schematic Fusion: An Essay on the Aesthetics of Leroi Jones (Imamu Amiri Baraka): A Marxist Approach.* Diss.; U of Wisconsin, Madison, 1993
MacAdams, L., interviewer. *Amiri Baraka*. Videocassette.
Olaniyan, T. "The Poetics and Politics of 'Othering': Contemporary African, African-American, and Caribbean Drama and the Invention of Cultural Identities," (#DA9203968; Cornell U) *DAI* 52(8):2922A, Feb. 1992
Rowden, T. J. *Bodies in Collision: African-American Fiction and the Sexual Politics of Narrative.* Diss.; Cornell U, 1992
Russell, D. A. *An Analysis of the Black Revolutionary Plays of Amiri Baraka and the Black Consciousness Plays of Ed Bullins.* M.A. Thesis; U of Oregon, 1993
Shapiro, L., producer. *Literatti*. Videocassette.
Simmons, R. "Some Thoughts on the Challenges Facing Black Gay Intellectuals," 211–28 in E. Hemphill, ed. *Brother to Brother: New Writings by Black Gay Men*

Dutchman, 1964
    McKelly, J. C. "Hymns of Sedition: Portraits of the Artist in Contemporary African-American Drama," *Arizona Quarterly* 48(1):87–107, Sprg. 1992

The Slave, 1964
    McKelly, J. C. "Hymns of Sedition: Portraits of the Artist in Contemporary African-American Drama," *Arizona Quarterly* 48(1):87–107, Sprg. 1992

BARNES, DJUNA

Altman, M. "The Antiphon: 'No Audience at All'?" 271–84 in M. L. Broe, ed. *Silence and Power: A Reevaluation of Djuna Barnes*
Dalton, A. B. " 'This Is Obscene': Female Voyeurism, Sexual Abuse, and Maternal Power in *The Dove*," *Review of Contemporary Fiction* 13:117–39, Fall 1993
Larabee, A. "The Early Attic Stage of Djuna Barnes," 37–44 in M. L. Broe, ed. *Silence and Power: A Reevaluation of Djuna Barnes*
Retallack, J. "One Acts: Early Plays of Djuna Barnes," 46–52 in M. L. Broe, ed. *Silence and Power: A Reevaluation of Djuna Barnes*
Stevens, J. "Djuna Barnes: An Updated Bibliography," *Review of Contemporary Fiction* 13(3):201–04, Fall 1993

BARRY, LYNDA

Barry, L. "Guardian Neighbor," *Newsweek* 117:70–3, Summ. 1991
———. "My First Job . . . ," *Glamour* 89:116, Oct. 1991
———. "Picturing Happiness," *Life* 14:87, Sept. 1991
———. "War," *Mother Jones* 16:92, Mar/Apr. 1991
Simpson, J. C. "The Good Times of Lynda Barry," *TheaterWeek* 5(2):16–19, 19 Aug. 1991

The Good Times Are Killing Me (dramatization of her novel), 1989
    Gates, D. *Newsweek* 118:54, 19 Aug. 1991
    Oliver, E. *New Yorker* 67:81, 6 May 1991
    Resnikova, E. *National Review* 43:54–5, 12 Aug. 1991
    Simon, J. *New York* 24:84, 29 Apr. 1991
    Simonson, R. *TheaterWeek* 4(39):30, 6 May 1991
    Torrens, J. S. *America* 165(14):344, 9 Nov. 1991

BARTEL, PAUL

Eating Raoul (adaptation of the film), 1992
    Provenzano, J. "Chewing Scenery," *Advocate* (603):73, 19 May 1992
    Simon, J. *New York* 25(22):61, 1 Jun. 1992
    Wontorek, P. "Raoul's Return: Paul Bartel Turns His Kinky Movie into a Musical," *TheaterWeek* 5(42):31–34, 25 May 1992

BASTION, JON

Noah Johnson Had a Whore, 1991
    Marowitz, C. *TheaterWeek* 5(27):37, 24 Feb. 1992

BATEMAN, MRS. SIDNEY

The Golden Calf, 1857
    Woods, L. "*The Golden Calf*: Noted American Vaudeville, 1904–1916," *Journal of American Culture* 15(3):61, Fall 1992

Self, 1856–57
    Wolter, J. C. *The Dawning of American Drama: American Dramatic Criticism 1746–1915.* 255

BEANE, DOUGLAS CARTER

Advice from a Caterpillar, 1991
    Kramer, M. *New Yorker* 67:77, 15 Apr. 1991
    Variety 342(13):74, 8 Apr. 1991

BEHRMAN, S. N.

Gross, R. F. *S. N. Behrman: A Research and Production Sourcebook*

End of Summer, 1936
> Fordyce, W. "S. N. Behrman's *End of Summer* in the Context of Moliére's *Tartuffe*," *American Drama* 2(1):2–25, Fall 1992

First Is Supper
> Evans, G. *Variety* 346(10):113, 23 Mar. 1992
> Filichia, P. *TheaterWeek* 5(34):11, 30 Mar. 1992

Jacobowsky and the Colonel (adaptation of play by F. Werfel), 1944
> Isser, E. "The Antecedents of American Holocaust Drama and the Transformation of Werfel's *Jacobowsky and the Colonel*," *Modern Drama* 34(4):513–21, Dec. 1991

BELASCO, DAVID

Atlas, A. W. "Belasco and Puccini: Old Dog Tay and the Zuni Indians," *Musical Quarterly* 75:362–98, Fall 1991

The Girl of the Golden West, 1905
> "Reversal of Fortune," *Opera News* 57(12):18, 27 Feb. 1993
> Russo, J. P. "Puccini, the Immigrants, and the Golden West," *Opera Quarterly* 7:4–27, Autm. 1990
> Wattenberg, R. " 'Local Colour' Plus 'Frontier Myth': The Belasco Formula in *The Girl of the Golden West*," *Essays in Theatre* 11(1):85, 1 Nov. 1992

BELL, NEAL

Golden Streets of San Francisco (adaptation of Frank Norris's novel *McTeague*)
> Metzker, J. *American Theatre* 8(11):11, Feb. 1992

On the Bum, Or the Next Train Through, 1992
> Harris, W. "Life May Not Stink, Says a Playwright, But It Sure Is Hard," *New York Times* 142:H5, 15 Nov. 1992
> Simon, J. *New York* 25(47):125, 30 Nov. 1992

BENNERT, ALAN. *SEE* MENKEN, ALAN, ALAN BENNERT, and DAVID SPENCER

BENNETT, MARK. *SEE* QUINTON, EVERETT, and MARK BENNETT

BENTLEY, ERIC

Bentley, E. "A Preface to Modern Drama," *TheaterWeek* 5(41):29, 18 May 1992
DiGaetani, J. L. "The Thinker as Playwright: An Interview with Eric Bentley," *Drama Review* 35:85–92, Fall 1991

Morgan, R. "Eric Bentley: Playwright," *TheaterWeek* 5(41):27–28, 18 May 1992
  "The Voice of America and the Voice of Eric Bentley," 293–305 in R. Kostelanetz, ed. *American Writing Today*
Wilson, E., interviewer. *Eric Bentley*. Videocassette.
———, producer. *Spotlight IV, 407 & 408*. Videocassette.

The First Lulu (a translation of Frank Wedekind's original 1890 play), 1993
  Bentley, E. "The Original Lulu," *TheaterWeek* 7(5):31–33, 6 Sep. 1993
  Hampton, W. *New York Times* 142:B4(N), 3 Sep. 1993

BERKOFF, STEVEN

Acapulco, 1987
  Lochte, D. *Los Angeles Magazine* 35(10):237, Oct. 1990
  Williams, H. *TLS* (4666):18, 4 Sep. 1992

Kvetch, 1987
  Korn, E. *TLS* (4620):17, 18 Oct. 1991

One Man
  Tanitch, R. *TLS* (4730):20, 26 Nov. 1993

Salome (adapted from the story by O. Wilde), 1992
  Evans, G. *Variety* 347(11):69–70, 29 Jun. 1992
  Henry, W. A., III. *Time* 140(1):70, 6 Jul. 1992
  Kramer, M. *New Yorker* 68(20):57, 6 Jul. 1992

The Trial, 1988
  Campbell, J. *TLS* (4589):16, 15 Mar. 1991
  Reynolds, O. *TLS* (4702):20, 14 May 1993

BERNARD, KENNETH

Templeton, J. "An Interview with Kenneth Bernard," *Studies in American
  Drama, 1945–Present* 7(1):253–64, 1992

Or, and Therefore, 1992
  Lamont, R. C. *TheaterWeek* 6(21):30, 28 Dec. 1992

BERNHARD, THOMAS

Honegger, G. "Thomas Bernard," *Partisan Review* 58:493–505, Summ. 1991

The Showman, 1993
  Josipovici, G. *TLS* (4704):21, 28 May 1993
  Wolf, M. *Variety* 351(9):57–58, 12 Jul. 1993

BIRD, ROBERT MONTGOMERY

McConachie, B. A. *Melodramatic Formations.* 77, 85, 91, 99, 105. 108, 117, 124, 210

BIRKENHEAD, SUSAN. *SEE* SWEET, JEFFREY, SUSAN BIRKENHEAD, and HOWARD MARREN

BISHOP, CONRAD

Zinman, T. S. "Uncommonly Compact," *American Theatre* 9(7):13, Nov. 1992

BISHOP, CONRAD, and ELIZABETH FULLER

Rash Acts, 1991
　　Chansky, D. *TheaterWeek* 5(23):37, 13 Jan. 1992

BISHOP, THOM. *SEE* ROSEN, LOUIS, and THOM BISHOP

BITTERMAN, SHEM

Peephole, 1992
　　Chase, A. "Reflections: A New Play Series at Geva," *TheaterWeek* 5(51):21–23, 27 Jul. 1992

BLEASDALE, ALAN

Saynor, J. "Clogging Corruption," *Sight Sound* (1):24–5, Jul. 1991

On the Ledge
　　Kemp, P. *TLS* (4701):8, 7 May 1993

BLECHER, HILARY

Frida, 1992
　　Chansky, D. *TheaterWeek* 6(17):32, 30 Nov. 1992
　　Rockwell, J. *New York Times* 140:10(B), 13 Apr. 1991

BLESSING, LEE

Rice, J. G. "An Interview with Lee Blessing," *American Drama* 2(1):84–100, Fall 1992

Down the Road, 1989
　　Evans, G. *Variety* 351(8):27–28, 28 Jun. 1993
　　Greene, A. *TheaterWeek* 6(47):39–40, 28 Jun. 1993

Grode, E. "A Penchant for the Trenchant," *TheaterWeek* 6(47):20–22, 28 Jun. 1993
Gussow, M. *New York Times* 142:12(N), 19 Jun. 1993
Liston, W. T. *Theatre Journal* 43(4):526–27, Dec. 1991
Simon, J. *New York* 26(25):71–72, 21 Jun. 1993

Fortinbras, 1991
Henry, W. A. *Time* 138:66, 15 Jul. 1991
Tuck-Rozett, M. *"Fortinbras*, by Lee Blessing, Signature Theatre Company," *Shakespeare Bulletin* 11(4):21, Fall 1993
———. *"Fortinbras* by Lee Blessing," *Shakespeare Bulletin* 11(3):18, Summ. 1993

Patient A (based on the life of Kimberly Bergalis), 1993
Henry, W. A., III. *Time* 141(20):65, 17 May 1993
Gussow, M. *New York Times* 142:B5(N), 29 Apr. 1993

BLITZSTEIN, MARK. *SEE* STEIN, JOSEPH, and MARK BLITZSTEIN

BOCK, JERRY

Corman, A. "Curtain Call for the 'Ice Cream' Team," *New York Times* 143(H5), 3 Oct. 1993

SEE ALSO MASTEROFF, JOE, SHELDON HARNICK, and JERRY BOCK

SEE ALSO STEIN, JOSEPH, JERRY BOCK, and SHELDON HARNICK

BOGART, ANNE

Lampe, E. "Collaboration and Cultural Clashing: Anne Bogart and Tadashi Suzuki's Saratoga International Theater," *TDR* 37:147–56, Sprg. 1993

BOGOSIAN, ERIC

Clements, M. "Eric Bogosian As the Man Who Won't Shut Up," *Esquire* 116(3):184, Sep. 1991
Holden, S. "Two Solo Performace Artists Confront the Limits of Personal Experience," *New York Times* 141:C3, 17 Jul. 1992

Sex, Drugs, Rock & Roll, 1990
Blumenthal, S. "Straight Talk: Eric Bogosian Is Master of the Monologue in *Sex, Drugs, Rock and Roll*," *Rolling Stone* (613):61, 19 Sep. 1991
McDonagh, M. "Laughter in the Dark," *Film Comment* 27(2):68, 1 Mar. 1991
Travers, P. *"Sex, Drugs, Rock and Roll*," *Rolling Stone* (612):99, 5 Sep. 1991

BOKER, GEORGE HENRY

Kitts, T. M. "The Theatrical Life of George Henry Boker," (#DA9134666; New York U) *DAI* 52(6):2143A, Dec. 1991
McConachie, B. A. *Melodramatic Formations.* 210
Wolter, J. C. *The Dawning of American Drama: American Dramatic Criticism 1746–1915.* 243–245

Francesca da Rimini, 1853
    Zappulla, E. *Italian Journal* 6(2/3):37, 1992

BOLT, JONATHAN, DOUGLAS J. COHEN, and THOMAS TOCE

Columbus, 1991
    Filichia, P. "Theater Works," *TheaterWeek* 5(13):13, 4 Nov. 1991

BOND, EDWARD

Stuart, I. "Answering to the Dead: Edward Bond's Jackets, 1989–90," *New Theatre Quarterly* 7:171–83, May 1991

In the Company of Men, 1990
    Carlson, M. *Theatre Journal* 45:240–1, May 1993

Restoration, 1982
    Weeks, S. *Theatre Journal* 45:241–2, May 1993

The Sea, 1977
    Brady, P. *TLS* (4631):16, 3 Jan. 1992
    Brustein, R. *New Republic* 206(7):28–30, 17 Feb. 1992

BOOTHE, CLARE

The Women, 1936
    Maddock, M. "Social Darwinism in the Powder Room: Clare Boothe's *The Women*," *Journal of American Drama and Theatre* 2(2):81–97, Sprg. 1990

BOTTRELL, DAVID, and JESSIE JONES

Dearly Departed, 1991
    Simon, J. *New York* 25(2):61, 13 Jan. 1992
    Ungaro, J. *TheaterWeek* 5(26):39, 3 Feb. 1992

BOUCICAULT, DION

Flynn, J. "Sites and Sights: The Iconology of the Subterranean in Late Nineteenth-Century Irish-American Drama," *MELUS* 18(1):5, Sprg. 1993
McConachie, B. A. *Melodramatic Formations.* 200, 205 +

Roach, J. R. "Mardi Gras Indians and Others: Genealogies of American Performance," *Theatre Journal* 44:461–83, Dec. 1992

Belle Lamar, 1874
   Wolter, J. C. *The Dawning of American Drama: American Dramatic Criticism 1746–1915*. 313

The Octoroon; or, Life in Louisiana, 1859
   Erdman, H. "Caught in the 'Eye of the Eternal': Justice, Race, and the Camera, from *The Octoroon* to Rodney King," *Theatre Journal* 45(3):333–48, 1 Oct. 1993
   Roach, J. R. "Slave Spectacles and Tragic Octoroons: A Cultural Genealogy of Antebellum Performance," *Theatre Survey* 33(2):167–87, 1 Nov. 1992
   Wolter, J. C. *The Dawning of American Drama: American Dramatic Criticism 1746–1915*. 269–70

Old Heads and Young Hearts, 1844
   Wolter, J. C. *The Dawning of American Drama: American Dramatic Criticism 1746–1915*. 182

BOURNE, BETTE, PEGGY SHAW, PAUL SHAW, and LOIS WEAVER

Belle Reprieve, 1991
   Bourne, B., et al. *"Belle Reprieve,"* 3–38 in T. Helbing, ed. *Gay and Lesbian Plays Today*

BOVASSO, JULIE

Rothstein, M. "Julie Bovasso, a Dramatist, 61; Active in Avant-garde Theater," *New York Times* 140:A17, 17 Sep. 1991
Tallmer, J. "A Life on the Edge: Julie Bovasso Remembered," *TheaterWeek* 5(10):30–31, 14 Oct. 1991

BOWLES, JANE AUER

In the Summer House (dramatization of her story "Two Serious Ladies"), 1953
   Bowles, P. *New York Times* 142:H5, 25 Jul. 1993
   Jaher, D. "Building the Summer House," *TheaterWeek* 7(2):23–27, 16 Aug. 1993
   Pearce, M. "Don't Tell Mother," *American Theatre* 10(9):11, Sep. 1993
   Rosen, C. *TheaterWeek* 7(3):32–35, 23 Aug. 1993
   Wyndham, F. *TLS* (4721):18, 24 Sep. 1993

BOWNE, ALAN

Forty Deuce, 1981
   Bell, J. "Forty Deuce Redux," *TheaterWeek* 6(12):16, 26 Oct. 1992

Snake in the Vein, 1992
    Holt, S. *TheaterWeek* 5(38):38, 27 Apr. 1992

BOYD, JULIANNE. *SEE* SILVER, JOAN MACKLIN, and JULIANNE BOYD

BOZZONE, BILL

Korea, 1991
    Evans, G. *Variety* 346(6):256–57, 24 Feb. 1992
    Holt, S. *TheaterWeek* 5(34):33, 30 Mar. 1992

BRASSARD, MARIE

Polygraph, 1991
    Macdougall, J. *Theatre Journal* 43:252–5, May 1991

BRENTON, HOWARD

Berlin Bertie, 1992
    Brady, P. *TLS* (4647):17, 24 Apr. 1992
    Lavender, A. *New Statesman & Society* 5(203):34, 22 May, 1992
    Pitman, J. *Variety* 347(2):88, 27 Apr. 1992

BREUER, LEE

Downey, R. "Hunkering Down with Mabou Mines," *American Theatre* 9(8):44–
    45, Dec. 1992
Gontarski, S. E. "Lee Breuer and Mabou Mines," 135–48 in B. King, ed. *Con-
    temporary American Theatre*

Lear (based on Shakespeare's tragedy *King Lear*), 1988
    Diamond, E. *Theatre Journal* 42:481–84, Dec. 1990

The Mahabharata, 1992
    Bell, J. "Ramayana and Ma Ha Bhar Ant a," *TheaterWeek* 6(16):15–16, 23
    Nov. 1992
    Nadler, P. *Theatre Journal* 45:373–5, Oct. 1993

BREUER, LEE, and BOB TELSON

Holden, S. "Lee Breuer and Bob Telson," *New York Times* 140:57, 26 May 1991

The Gospel at Colonus (based on Sophocles's play *Oedipus at Colonus*), 1983
    D'Aponte, M. G. "*The Gospel at Colonus* and Other Black Morality Plays,"
        Black American Literature Forum 25(1):101–11, Sprg. 1991
    Hill, A. D. "The Pulpit and Grease Paint: The Influence of Black Church

Ritual on Black Theatre," *Black American Literature Forum* 25(1):113–120, Sprg. 1991

BRODY, ALAN

Invention for Fathers and Sons, 1989
Evans, G. *Variety* 346(2):57, 27 Jan. 1992
Kanfer, S. *New Leader* 75(2):23, 10 Feb. 1992
Ungaro, J. *TheaterWeek* 5(27):34, 24 Feb. 1992

BROGGER, ERIK

A Normal Life (based on three autobiographical short stories by D. Schwartz), 1990
Weales, G. *Commonweal* 118(4):132, 22 Feb. 1991

BROOKS, COLETTE

Brooks, C. "The Speed of Light," *Georgia Review* 45:249–60, Summ. 1991

Democracy in America, 1991
Osborn, M. Elizabeth. "Letter from New Haven: Winterfest Features Experimental Plays by Women," *TheaterWeek* 5(32):21–23, 16 Mar. 1992
Taylor, M. *Variety* 346(6):257, 24 Feb. 1992

BROSIUS, PETER. *SEE* COOPER, DENNIS, ISHAMEL HOUSTON-JONES, and PETER BROSIUS

BROSSARD, CHANDLER

Saxon, W. "Chandler Brossard, Prolific Writer, 71, Was Self-Educated," *New York Times* 142:B11, 1 Sep. 1993

BROUGHAM, JOHN

McConachie, B. A. *Melodramatic Formations.* 241, 242, 253

BROWN, CARLYLE

The African Company Presents Richard III, 1993
Henry, W. A., III. *Time* 141(3):60, 18 Jan. 1993
Richards, D. *New York Times* 142:H5, 17 Jan. 1993
Sullivan, A. M. "Carlyle Brown and Douglas Wager: Griots of Our Time," *English Journal* 82(4):68, Apr. 1993

The Little Tommy Parker Celebrated Colored Minstrel Show, 1991
Oliver, E. *New Yorker* 67:75, 1 Apr. 1991
Variety 342(11):75, 1 Apr. 1991

BROWN, MICHAEL HENRY

Holloway, L. "Capturing the Complexities of a Working-Class Family," *New York Times* 142:H26, 4 Jul. 1993

Ascension Day, 1991
>Chansky, D. "The Ascension of the Working Theater," *TheaterWeek* 5(26):26–29, 3 Feb. 1992
>Ungaro, J. *TheaterWeek* 5(34):31, 30 Mar. 1992

Generations of the Dead in the Abyss of Coney Island Madness, 1990
>Spillane, M. *Nation* 252(3):101–2, 28 Jan. 1991

BROWN, TRISHA

Tobias, T. *Dance* 24:99–100, 8 Apr. 1991

BROWN, WILLIAM WELLS

The Escape: or, A Leap for Freedom, 1858
>"William Wells Brown," 38–95 in L. Hamalian and J. V. Hatch, eds. *The Roots of African American Drama*

BUCKSTONE, J. B.

McConachie, B. A. *Melodramatic Formations*. 241, 242

BULLINS, ED

Bullins, E. *New/Lost Plays by Ed Bullins: An Anthology*
Cohn, R. "Black on Black," in *New American Dramatists, 1960–1990*
Russell, D. A. *An Analysis of the Black Revolutionary Plays of Amiri Baraka and the Black Consciousness Plays of Ed Bullins*. M.A. Thesis; U of Oregon, 1993
St. Hill, Philip H. *Images of Afro-American Fathers Presented in Four Critically Acclaimed Plays Written by Afro-American Playwrights Since 1950*. M.A. Thesis; Florida State U, 1991

The Taking of Miss Janie, 1975
>Bullins, E. *The Taking of Miss Janie*, in W. B. Branch, ed., *Black Thunder: An Anthology of Contemporary African-American Drama*

SEE ALSO ACKAMOOR, IDRIS, and ED BULLINS

BUMBALO, VICTOR

Tell: A Play for Voices
>Bumbalo, V. *Tell*, 215–234 in T. Helbing, ed. *Gay and Lesbian Plays Today*

BURRILL, MARY

Aftermath, 1919
   "Mary Burrill," 134–151 in L. Hamalian and J. V. Hatch, eds. *The Roots of African American Drama*

BURROUGHS, WILLIAM S. *SEE* WILSON, ROBERT, TOM WAITS, and WILLIAM S. BURROUGHS

BURROWS, ABE, JO SWERLING, and FRANK LOESSER

Guys and Dolls (musical based on stories by D. Runyon), 1950
   Alexander, P. "Guys and Dollars," *New York* 25(18):36, 4 May 1992
   Asals, F. " 'Obediah,' 'Obadiah': *Guys and Dolls* and 'Parker's Back,' " *Flannery O'Connor Bulletin* 21:37–42, 1992
   "Best Theater of 1992," *Time* 141(1):67, 4 Jan. 1993
   Blum, D. "Who Is This Sky?" *New York* 25(14):68–78, 6 Apr. 1992
   Brustein, R. *New Republic* 206(23):34–35, 8 Jun. 1992
   Buckley, M. "The Guys of *Guys and Dolls*," *TheaterWeek* 5(36):23–28, 13 Apr. 1992
   Dalva, N. *Dance Magazine* 66(8):52, Aug. 1992
   ———. "William Ivey Long," *Dance Magazine* 66(9):45–47, Sep. 1992
   Davis, F. "Full of Foolish Song," *Atlantic* 271(3):108–112, Mar. 1993
   Disch, T. M. *Nation* 254(22):798–99, 8 Jun. 1992
   Evans, G. "*Guys and Dolls* Rolls Dice in Roadshow Crap Shoot," *Variety* 349(2):93, 2 Nov. 1992
   ———. " 'Guys' Crows Field, But a Few Break Away," *Variety* 347(3):297–98, 4 May 1992
   ———. "Season Waiting for Boost from Big Hits," *Variety* 348(6):69–70, 31 Aug. 1992
   ———. *Variety* 347(3):297, 4 May 1992
   Fein, E. B. "Rockin' for Runyon," *New York Times* 141:B2, 22 Apr. 1992
   Gerard, J. "B'way Directors Feel Heat at Center Stage," *Variety* 347(2):85, 27 Apr. 1992
   ———. "Dodgers from Brooklyn Play the Major Leagues," *Variety* 348(6):69–70, 31 Aug. 1992
   ———. *Variety* 347(1):50, 20 Apr. 1992
   Gordon, J. S. "Author's Choice: The 10 Greatest Musicals," *American Heritage* 44(1):62–68, Feb/Mar. 1993
   Grimes, W. "Designer's Versatility Is Displayed on Broadway," *New York Times* 141:B1, 9 Jun. 1992
   Henry, W. A., III. *Time* 139(21):64–66, 25 May 1992
   ———. *Time* 139(17):65, 27 Apr. 1992
   Hornby, R. "Musicals Revived," *Hudson Review* 45(3):452–58, Autm. 1992
   Kanfer, S. *New Leader* 75(6):20, 4 May 1992
   Kroll, J. *Newsweek* 119(17):67, 27 Apr. 1992

Kennedy, W. "The Runyonland Express Is Back in Town," *New York Times* 141:H1, 12 Apr. 1992

Murdoch, B. "Oz Legit Banks on Tried and True Tuners," *Variety* 349(6):91–92, 30 Nov. 1992

Newman, B. "Another Opening, Another Show," *Dancing Times* 83(994):980, 1 Jul. 1993

Oliver, E. *New Yorker* 68(10):84, 27 Apr. 1992

"Recycled: Broadway Musicals," *Economist* 323(7761):92, 30 May 1992

Rich, F. *New York Times* 141:B1(N), 15 Apr. 1992

————. *New York Times* 142:H5, 27 Dec. 1992

Richards, D. "A Bushel and a Peck for Adelaide," *New York Times* 141:H5, 26 Apr. 1992

Sandla, R. "Faith Prince, Denise Faye, Scott Wise, Gary Chryst, and Joann M. Hunter," *Dance Magazine* 66(9):40–43, Sep. 1992

————. "Songs of the Open Road," *Dance Magazine* 67(1):80, Jan. 1993

Sidnell, M. J. *Journal of Canadian Studies* 25(4):139–140, Wntr. 1991

Simon, J. *New York* 25(17):82, 27 Apr. 1992

Sobran, J. *National Review* 44(10):46–48, 25 May 1992

Taylor, M. "Guys and Dolls," *Variety* 348(9):94, 21 Sep. 1992

Torrens, J. S. *America* 168(5):120–21, 29 Aug. 1992

Weales, G. *Commonweal* 119(10):12–13, 22 May 1992

Weber, B. "How to Turn Audacity into Song and Dance," *New York Times* 142:13, 5 Dec. 1992

Wetzsteon, R. "The Great New York Show: *Guys and Dolls* Lights Up Broadway All Over Again," *New York* 25(18):28–36, 4 May 1992

Witchel, A. "Lorna Luft, On the Road Again," *New York Times* 142:H1, 22 Nov. 1992

————. "Yesterday a Tony, Today the Chorus: A Dancer's Tale," *New York Times* 141:B1, 13 Apr. 1992

BURROWS, ABE, JACK WEINSTOCK, WILLIE GILBERT, and FRANK LOESSER

How to Succeed in Business Without Really Trying (musical version of novel by S. Mead), 1961

Murdoch, B. *Variety* 349(12):83, 18 Jan. 1993

BUSCEMI, STEVE

Bellafante, G. "People," *Time* 140(19):91, 9 Nov. 1992

BUSCH, CHARLES

Holden, S. "The Charles Busch Revue," *New York Times* 142:13, 22 May 1993

Loud, L. "Out Loud: Charles Busch," *Advocate* (627):81, 20 Apr. 1993

Mendelsohn, D. "Charles Busch: Some Kind of Diva," *American Theatre* 10(12):44–45, Dec. 1993

Psycho Beach Party, 1987
  Loynd, R. *Variety* 352(6):32, 20 Sep. 1993

Red Scare on Sunset, 1991
  Anderson, P. "Pretty in Pink," *TheaterWeek* 4(38):22–25, 29 Apr. 1991
  Garther, R. "Two in the Busch," *New York* 24:26, 25 Mar. 1991
  Gussow, M. *New York Times* 140:C10, 24 Apr. 1991
  Kramer, M. *New Yorker* 67(24):67, 5 Aug. 1991
  Leslie, G. *TheaterWeek* 4(39):38–39, 6 May 1991
  Variety 343(3):98, 29 Apr. 1991

BUTTERFIELD, CATHERINE

Joined at the Head, 1992
  Gerard, J. *Variety* 349(4):70, 16 Nov. 1992
  Gussow, M. *New York Times* 142:C16(L), 16 Nov. 1992
  Karlin, S. "Actress/Playwright," *TheaterWeek* 6(15):42–43, 16 Nov. 1992
  Oliver, E. *New Yorker* 68(42):154–55, 7 Dec. 1992
  Simon, J. *New York* 25(47):125–26, 30 Nov. 1992

Snowing at Delphi, 1993
  Brantley, B. *New York Times* 143:C17, 20 Oct. 1993
  Collins, G. "A Playwright-Actress Puts Herself on Stage in Fact and Fiction," *New York Times* 143:H5, 10 Oct. 1993
  Gerard, J. *Variety* 352(12):35, 1 Nov. 1993
  Kirkpatrick, M. *Wall Street Journal* A14, 26 Oct. 1993

CARLOS, LAURIE

Outlaw, M. D. "New Tracks on Tobacco Road," *American Theatre* 10(10):100, Oct. 1993

CARLOS, LAURIE, and ROBBIE McCAULEY

Persimmon Peel, 1993
  Chansky, D. *TheaterWeek* 6(27):29, 8 Feb. 1993

CARLTON, BOB

Return to the Forbidden Planet (loosely based on *The Tempest* and the 1956 film *Forbidden Planet*), 1989
  Stephens, L. "Shakespeare-a-Go-Go," *TheaterWeek* 5(8):19–21, 30 Sep. 1991

CAROTHERS, A. J., RICHARD SHERMAN, and ROBERT SHERMAN

Busker Alley, 1991
  Gerard, J. "Busted 'Busker' Zings Tune," *Variety* 346(8):1–2, 9 Mar. 1992

———. ''Tune Sings Bye, Bye, 'Busker,' '' *Variety* 344(5):1–2, 12 Aug. 1991

Mandelbaum, K. ''Season Preview: The Musicals,'' *TheaterWeek* 5(1):18, 12 Aug. 1991

CARROLL, BAIKIDA. *SEE* SHANGE, NTOZAKE, EMILY MANN, and BAIKIDA CARROLL

CARTER, LONNIE

Gulliver (suggested by J. Swift's *Gulliver's Travels*), 1989
Bruckner, D. J. R. *New York Times* 143:C20, 13 Oct. 1993

CARTEY, WILFRED

Asante, M. K. ''Wilfred Cartey: In Memoriam,'' *Journal of Black Studies* 23(1):5, 1 Sep. 1992

CHAIKIN, JOSEPH

Blumenthal, E. ''The Voyage Back: Joseph Chaikin and Sam Shepard Collaborate Across the Chasm of Language Disability,'' *American Theatre* 8(3):12, 1 Jun. 1991

Gilman, R. ''Seeking the Works to Recapture a Past and Shape a Future,'' *New York Times,* 140:H5, 19 May 1991

van Itallie, J. C. ''Speaking from the Heart,'' *Performing Arts Journal* 15:110–14, May 1993

CHAIKIN, JOSEPH, and JEAN-CLAUDE VAN ITALLIE

Struck Dumb, 1991
Tallmer, J. ''*Struck Dumb*,'' *TheaterWeek* 4(34):31–33, 1 Apr. 1991
Weales, G. *Commonweal* 119(1):18–19, 17 Jan. 1992

CHAMBERS, JANE

Morgan-Bowstead, L. ''Remembrances of Jane Chambers and Beth Allen,'' *Visibilities* 4(2):12, 1 Mar. 1990

Eye of the Gull (as revised by Vita Dennis in 1991), 1971
Chambers, J. ''*Eye of the Gull*,'' 41–107 in T. Helbing, ed. *Gay and Lesbian Plays Today*

CHAMPAGNE, LENORA

Dr. Charcot's Hysteria Shows, 1990
Schneider, R. *Theatre Journal* 42:488–91, Dec. 1990

CHARLAP, MOOSE. *SEE* COMDEN, BETTY, ADOLPH GREEN, MOOSE
CHARLAP, and CAROLYN LEE

CHARNIN, MARTIN. *SEE* MEEHAN, THOMAS, MARTIN CHARNIN, and
CHARLES STROUSE

CHASNOFF, SALOME

The Gradual Making of the Autobiography of Alice B. Toklas
    King, T. A. *Theatre Journal* 43:391–2, Oct. 1991

CHÁVEZ, DENISE

Castillo, D. A. "The Daily Shape of Horses: Denise Chávez and Maxine Hong
    Kingston," *Dispositio* 16(41):29, 1991

CHAYEFSKY, PADDY

"Network Radio: What Does Paddy Chayefsky Have to Do with Consumer Be-
    havior in 1992?" *Mediaweek* 2(45):17, 30 Nov. 1992

CHIHARA, PAUL. *SEE* DRIVER, JOHN, and PAUL CHIHARA

CHILDRESS, ALICE

Gebhard, A. O. "The Emerging Self: Young-Adult and Classic Novels of the
    Black Experience," *English Journal* 82(5):50, Sep. 1993
Shinn, T. J. "Living the Answer: The Emergence of African American Feminist
    Drama," *Studies in the Humanities* 17(2):149–59, Dec. 1990
Staub, D. "NCTE to You," *College English* 55(2):279, Feb. 1993

CHIN, FRANK

Davis, R. M. "Frank Chin: Iconoclastic Icon," *Redneck Review of Literature*
    23:75–78, Fall 1992
Feldman, G. "Spring's Five Fictional Encounters of the Chinese American
    Kind," *Publishers Weekly* 238(8):25, 8 Feb. 1991
"Lannan Foundation Awards $360,000 to Nine Writers," *Publishers Weekly*
    239(47):8, 26 Oct. 1992

CHONG, PING

Sandla, R. "Downtown Time Warp," *Dance Magazine* 65:66, Dec. 1991
"Writing Homes: Interviews with Suzan-Lori Parks, Christopher Durango, Edu-
    ardo Machado, Ping Chong and Migdalia Cruz," *American Theatre* 8(7):36, 1
    Oct. 1991

Westfall, S. R. "Ping Chong's Terra In/Cognita: Monsters on Stage," 359–74 in S. G. Lim and A. Ling, eds. *Reading the Literatures of Asian America.*

Brightness, 1989
   Woertendyke, R. *Theatre Journal* 42:491–95, Dec. 1990

Nosferatu, 1985
   Neely, K. "Ping Chong's Theatre of Simultaneous Consciousness," *Journal of Dramatic Theory and Criticism* 7(1):121–35, Fall 1992

CHONG, PING, and OTHERS

4 A.M. America, 1990
   Variety 341(13):98, 7 Jan. 1991

CLARKE, MARTHA

Dunning, J. "Bouncing Back from an Elephantine Disaster," *New York Times* 142:H8, 11 Jul. 1993

CLARKE, MARTHA, RICHARD COE, RICHARD PEASLEE, and STANLEY WALDEN

Endangered Species, 1990
   Acocella, J. "Exits and Entrances: On Martha Clarke's Endangered Species," *Artforum* 30(29):27–8, Dec. 1990
   Garafola, L. *Dance Magazine* 65:90–91, Jan. 1991

CLARVOE, ANTHONY

Let's Play Two, 1992
   Rubio, J. "So Much in Common," *American Theatre* 9(6):12, Oct. 1992

The Living, 1993
   Clarvoe, A. "From *The Living*," *Kenyon Review* (15):40–58, Sprg. 1993
   ———. "*The Living*," *American Theatre* 10(12):25–42, 1 Dec. 1993

CLEAGE, PEARL

Cleage, P. "Hairpeace," *African American Review* 27:37–41, Sprg. 1993

Chain (a companion piece to *Late Bus to Mecca*), 1991
   Evans, G. *Variety* 346(8):61, 9 Mar. 1992
   Miles, J. ed. *Playwriting Women: 7 Plays from the Women's Project*

Flyin' West, 1992
   Madison, C. "Home Sweet Homestead," *American Theatre* 9(8):11, Dec. 1992

Late Bus to Mecca (a companion piece to *Chain*), 1991
    Evans, G. *Variety* 346(8):61, 9 Mar. 1992
    Miles, J., ed. *Playwriting Women: 7 Plays from the Women's Project*

CLEMENS, SAMUEL LANGHORNE. *SEE* TWAIN, MARK

CLOUD, DARRAH

O Pioneers! (dramatization of a novel by W. Cather), 1990
    Miles, J., ed. *Playwriting Women: 7 Plays from the Women's Project*

The Stick Wife, 1991
    Oliver, E. *New Yorker* 67:94, 20 May 1991
    Simon, J. *New York* 24:71–72, 27 May 1991

COATES, GEORGE

DiNucci, D. "The Art of Multimedia," *Publish* 7(8):96, Aug. 1992

George Coates Performance Works, 1992
    Harvey, D. *Variety* 353(4):33, 29 Nov. 1993
    ———. *Variety* 346(3):87, 3 Feb. 1992
    Stout, F. C. "The Desert Music: A Live Sho," *Theatre Journal* 45(4):545,
        Dec. 1993
    Wilder, C. "High Tech Takes to Theater Stage," *Computerworld*, 26(13):31,
        30 Mar. 1992

COE, RICHARD. *SEE* CLARKE, MARTHA, RICHARD COE, RICHARD
PEASLEY, and STANLEY WALDEN

COHEN, DOUGLAS J. *SEE* BOLT, JONATHAN, DOUGLAS J. COHEN, and
THOMAS TOCE

COHEN, MICHAEL

Bonami, F. "Cohen, Michael," *Flash Art* 26(170):81, 1 May 1993

COLEMAN, CY

Sheed, W. "With a Song in His Heart," *Time* 139(8):66, 24 Feb. 1992

The Will Rogers Follies, 1991
    Filichia, P. *TheaterWeek* 4(46):13, 24 Jun. 1991
    Gerard, J. *Vanity Fair* 54:152–55, May 1991
    Gottfried, M. "The Last American Musical?" *TheaterWeek* 4(48):18–23, 8
        Jul. 1991
    Greskovic, R. *Dance Magazine* 65:52, Aug. 1991

Heilpern, J. *Vogue* 181:262–65, May 1991
Kanfer, S. *New Leader* 74:23, 6 May 1991
Kroll, J. *Newsweek* 117(19):68, 13 May 1991
Oliver, E. *New Yorker* 67:84, 13 May 1991
Sandla, R. *Theatre Crafts* 25:44–47, Aug/Sep. 1991
Simon, J. *New York* 24:88, 13 May 1991
Simonson, R. *TheaterWeek* 4(48):17, 8 Jul. 1991
Weales, G. *Commonweal* 118:515–16, 13 Sep. 1991
Wong, W. "Willa-Mania!" *TheaterWeek* 4(48):18–23, 8 Jul. 1991

SEE ALSO GELBART, LARRY, CY COLEMAN, and DAVID ZIPPEL

COMDEN, BETTY, and ADOLPH GREEN

Heilpern, J. "Broadway's Dream Team," *Vogue* 181(5):262, May 1991
Laffel, J. "Betty Comden and Adolph Green, Part 1," *Films in Review*
   43(3–4):75, Mar/Apr. 1992
———. "Betty Comden and Adolph Green, Part 2," *Films in Review*
   43(5–6):154, May/Jun. 1992
Zippel, D. "Together Again . . . and Again . . . and Again," *New York Times*
   142:H8, 20 Jun. 1993

COMDEN, BETTY, ADOLPH GREEN, and JULE STYNE

Subways Are for Sleeping
   Filichia, P. "Elevators Are for Asking," *TheaterWeek* 5(11):19, 21 Oct. 1991

COMDEN, BETTY, ADOLPH GREEN, JULE STYNE, MOOSE CHARLAP, and
CAROLYN LEE

Peter Pan (based on the play by J. M. Barrie), 1992
   Walker, S. *TheaterWeek* 6(4):26–27, 31 Aug. 1992

CONDON, FRANK

The Chicago Conspiracy Trial, 1991
   Adler, A. *Chicago* 40(12):93–95, Dec. 1991
   Abarbanel, J. *TheaterWeek* 5(13):31–32, 4 Nov. 1991
   Hanson, H. "Chicago Law: Replaying the Courtroom Riot on Stage," *Chi-
      cago* 40(10):26, Oct. 1991
   Ingram, B. *Variety* 344(13):204, 7 Oct. 1991

CONGDON, CONSTANCE

Casanova, 1991
   Osborn, M. E. "Connie's *Casanova*," *TheaterWeek* 4(43):37–39, 3 Jun.
      1991

Simon, J. *New York* 24:57–8, 10 Jun. 1991
Weales, G. *Commonweal* 118:484–5, 9 Aug. 1991

Tales of the Lost Formicans, 1988
Osborn, M. E. *TheaterWeek* 4(42):31, 27 May, 1991

CONKLIN, JOHN

The Carving of Mount Rushmore, 1992
Osborn, M. E. "Letter from Louisville," *TheaterWeek* 5(38):31, 27 Apr. 1992

COOKE, ROSE TERRY

Makosky, D. R. "*Introduction to Diego* by Rose Terry Cooke: An Edition of the Previously Unpublished Manuscript," *Connecticut Historical Society Bulletin* 54(3/4):212, Summ. 1989
Walker, C. "Rose Terry Cooke, 1827–1892," *Legacy* 9(2):143, Fall 1992

COONS, CHERI. *SEE* HOLLANDER, NICOLE, ARNOLD APRILL, TOM MULA, STEVE RASHID, and CHERI COONS

COOPER, DENNIS, ISHMAEL HOUSTON-JONES, and PETER BROSIUS

The Undead, 1991
Cole, C. B. *TheaterWeek* 5(21):33, 30 Dec. 1991

COPLAND, AARON

Biemiller, L. "A Touring Company Reclaims America's Musical World at the Farmhouses of Minnesota," *Chronicle of Higher Education* 39(43):A39, 30 Jun. 1993
"Copland Remembered," *Opera News* 55:33, 2 Feb. 1991

COUSINS, NORMAN

McCray, N. "Self Healing: An Interview with Norman Cousins," (audio-visual), *Booklist* 90(5):544–45, 1 Nov. 1993
"Norman Cousins," *Current Biography* 52(1):58, Jan. 1991

CREGAN, DAVID

Nice Dorothy, 1993
O'Connor, P. *TLS* (4705):19, 4 Jun. 1993

CREWS, HARRY

Shelton, F. W. "Harry Crews After a Childhood," *Southern Literary Journal* 24(2):3, Sprg. 1992

CROWLEY, MART

Boys in the Band, 1968
Kramer, R. E. "A Play of Words About a Play," *New York Times* 143:H1, 31 Oct. 1993

CRYTON, SARA

She's a Real Dyke, 1991
Chansky, D. *TheaterWeek* 4(44):35, 10 Jun. 1991

CURRAN, KEITH

Walking the Dead, 1991
Leslie, G. *TheaterWeek* 4(42):40–41, 27 May 1991
Miller, S. "Night of the Living Dread," *TheaterWeek* 4(41):22- 23, 20 May 1991
Simon, J. *New York* 24:72–3, 27 May 1991

CUSH, GEOFFREY

The Criminal Prosecution and Capital Punishment of Animals, 1993
Turner, E. S. *TLS* (4715):16, 13 Aug. 1993

DAHL, ROALD

The BFG, 1991
Treglown, J. *TLS* (4629):19, 20 Dec. 1991

DALY, AUGUSTIN

Carroll, K. L. "The Americanization of Beatrice: Nineteenth-Century Style," *Theatre Survey* 31:67–84, May 1990
Flynn, J. "Sites and Sights: The Iconology of the Subterranean in Late Nineteenth-Century Irish-American Drama," *MELUS* 18(1):5, Sprg. 1993
Mason, J. D. "The Face of Fear," 213–21 in J. Redmond, ed. *Melodrama*
Wolter, J. C. *The Dawning of American Drama: American Dramatic Criticism 1746–1915*. 339, 344,348, 383, 392

DAMASHEK, BARBARA

Schiffman, J. "Barbara Damashek: A Moving Target," *American Theatre* 10(12):46–47, Dec. 1993

DANIELE, GRACIELA

Dalva, N. "Dance Show Moves to Broadway," *Dance Magazine* 64(10):15
"Graciela Danielle," *Dance Pages Magazine* 9(3):20, Wntr. 1992

DAVIS, BILL C.

Spine, 1993
    Daniels, R. L. *Variety* 349(13):142, 25 Jan. 1993
    Scasserra, M. P. *TheaterWeek* 6(29):28, 22 Feb. 1993

DAVIS, LUTHER, ROBERT WRIGHT, GEORGE FOREST, and MAURY YESTON

Grand Hotel: The Musical (musical version of V. Baum's novel; revision of Davis,
    Wright, and Forest's 1958 musical *At the Grand*), 1989
    Lochte, D. *Los Angeles Magazine* 36(7):123, Jul. 1991
    Pitman, J. *Variety* 347(12):48, 13 Jul. 1992
    Simon, J. *New York* 25(4):57, 27 Jan. 1992
    Witchel, A. "Strings Strike Back," *New York Times* 140:B2(N), 13 Sep.
    1991

DAVIS, OSSIE

Anderson, W. C. "One Miracle at a Time," *American Visions* 7(2):20–24, Apr/
    May. 1992

DAVIS, OWEN

Wolter, J. C. *The Dawning of American Drama: American Drama Criticism
    1746–1915.* 484+

DAVY, BABS

Women and Children First: Outstanding Perk or Tool of Oppression?, 1992
    Chansky D. *TheaterWeek* 6(19):33, 14 Dec. 1992

DEAKIN, RICHARD

Angels Still Falling, 1991
    Baker, P. *TLS* (4611):19, 16 Aug. 1991

DEE, RUBY

The Disappearance (an adaptation of the novel by Rosa Guy), 1993
    Scasserra, M. P. "Ruby Dee: Walking Words," *American Theatre* 9(9):27–
    28, Jan. 1993
    ———. *TheaterWeek* 6(29):29, 22 Feb. 1993

DELGADO, LOUIS

A Better Life for You and Me, 1991
    Filichia, P. *TheaterWeek* 4(29):13, 25 Feb. 1991
    ———. "It's Not Where You Start, It's Where You Finish," *TheaterWeek*
       6(10):11–12, 12 Oct. 1992
    ———. *TheaterWeek* 7(4):9–10, 30 Aug. 1993

DeLILLO, DON

Begley, A. "Don DeLillo: Interview," *Paris Review* 35:274–306, Fall 1993
DeLillo, D. "The Rapture of the Athlete Assumed into Heaven," *South Atlantic
    Quarterly* 91(2):241–42, Sprg. 1992
Zinman, T. S. "Gone Fission: The Holocaustic Wit of Don DeLillo," *Modern
    Drama* 34(1):74–87, Mar. 1991

DePOY, PHILLIP

Hall, P. "Hellish Music," *American Theatre* 9(10):11, Feb. 1993

DEWHURST, KEITH

Woddis, C. "Snowed Under: Carole Woddis Talks to Keith Dewhurst . . . ," *Plays
    and Players* (449):10, 1 May 1991

Black Snow, 1991
    Graffy, J. *TLS* (4596):17, 3 May 1991
    Henning, J. *Wall Street Journal* A8(W), 21 May 1993
    Lahr, J. *New Yorker* 68(44):123–126, 21 Dec. 1992
    Simon, J. *New York* 24(35):50, 9 Sep. 1991
    Wilson, E. *Wall Street Journal* A8(W), 15 Jan. 1993

DIAMOND, DAVID

"Award for Diamond," *New York Times* 140:B3, 22 Jul. 1991
DiPalma, M. "David Diamond: An American Treasure," *Guitar Review* (94):1,
    Summ. 1993
Kozinn, A. "A Season of Concerts with Firsts," *New York Times* 141:12, 6 Jun.
    1992

DIAMOND, THERESA MARIE

Relationship Jones, 1991
    Chansky, D. *TheaterWeek* 5(12):40, 28 Oct. 1991

Di DONATO, PIETRO

Napolitano, L. M. *A Study of Pietro DiDonato's Christ in Concrete.*
    (#DA9104075; State U of New York, Stony Brook) *DAI* 51(9):3074–75A, Mar.
    1991
"Pietro Di Donato," (Obituary), *Facts on File* 52(2670):4B, 23 Jan. 1992

DIETZ, STEVEN

Halcyon Days, 1993
   Weales, G. *Commonweal* 120(1):20, 15 Jan. 1993

DI PAOLO, ELVIRA J.

Bricklayers, 1992
   George, K. *Theatre Journal* 44:544–5, Dec. 1992

The Cardinal Detoxes, 1990
   Disch, T. M. *"The Cardinal Detoxes*: A Play in One Act," *Hudson Review*
   46:57–76, Sprg. 1993
   Gahr, E. "N.Y. Archdiocese Threatens Theater Group Over Play," *National
   Catholic Reporter* 26(42):7, 28 Sep. 1990

DODSON, OWEN VINCENT

Hatch, J. V. *Sorrow Is the Only Faithful One: The Life of Owen Dodson*
Madison, C. "Dodson's Dilemma," *American Theatre* 10(12):60, Dec. 1993

The Shining Town, 1937
   "Owen Vincent Dodson," 328–352 in L. Hamalian and J. V. Hatch, eds. *The
   Roots of African American Drama*

DONAGHY, TOM

Northeast Local, 1993
   Taylor, M. *Variety* 349(13):142, 25 Jan. 1993
   Ungaro, J. *TheaterWeek* 6(29):32, 22 Feb. 1993

DORSEY, JEANNE

At the Movies with Vera and Vivien Vigilante, 1992
   Moran, T. *TheaterWeek* 6(9):37, 5 Oct. 1992

Gideon and Josephine, 1992
   Moran, T. *TheaterWeek* 6(9):37, 5 Oct. 1992

DOUGHERTY, JOSEPH. *SEE* AHRENS, LYNN, STEPHEN FLAHERTY, and JOSEPH DOUGHERTY

DRAKE, DAVID

Harris, J. "Gay Activist or Beauty Queen?" *TheaterWeek* 4(52):18–23, 5 Aug.
   1991
Weiss, P. "Going Solo," *Vogue* 183(4):242–44, Apr. 1993

The Night Larry Kramer Kissed Me, 1992
    Bell, J. "Sheros," *TheaterWeek* 6(14):15, 2 Nov. 1992
    Bruckner, D. J. R. *New York Times* 141:B4, 25 Jun. 1992
    Evans, G. *Variety* 347(12):48, 13 Jul. 1992
    Provenzano, J. *Advocate* (608):71, 30 Jul. 1992
    Richards, D. *New York Times* 141:H5, 12 Jul. 1992
    Time 140(2):81, 13 Jul. 1992

DREISER, THEODORE

Newlin, K. "Expressionism Takes the Stage: Dreiser's *Laughing Gas*," *Journal of American Drama and Theatre* 4(1):5, Wntr. 1992
———. "Melodramatic Naturalism: London, Garland, Dreiser, and the Campaign to Reform the American Theater," (#DA9203442; Indiana U) *DAI* 52(8):2925A, Feb. 1992

DREXLER, ROSALYN

The Flood, 1992
    Bell, J. *TheaterWeek* 5(28):11–12, 17 Feb. 1992

Occupational Hazard
    Lamont, R. C., ed. *Women on the Verge: 7 Avant-Garde Plays*

DRIVER, JOHN, and PAUL CHIHARA

James Clavell's Shogun: The Musical (musical version of novel by J. Clavell), 1990
    Disch, T. M. *Nation* 252(1):26, 7 Jan. 1991
    Hering, D. *Dance Magazine* 65(2):84, Feb. 1991

DUBAY, BRENDA JOYCE

Secrets, 1991
    Thompson, D. *Theatre Journal* 43:115–16, Mar. 1991

DULAK, TOM

Breaking Legs, 1989
    Evans, G. "Off B'way Thumbs Ride Along a Rocky Road," *Variety* 348(12):191–92, 12 Oct. 1992
    Oliver, E. *New Yorker* 67(15):78, 3 Jun. 1991
    Rich, F. *New York Times* 140:B4(N), 20 May 1991
    Richards, D. *New York Times* 140:H20(N), 26 May 1991
    Simon, J. *New York* 24(22):53, 3 Jun. 1991
    Taylor, M. *Variety* 348(12):194, 12 Oct. 1992
    ———. *Variety* 349(2):99, 2 Nov. 1992

Incommunicado (about Ezra Pound), 1989
    Lochte, D. *Los Angeles Magazine* 38(5):166–67, May 1993
    Schlatter, J. F. *Theatre Journal* 42:505–06, Dec. 1990

Just Deserts, 1992
    M. R. *TheaterWeek* 5(33):14, 23 Mar. 1992

DURANG, CHRISTOPHER

Carroll, D. "Not-Quite Mainstream Male Playwrights: Guare, Durang, and
    Rabe," 41–61 in B. King, ed. *Contemporary American Theatre*
Dieckman, S. B. "Metatheatre as Antitheatre: Durang's Actor's Nightmare,"
    American Drama 1(2):26–41, Sprg. 1992
Durang, C. "Naomi in the Living Room," *Antaeus* 66:69–74, Sprg. 1991
Spivak, R. *Christopher Durang: Satire and Beyond.* Canadian Theses: Biblio-
    theque Nationale du Canada, 1993
Wilson, E., Interviewer. *Jerry Zaks; Christopher Durang; Walter Kerr; Tommy
    Tune.* Videocassette

TV or Not TV, 1991
    Durang, C. *"TV or Not TV,"* *TheaterWeek* 4(41):26–28, 20 May 1991

EBB, FRED. *SEE* KANDER, JOHN, and FRED EBB

SEE ALSO McNALLY, TERRENCE, JOHN KANDER, and FRED EBB

EDGAR, DAVID

The Strange Case of Dr. Jekyll and Mr. Hyde, 1991
    Duguid, L. *TLS* (4627):18, 6 Dec. 1991

EDWARDS, JODIE, and SUSIE (BUTTERBEANS and SUSIE)

"Butterbeans and Susie," 152–58 in L. Hamalian and J. V. Hatch, eds. *The Roots
    of African American Drama*

EDWARDS, SHERMAN. *SEE* STONE, PETER, and SHERMAN EDWARDS

EGLOFF, ELIZABETH

The Swan, 1988 (revised 1990)
    Evans, G. *Variety* 353(4):33, 29 Nov. 1993
    Holden, S. *New York Times* 143:B3(N), 16 Nov. 1993
    Kirkpatrick, M. *Wall Street Journal* A12, 29 Nov. 1993
    Simon, J. *New York* 26(47):81, 29 Nov. 1993
    Variety 343(8):60, 3 Jun. 1991

EICHELBERGER, ETHYL

Jeffreys, J. E. "In Memory: Ethyl Eichelberger 1945–1990," *TDR* 35(1):10–12, Sprg. 1991
Oxman, S. "Marzipan Upon a Birthday Cake, A Talk with Ethyl Eichelberger," *Theater* 21(3):66, Summ. 1990

ELLIS, BRAD. *SEE* MORRIS, PETER, and BRAD ELLIS

EMERSON, JOHN

Bruce-Novoa, J. "From Paragonia to Parador: Hollywood's Strategy for Saving Latin America," *Gestos: Teoria y Practica del Teatro Hispanico* 6(11):175–85, Apr. 1991

EPHRON, HENRY

"Henry Ephron, 81, Screenwriter of *The Desk Set* with His Wife," *New York Times* 141:16, 7 Sep. 1992

EPP, STEVEN, FELICITY JONES, and DOMINIQUE SERRAND

Children of Paradise: Shooting a Dream (based in part on Marcel Carne's film *Les Enfants du Paradis*), 1992
    Gussow, M. *New York Times* 142:B3(N), 20 Jan. 1993
    Henry, W. A., III. *Time* 140(23):71, 7 Dec. 1992
    Hornby, R. "Regional Theatre Comes of Age," *Hudson Review* 46(3):529–36, Autm. 1993
    Kroll, J. *Newsweek* 121(6):64, 8 Feb. 1993
    Szekrenyi, L. *TheaterWeek* 6(29):26–27, 22 Feb. 1993
    Taylor, M. *Variety* 349(13):140–41, 25 Jan. 1993

Crusoe, Friday, and the Island of Hope, 1991
    Chase, T. "The Guthrie and the Theatre de la Jeune Lune," *TheaterWeek* 4(52):16–17, 5 Aug. 1991

ESSMAN, JEFFREY, and MICHAEL JOHN LaCHUISA

Bella, Belle of Byelorussia, 1992
    Evans, G. *Variety* 346(2):57, 27 Jan. 1992
    Simonson, R. *TheaterWeek* 5(30):37, 2 Mar. 1992

EVANS, ROSS. *SEE* PARKER, DOROTHY (with ROSS EVANS)

EWING, GEOFFREY C.

Ali, 1992
    Evans, G. *Variety* 348(6)64, 31 Aug. 1992

Gussow, M. *New York Times* 141:B3(N), 13 Aug. 1992
Kanfer, S. *New Leader* 75(13):22, 5 Oct. 1992
Kirkpatrick, M. *Wall Street Journal* A14(W), 30 Sep. 1992
Lipsyte, R. *New York Times* 141:29(N), 16 Aug. 1992
TheaterWeek 6(7):10, 21 Sep. 1992

EYEN, TOM

Holden, S. "Tom Eyen, 50, Off Off Broadway Playwright, Dies," *New York Times* 140:A13, 28 May 1991

FAULKNER, WILLIAM

Brodsky, L. D., and R. W. Hamblin. *Faulkner: A Comprehensive Guide to the Brodsky Collection: Volume IV: Battle Cry: A Screenplay by William Faulkner*

FEIBLEMAN, PETER

Cakewalk, 1993
Hartigan, P. "Intruding on Lillian," *American Theatre* 20(7–8):10–12, Jul/ Aug. 1993
Lahr, J. *New Yorker* 69(18):93–95, 21 Jun. 1993
Taylor, M. *Variety* 351(8):32, 28 Jun. 1993

FEIFFER, JULES

"The Forbidden Books of Youth: After the First Furtive Peek, There Was No Turning Back," *New York Times Book Review* 13, 6 Jun. 1993
"Theater—the Artist," *Nieman Reports* 46(3):29, Fall 1992

Grownups, 1981
Simonson, R. *TheaterWeek* 4(28):36, 18 Feb. 1991

FELDSHUH, DAVID

Miss Evers' Boys (suggested by, among other things, the book *Bad Blood* by J. H. Jones), 1989
Abarbanel, J. *TheaterWeek* 5(13):32, 4 Nov. 1991
Urquhart, S. "Confronting Campus Racism from Day One," *Time* 138(8):15, 26 Aug. 1991
Weales, G. *Commonweal* 118(22):750–51, 20 Dec. 1991

FIELD, BARBARA

Playing with Fire (After Frankenstein), 1993
Koren-Deutsch, I. S. *Theatre Journal* 44(3):392–94, Oct. 1992
Van Gelder, L. *New York Times* 142:C18(L)

FIERSTEIN, HARVEY

Cohen, J. R. "Intersecting and Competing Discourses in Harvey Fierstein's *Tidy Endings*," *Quarterly Journal of Speech* 77(2):196, 1 May 1991
"Fierstein Sues Over *Torch Song* B'Cast," *Variety* 347(4):143, 11 May 1992
Horwitz, S. "The Substance of Fierstein," *TheaterWeek* 4(42):17–23, 27 May 1991
Loud, L. "Out Loud," *Advocate* (626):79, 6 Apr. 1993

Safe Sex (three one-acts: *Manny and Jake*, *Safe Sex*, and *On Tidy Endings*), 1987
    Gross, G. D. "Coming Up for Air: Three AIDS Plays," *Journal of American Culture* 15(2):63, Summ. 1992

FINDLEY, TIMOTHY

Roberts, C. "The Perfection of Gesture: Timothy Findley and Canadian Theatre," *Theatre History in Canada* 12(1):22–36, Sprg. 1991

The Stillborn Lover, 1993
    Bemrose, J. "Two Spring Hits: Timothy Findley Visits the Heart of Darkness," *Maclean's* 106(16):49–50, 19 Apr. 1993

FINLEY, KAREN

de Grazia, E. "Indecency Exposed," *Nation* 255(1):4, 6 Jul. 1992
"Endowment to Pay Four Artists Is Rejected," *New York Times*, 142:13, 5 Jun. 1993
Gandee, C. "People Are Talking About the Dumbest Things Men Ever Said About Women," *Vogue* 183(10):139, 1 Oct. 1993
Hart, L. "Karen Finley's Dirty Work: Censorship, Homophobia, and the NEA," *Genders* (14):1, Fall 1992
———. "Motherhood According to Finley: 'The Theory of Total Blame,' " *TDR* 36(1):124, Sprg. 1991
Heins, M. "Portrait of a Much Abused Lady," *Index on Censorship* 22(1):9, Jan. 1993
Holden, S. "Karen Finley," *New York Times* 141:C3, 17 Jul. 1992
———. "Two Solo Performance Artists Confront the Limits of Personal Experience," *New York Times* 141:C3, 17 Jul. 1992
Kozinn, A. "Karen Finley," *New York Times* 141:17, 13 Jun. 1992
Licata, E. "Let Us Now Praise Infamous Women," *Humanist* 51(3):15, 1 May 1991
Mifflin, M. "Performance Art: What Is It and Where Is It Going?" *ARTnews* 91(4):84, Apr. 1992
Muse, J. "War on War: Karen Finley/Desert Storm/Masochism," *Artspace* 15(6):60, Fall 1991
Nesbitt, L. "Karen Finley," *Artforum*, 31(7):98, Mar. 1993
Vanden Heuvel, M. "Complementary Spaces: Realism, Performance and a New Dialogics of Theatre," *Theatre Journal* 44(1):47, Mar. 1992
Wei, L., et. al. "On Nationality: 13 Artists," *Art in America* 79(9):124, Sep. 1991

The Constant State of Desire, 1986
> Pramaggiore, M. T. "Resisting/Performing/Femininity: Words, Flesh, and
> Feminism in Karen Finley's *The Constant State of Desire*," *Theatre Jour-*
> *nal* 44(3):269–90, 1 Oct. 1992

We Keep Our Victims Ready, 1989
> Leo, A. "Karen Finley's *We Keep Our Victims Ready*," *Feminisms* 4(3):3, 1
> May 1991
> Marowitz, C. *TheaterWeek* 5(23):34–35, 13 Jan. 1992

FINN, WILLIAM

Helbing, T. "Truth and Falsettos: William Finn's Moving Saga Puts the Story of
> One Gay Man's Life and Loss on Broadway," *Advocate* (602):70, 5 May 1992
Henry, W. A., III. "The Quirky William Finn," *Time* 139(19):57, 11 May 1992
Richards, D. "An Ode to Joy on Broadway," *New York Times* 141:H1, 10 May
> 1992
Scher, H. "William Finn." *American Theatre* 10(3):27, Mar. 1993
"Stage," *People Weekly* 37(25):45, 29 Jun. 1992
"Theater—Sister Act," *Vogue* 182(9):360, 1 Sep. 1992

March of the Falsettos (second play of *Marvin's Trilogy*; the first is *In Trousers*;
> the third is *Falsettoland*, by James Lapine and Finn, which see), 1981
> Mandelbaum, K. *TheaterWeek* 5(13):38–39, 4 Nov. 1991
> Taylor, M. *Variety* 345(2):79, 21 Oct. 1991

SEE ALSO LAPINE, JAMES, and WILLIAM FINN

FITCH, CLYDE

Marra, K. "Clara Bloodgood (1870–1907), Exemplary Subject of Broadway Gen-
> der Tyranny," *ATQ* 7(3):193, Sep. 1993

FITZSIMMONS, RAYMUND

Kean, 1991
> Raw, L. *Theatre Journal* 43:525–6, Dec. 1991

FLAHERTY, STEPHEN. *SEE* AHRENS, LYNN, STEPHEN FLAHERTY, and
JOSEPH DOUGHERTY

FLECK, JOHN

Burnham, L. F. "An Unclassified Number: An Interview with John Fleck,"
> *Drama Review* 35:192–97, Fall 1991

Fleck, J. "Blessed Are All the Little Fishes," *Drama Review* 35:178–91, Fall 1991
"John Fleck," *Mime Journal* 91/92:28, 1991

FOOTE, HORTON

Briley, R. L. *You Can Go Home Again: The Focus on Family in the Works of Horton Foote*
Buckley, M. "The Life and Times of Horton Foote," *TheaterWeek* 6(7):33–35, 21 Sep. 1992
Castleberry, M. *Voices from Home: Familial Bonds in the Works of Horton Foote.* Diss.; Louisiana State U, 1993
Charlotte, S. *Creativity in Film: Conversations with 14 Who Excel*
"Conversation with Horton Foote," *Dramatists Guild Quarterly* 29(4):17, Wntr. 1993
"Horton Foote: Four New Plays," *Publisher's Weekly* 240(50):67, 13 Dec. 1993
Porter, L. R. "An Interview with Horton Foote," *Studies in American Drama, 1945–Present* 6(2):177, 1991
Reinert, A. "Tender Foote," *Texas Monthly* 19(7):110–11, Jul. 1991
Richards, D. "The Secret Aches of Broken Families," *New York Times* 142:H5, 4 Oct. 1992
Smelstor, M. "The World's an Orphans' Home: Horton Foote's Social and Moral History," *Southern Quarterly* 29(2):7–16, Wntr. 1991
Watson, C. S. "Beyond the Commercial Media: Horton Foote's Procession of Defeated Men," *Studies in American Drama, 1945–Present* 8(2):175, 1993
Wood, G. "Horton Foote: An Interview," *PostScript: Essays in Film and the Humanities* 10(3):3–12, Summ. 1991

The Roads to Home (includes *The Dearest of Friends*, *A Nightingale*, and *Spring Dance*), published 1982
    Rich, F. *New York Times* 142:B3(N), 18 Sep. 1992
    Ungaro, J. *TheaterWeek* 6(10):27, 12 Oct. 1992

The Trip to Bountiful, 1954
    Jayroe, T. *Footeprints: A Comparison of the Teleplay and Stage Play Versions of The Trip to Bountiful.* M.S. Thesis; East Texas State U, 1991
    Moore, B. and D. G. Yellin. *Horton Foote's Three Trips to Bountiful*

FORD, RICHARD

Ford, R. *"American Tropical,"* *Antaeus* (66):75–80, Sprg. 1991
Schneider, W. "Richard Ford Ups the Ante," *American Film* 16:50–51, May 1991

FOREMAN, RICHARD

Bernstein, C. "A Conversation with Richard Foreman," *TDR* 36(3):103, Fall 1992
Goldberg, R. "Richard Foreman," *Art Forum* 29(10):116, Summ. 1991

Gussow, M. "The Richard Foreman Trilogy," *New York Times* 141:C15, 27 May 1992

Halstead, J. "Re-Viewing Richard Foreman," *Journal of Dramatic Theory and Criticism* 6(2):61–79, Sprg. 1992

Kostelanetz, R. "Writing and Performance: A Conversation Among Linda Mussman, Richard Foreman, Robert Wilson, and Richard Kostelanetz," 489–509 in R. Kostelanetz, ed., *American Writing Today*

MacDonald, E. "Richard Foreman and the Closure of Representation," *Essays in Theatre* 9(1):19, 1 Nov. 1990

Eddie Goes to Poetry City, 1991
Bell, J. *TheaterWeek* 4(37):14, 22 Apr. 1991
Gussow, M. *New York Times* 140:B4(N), 10 Apr. 1991

Samuel's Major Problems, 1992
Bell, J. *TheaterWeek* 6(26):11–12, 1 Feb. 1993
Gussow, M. *New York Times* 142:C15(L), 12 Jan. 1993

FOREST, GEORGE. *SEE* DAVIS, LUTHER, ROBERT WRIGHT, GEORGE FOREST, and MAURY YESTON

FORNÉS, MARÍA IRENE

Fornés, M. I. "Springtime," *Antaeus* (66):81–90, Sprg. 1991

———. "Terra Incognita," *Theater* 24(2):99–112, Sprg. 1993

Kintz, L. "Gendering the Critique of Representation: Fascism, the Purified Body, and Theater in Adorno, Artaud, and María Irene Fornés," *Rethinking Marxism* 4(3):83, Fall 1991

———. "Permeable Boundaries, Femininity, Fascism, and Violence: Fornés' *The Conduct of Life*," *Gestos* 6(11):79–89, Apr. 1991

"María Irene Fornés: Q & A," *Theatre Insight* 4(1/2):14, Summ. 1993

Marranca, B. "The State of Grace. María Irene Fornés at Sixty-Two," *Performing Arts Journal* (41):24–31, 1 May 1992

Schechner, R. "Toward the 21st Century," *TDR* 37(4):7–8, Wntr. 1993

Watson, M. "The Search for Identity in the Theater of Three Cuban American Female Dramatists," *Bilingual Review* 16(2/3):188–96, May–Dec. 1991

Wolf, S. "Re/Presenting Gender, Re/Presenting Violence: Feminism, Form and the Plays of María Irene Fornés," *Theatre Studies* 37:17–31, 1992

And What of the Night? (four parts: *Charlie, Lust, Springtime,* and *Hunger*), 1989
Kent, A. "*And What of the Night?*: Fornés' Apocalyptic Vision of American Greed and Poverty," *Journal of Dramatic Theory and Criticism* 7(2):133, Sprg. 1993

Lamont, R. C., ed. *Women on the Verge: 7 Avant-Garde American Plays*

Fefu and Her Friends, 1977
Keyssar, H. "Drama and the Dialogic Imagination: *The Heidi Chronicles* and *Fefu and Her Friends*," *Modern Drama* 34(1):88–106, Mar. 1991

Osborn, M. E. "Letter from New Haven: Winterfest Features Experimental Plays by Women," *TheaterWeek* 5(32):21–23, 16 Mar. 1992

Oscar and Bertha
Harvey, D. *Variety* 346(10):113–14, 23 Mar. 1992

FRANDSEN, ERIK, MICHAEL GARIN, ROBERT HIPKENS, and PAULA LOCKHEART

Song of Singapore, 1991
Borowski, M. "Drinking, Dancing, Murder, and a Stolen Fish," *Theater-Week* 5(3):18–21, 26 Aug. 1991
Simon, J. *New York* 24(23):57–58, 10 Jun. 1991

FRANKLIN, J. E.

Christchild, 1992
Evans, G. *Variety* 349(7):76, 7 Dec. 1992
Holden, S. *New York Times* 142:C18(L), 2 Dec. 1992
Ungaro, J. *TheaterWeek* 6(20):33, 21 Dec. 1992

FRASER, BRAD

Morison, S. "Rebel Without a Pause," *Saturday Night* 107(4):44, 1 May 1992

Unidentified Human Remains and the Nature of Love, 1990
Filichia, P. "Clark Gregg: Serial Artist," *TheaterWeek* 5(11):17, 21 Oct. 1991
Gerard, J. *Variety* 344(11):82, 23 Sep. 1991
Henry, W. A., III. *Time* 138(13):81, 30 Sep. 1991
James, P. *TheaterWeek* 5(9):38, 7 Oct. 1991
Kramer, M. *New Yorker* 67(32):73, 30 Sep. 1991
Leslie, G. *TheaterWeek* 5(9):38, 7 Oct. 1991
Raymond, G. "Sex and the Serial Killer," *TheaterWeek* 5(7):25-27, 23 Sep. 1991
Richards, D. "What Would Sally and Geraldo Say?" *New York Times* 141:H5(N), 29 Sep. 1991
Simon, J. *New York* 24(38):65, 30 Sep. 1991
Variety 344(5):49, 12 Aug. 1991
Weales, G. *Commonweal* 119(2):27, 31 Jan. 1992

FRAYN, MICHAEL

Glaap, A. "Short Plays im Englischunterricht: Playdoyer für ein immer noch ver-nachlässigtes Genre," *Die Neueren Sprachen* 90(4):368–88, Aug. 1991
Gottlieb, V. "Why This Farce? From Chekhov to Frayn—and Frayn's *Chekov*," *New Theatre Quarterly* 7(27):217–28, 1 Aug. 1991

Here, 1993
  Duguid, L. *TLS* (4715):17, 13 Aug. 1993
  Wolf, M. *Variety* 352(3):29, 30 Aug. 1993

FRAZIER, LEVI, JR.

Frazier, L. "You're Different," *African American Review* 27(1):67–77, Sprg. 1993

FREED, DONALD

Spoo, R. "An Interview with Donald Freed," *James Joyce Quarterly* 28(1):71–9, Fall 1990

FRIEDMAN, BRUCE JAY

Friedman, B. J. "The Man They Threw Out of Jets," *Antioch Review* 50(1–2):132, Wntr/Sprg. 1992

FULLER, CHARLES

Carter, S. R. "The Detective as Solution: Charles Fuller's *A Soldier's Play*," *Clues* 12(1):33–42, Sprg/Summ. 1991
Kunz, D. "Singing the Blues in *A Soldier's Story*," *Literature-Film Quarterly* 19(1):27, Jan. 1991
Storhoff, G. P. "Reflections of Identity in *A Soldier's Story*," *Literature-Film Quarterly* 19(1):21, Jan. 1991

FULLER, ELIZABETH

Zinman, T. S. "Uncommonly Compact," *American Theatre* 9(7):13, Nov. 1992

SEE ALSO BISHOP, CONRAD, and ELIZABETH FULLER

FURTH, GEORGE, and STEPHEN SONDHEIM

Company (musical version of some short plays by Furth), 1970
  Filichia, P. "Everybody Rise," *TheaterWeek* 5(17):16, 2 Dec. 1991

GALATI, FRANK

Earthly Possessions (adaptation of Anne Tyler's work), 1991
  Simonson, R. *TheaterWeek* 5(6):36, 16 Sep. 1991

GANZ, LOWELL. *SEE* MARSHALL, GARRY, and LOWELL GANZ

GARDNER, HERB

Filichia, P. "Stagestruck: Conversation with the Playwright," *TheaterWeek* 6(7):16–17, 21 Sep. 1992

Conversations with My Father, 1990
   Dwyer, V. *Maclean's* 105(20):56–57, 18 May 1992
   Gardner, H. "Conversations," in J. Beard, ed. *The Best Men's Stage Monologues of 1993*
   Gerard, J. *Variety* 346(11):84, 30 Mar. 1992
   Kanfer, S. *Time* 139(15):70, 13 Apr. 1992
   Kramer, M. *New Yorker* 68(8):82, 13 Apr. 1992
   Kroll, J. *Newsweek* 119(15):68, 13 Apr. 1992
   Richards, D. *New York Times* 141:H5(N), 12 Apr. 1992
   Simon, J. *New York* 25(15):70, 13 Apr. 1992
   Snow, L. "Conversations with Judd Hirsch," *TheaterWeek* 5(33):17–19, 23 Mar. 1992
   Wetzsteon, R. "Ghost Story," *New York* 25(13):50, 30 Mar. 1992
   Wolf, W. "Conversations with Herb Gardner," *Playbill* 10(7):54, 30 Apr. 1992

I'm Not Rappaport, 1985
   Terry, P. S. *Shared Comedic Elements of Three Plays in Modern American Theater: Six Degrees of Separation, I'm Not Rappaport, and Broadway Bound.* M.A. Thesis; U of Nevada, Las Vegas, 1992

GARIN, MICHAEL. *SEE* FRANDSEN, ERIK, MICHAEL GARIN, ROBERT HIPKINS, and PAULA LOCKHEART

GARLAND, HAMLIN

Bovey, S., and G. Scharnhorst. "Hamlin Garland's First Published Essay," *ANQ* 5(1):20, Jan. 1992
Newlin, K. "Melodramatic Naturalism: London, Garland, Dreiser, and the Campaign to Reform the American Theater," (#DA9203442; Indiana U) *DAI* 52(8):2925A, Feb. 1992
———. "Melodramatist of the Middle Border: Hamlin Garland's Early Work Reconsidered," *Studies in American Fiction* 21(2):153–69, Autm. 1993
Wolter, J. C. *The Dawning of American Drama: American Dramatic Criticism 1746–1915.* 469–70

GARRETT-GROAG, LILLIAN

The White Rose, 1991
   Garrett-Groag, L. *The White Rose*
   Gerard, J. *Variety* 345(4):66, 4 Nov. 1991
   Simon, J. *New York* 24(44):120, 11 Nov. 1991

GELBART, LARRY

Bowman, D. "A Little Hyperkinetic Above the Eyebrows," *Performing Arts* 25(7):21, 1 Jul. 1991
Collins, G. "Neil Simon Opens a Door to the Past and Finds a Roomful of Vying Jokesters," *New York Times* 143:H5, 21 Nov. 1993

GELBART, LARRY, CY COLEMAN, and DAVID ZIPPEL

City of Angels (originally titled *Death Is for Suckers* and *Double Exposure*), 1989
    Harry, L. *Philadelphia Magazine* 83(11):17, Nov. 1992
    Lochte, D. *Los Angeles Magazine* 36(7):120–22, Jul. 1991
    Wolf, M. *Variety* 350(11):82, 12 Apr. 1993

GERSHWIN, GEORGE. *SEE* KAUFMAN, GEORGE S., MORRIE RYSKIND, GEORGE GERSHWIN, and IRA GERSHWIN

SEE ALSO LUDWIG, KEN, GEORGE GERSHWIN, and IRA GERSHWIN

GERSHWIN, IRA. *SEE* KAUFMAN, GEORGE S., MORRIE RYSKIND, GEORGE GERSHWIN, and IRA GERSHWIN

SEE ALSO LUDWIG, KEN, GEORGE GERSHWIN, and IRA GERSHWIN

GERSTENBERG, ALICE

Hecht, S. J. "The Plays of Alice Gerstenberg: Cultural Hegemony in the American Little Theatre," *Journal of Popular Culture* 26(1):1–16, Summ. 1992

GIBBONS, LEWIS GRASSIC

A Scots Quair, 1993
    Stevenson, R. *TLS* (4717):18, 27 Aug. 1993

GIBBONS, TOM

6221:Prophecy and Tragedy, 1993
    Hammer, K. "This Is the House," *American Theatre* 10(10):10, Oct. 1993
    Weales, G. *Commonweal* 120(9):19–20, 7 May 1993
    Zinman, T. S. *Variety* 353(1):30, 8 Nov. 1993

GILBERT, SKY

"Towards a Director-Centered Theatre," *Canadian Theatre Review* (76):59, Fall 1993

GILBERT, WILLIE. *SEE* BURROWS, ABE, JACK WEINSTOCK, WILLIE
GILBERT, and FRANK LOESSER

GILLETTE, WILLIAM

Gill, B. "Gillette Castle: An Actor's Folly on a Connecticut Hilltop," *Architectural Digest* 50(11):32, Nov. 1993

GILROY, FRANK D.

Any Given Day, 1993
> Brantley, B. *New York Times* 143:B3(N), 17 Nov. 1993
> Clarke, E. *New York* 26(36):46–47, 13 Sep. 1993
> Collins, G. "New Test of Broadway Alliance Arrives with *Any Given Day*," *New York Times* 143:B1(N), 16 Nov. 1993
> Gerard, J. *Variety* 353(4):32, 29, Nov. 1993
> Henry, W. A., III. *Time* 142(25):82, 13 Dec. 1993
> Simon, J. *New York* 26(47):80–81, 29 Nov. 1993

The Subject Was Roses, 1964
> Buckley, M. "The Subject Is Dempsey," *TheaterWeek* 4(45):26–27, 10 Jun. 1991
> Rothstein, M. "The 'Roses' Man," *New York Times* 140:H7, 2 Jun. 1991
> Simonson, R. *TheaterWeek* 4(47):41, 1 Jul. 1991

GINSBERG, ALLEN, AND PHILIP GLASS

Hydrogen Jukebox, 1990
> Tallmer, J. "The Fall of America, Part II," *TheaterWeek* 4(40):3–27, 13 May 1991

GLASPELL, SUSAN KEATING

Bzowski, F. D. *American Women Playwrights, 1900–1930: A Checklist*. 149
Carroll, K. L. "Centering Women Onstage: Susan Glaspell's Dialogic Strategy of Resistance," (#DA9121323; U of Maryland, College Park) *DAI* 52(3):914A, Sep. 1991
Corey, A. S. "Susan Glaspell, Playwright of Social Consciousness," (#DA9113087; New York U) *DAI* 51(12):4119A, Jun. 1991
Ferguson, M. A. *Images of Women in Literature*
Heller, A., and L. Rudnick, directors. *Beginnings*. Videocassette
————. *1915, The Cultural Moment: The New Politics, the New Woman, the New Psychology, the New Art & the New Theatre in America*
Makowsky, V. *Susan Glaspell's Century of American Women: A Critical Interpretation of Her Work*
Papke, M. E. *Susan Glaspell: A Research and Production Sourcebook*
Rabkin, E. S. *Lifted Masks and Other Works*

Trifles, 1916
>Ben-Zvi, L. ''Murder, She Wrote: The Genesis of Susan Glaspell's *Trifles*,'' *Theatre Journal* 44(2):141–62, May 1992
>Brodkin, S. Z. *Seven Plays of Mystery & Suspense*

The Verge, 1921
>Bach, G., and C. Harris. *The Verge*, *Theatre Journal* 44(1):94–96, Mar. 1992
>Diederich, L. *I or We?: Susan Glaspell's The Verge and Ethical Theory.* M.A. Thesis; U of South Carolina, 1992

GLASS, PHILIP

Charlotte, S. *Creativity: Conversations with 28 Who Excel*
Frandsen, P. J. ''Philip Glass's *Akhnaten*,'' *Musical Quarterly* 77:241–67, Summ. 1993
Harris, J. ''The Secret of Surviving Bad Art,'' *Christopher Street* (192):4, 23 Nov. 1992
Loney, G. ''Beyond the Broadway Musical: Crossovers, Confusions and Crisis,'' 151–76 in B. King, ed. *Contemporary American Theatre*
Pearce, M. ''Don't Tell Mother,'' *American Theatre* 10(9):11, Sep. 1993

GLASS, PHILIP, and DAVID HWANG

Loney, G. ''Playwrights at the Met,'' *New Theatre Quarterly* 9(36):392, Nov. 1993
Marx, R. ''Hwang's World,'' *Opera News* 57(4):14, Oct. 1992

The Voyage, 1992
>Clark, R. S. *Hudson Review* 46:201–03, Sprg. 1993
>Croyden, M. ''To Boldly Go Where No Team Has Gone Before,'' *Theater-Week* 9(11):24–26, 19 Oct. 1992

GLASS, PHILIP, DAVID GORDON, and RED GROOM

The Mysteries, 1992
>Bell, J. *TheaterWeek* 6(22):12, 4 Jan. 1993

SEE ALSO GINSBERG, ALLEN, and PHILIP GLASS

SEE ALSO WILSON, ROBERT, and PHILIP GLASS

GLAZER, BENJAMIN F. *SEE* HAMMERSTEIN, OSCAR, II, BENJAMIN F. GLAZER, and RICHARD RODGERS

GLINES, JOHN

Body and Soul, 1991
　　Anderson, P. *TheaterWeek* 5(13):12, 4 Nov. 1991

GOETZ, RUTH

Hamburger, P. "On the Whole," *New Yorker* 69(3):35, 8 Mar. 1993

GOMEZ, MARGA

Memory Tricks, 1992
　　Evans, G. *Variety* 350(13):74–75, 26 Apr. 1993
　　Gussow, M. *New York Times* 142:C19(L), 16 Apr. 1993
　　Lahr, J. *New Yorker* 69(10):113, 26 Apr. 1993
　　Weiss, P. "Going Solo," *Vogue* 183(4):242–44, Apr. 1993

GÓMEZ-PEÑA, GUILLERMO

"Crossing All Borders," *Americas* 44(6):4, Nov/Dec. 1992
"Guillermo Gómez-Peña," *Mime Journal* 91/92:42, 1991
Thompson, M. "Interview: Guillermo Gómez-Peña/Keith Antar Mason," *Art Papers* 17(1):3, 1 Jan. 1993
Wei, L., et. al. "On Nationality: 13 Artists," *Art in America* 79(9):124, Sep. 1991
Weiss, J. "An Interview with Guillermo Gómez-Peña," *Latin American Literature and Arts* (45):8–13, 1 Jul. 1991

Border Brujo, 1990
　　"A Binational Performance Pilgrimage," *TDR* 35:22–45, Fall 1991
　　"Border Brujo," *TDR* 35:48–66, Fall, 1991
　　Fusco, C. "Introduction to Border Brujo," *TDR* 35:46–7, Fall 1991

New World Order/El Nuevo Order Mundial, 1993
　　Moy, J. S. *Theatre Journal* 45:378–79, Oct. 1993

1991-A Performance Chronicle, 1991
　　Bell, J. *TheaterWeek* 5(14):12, 11 Nov. 1991

GONZALEZ, REUBEN

Weber, B. "Life in *The Boiler Room*," *New York Times* 142:B4, 29 Jan. 1993

GOODMAN, ALICE, and JOHN ADAMS

The Death of Klinghoffer, 1991
　　Kennicott, P. *Dance Magazine* 65(12):91–92, Dec. 1991
　　Leslie, G. *TheaterWeek* 5(8):32–33, 30 Sep. 1991

Lipman, S. "The Second Death of Leon Klinghoffer," *Commentary* 92(5):46–49, Nov. 1991

Porter, A. *New Yorker* 67(32):82–84, 30 Sep. 1991

Said, E. W. *Nation* 253(16):597–99, 11 Nov. 1991

Smith, P. J. "The Birth of Klinghoffer," *Opera News* 55:21–2, 16 Mar. 1991

GOODMAN, PAUL

Kirby, K. M. "The Personal and the Political: Rearticulating the Difference," *New Orleans Review* 19(2):9–17, Summ. 1992

Smith, J. "Allan Bloom, Mike Rose, and Paul Goodman: In Search of a Lost Pedagogical Synthesis," *College English* 55(7):721, Nov. 1993

Stoehr, T. "Growing Up Absurd—Again: Rereading Paul Goodman in the Nineties," *Dissent* 37(4):486, Fall 1990

GORDON, CHARLES. *SEE* OYAMO

GORDON, DAVID

The Mysteries and What's So Funny?, 1991

Gussow, M. *New York Times* 142:C3(L), 18 Dec. 1992

Hering, D. *Dance Magazine* 67(3):91–92, Mar. 1993

Holbrook, C. *TheaterWeek* 4(51):34, 29 Jul. 1991

Tobias, T. *New York* 26(1):53, 4 Jan. 1993

SEE ALSO GLASS, PHILIP, DAVID GORDON, and RED GROOM

GOTANDA, PHILIP KAN

"Race and Relationships," [Panel Discussion], *American Theatre* 9(5):24, Sep. 1992

GOULD, ELLEN

Bubbes, 1992

Ungaro, J. *TheaterWeek* 6(17):31, 30 Nov. 1992

GRACZYK, ED

Come Back to the 5 and Dime, Jimmy Dean, Jimmy Dean, 1982

Filichia, P. *TheaterWeek* 5(9):13, 7 Oct. 1991

GRAFF, TODD

"Graff, Kazdin 'Woke Up' at Caravan," *Variety* 353(8):32, 27 Dec. 1993

GRAHAM, BARBARA

Camp Paradox, 1992

Evans, G. *Variety* 349(3):70, 9 Nov. 1992

Gussow, M. *New York Times* 142:C14(L), 9 Nov. 1992
Simon, J. *New York* 25(45):97–98, 16 Nov. 1992
Ungaro, J. *TheaterWeek* 6(17):31, 30 Nov. 1992

GRAHAM, SHIRLEY

Tom-Tom, 1932
"Shirley Graham," 231–286 in L. Hamalian and J. V. Hatch, eds. *The Roots of African American Drama*

GRAHN, JUDY

Donnelly, N. "An Uncommon Woman," *Advocate* (643):56, 30 Nov. 1993
"Isn't It Grahn," *Advocate* (643):56, 30 Nov. 1993

GRANGER, PERCY

The Dolphin Position, 1992
Gussow, M. *New York Times* 142:C3(L), 9 Oct. 1992
Simonson, R. *TheaterWeek* 6(21):32, 28 Dec. 1992

GRANT, BEN Z. *SEE* KING, LARRY, and BEN Z. GRANT

GRAY, SPALDING

Georgakas, D., and R. Porton. "The Art of Autobiography: An Interview with Spalding Gray," *Cineaste* 19(4):34, 1993
Goldman, J. "Dancing with the Audience," *Dramatics* 63(3):24, 1 Nov. 1991
"Inside Culture," *Harper's Bazaar* (3365):46, 1 May 1992
Johnson, B. D. "The Talking Cure: A Performer Bases His Career on Confession," *Maclean's* 105(28):44, 13 Jul. 1992
Kauffmann, S. "On Films: Gray Power," *New Republic* 207(2):26, 13 Jul. 1992
Rasminsky, S. "From 52nd Street to Virginia Avenue," *American Theatre* 10(9): 56, Sep. 1993
Richards, D. "Secret Sharers: Solo Acts in a Confessional Age," *New York Times* 140:H1, 14 Apr. 1991
Weber, B. "Spalding Gray's Life, as Based on a True Story," *New York Times* 143:B2, 9 Dec. 1993
Wilder, J. B. "Under the Psychic Knife," *American Theatre* 10(9):10, Sep. 1993

Swimming to Cambodia, 1984
Prinz, J. "Spalding Gray's *Swimming to Cambodia*: A Performance Gesture," 156–68 in P. D. Murphy, ed. *Staging the Impossible: The Fantastic Mode in Modern Drama*

GREEN, ADOLPH. *SEE* COMDEN, BETTY, and ADOLPH GREEN

SEE ALSO COMDEN, BETTY, ADOLPH GREEN, and JULE STYNE

SEE ALSO COMDEN, BETTY, ADOLPH GREEN, JULE STYNE, MOOSE CHARLAP, and CAROLYN LEE

GREEN, PAUL

Sanders, L. M. "The People Who Seem to Matter Most to Me: Folklore as an Agent of Social Change in the Work of Howard W. Odum and Paul Green," *Southern Literary Journal* 24(2):62–75, Sprg. 1992

GREENBERG, ALBERT

The Fatherless Sky, 1993
    Mackey, H. "Rich and Smart?" *American Theatre* 10(11):9, Nov. 1993

GREENBERG, RICHARD

Karam, E. "Richard Greenberg: Now He's Pals with Joey," *American Theatre* 9(9):29, Jan. 1993

The Author's Voice, 1991
    Holbrook, C. *TheaterWeek* 5(4):42, 2 Sep. 1991

Life Under Water, 1991
    Greenberg, R. *"Life Under Water,"* *Antaeus* 66:92–114, Sprg. 1991

GREENSPAN, DAVID

Robinson, M. "Four Writers," *Theater* 24(1):31, Wntr. 1993
Witchel, A. "4 Directors to Stay," *New York Times* 140:B4, 26 Apr. 1991

Dead Mother or Shirley Not All in Vain, 1991
    Leslie, G. *TheaterWeek* 4(27):34–35, 11 Feb. 1991

GREIF, MICHAEL

What the Butler Saw, 1992
    Marowitz, C. *TheaterWeek* 6(4):31, 31 Aug. 1992

GRIFFIN, SUSAN

Rhoads, H. "The Deadly Denial: An Interview with Feminist Susan Griffin," *On the Issues* 2(3):44, Summ. 1993

GRIFFITHS, ROBERT

Souls, 1993
    Hughes, L. *TLS* (4689):19, 12 Feb. 1993

GRIMKÉ, ANGELINA WELD

Smith, J. C. *Epic Lives: One Hundred Black Women Who Made a Difference*

Rachel, 1920
>   Anderson, A. A. *Theatre Journal* 43:385–6, Oct. 1991
>   Storm, W. "Reactions of a 'Highly-Strung Girl': Psychology and Dramatic Representation in Angelina W. Grimké's *Rachel*," *African American Review* 27(3):461–71, Fall, 1993
>   Young, P. "Shackled: Angelina Weld Grimké," *Women and Language* 15(2):25–31, Fall 1992

GROOM, RED. *SEE* GLASS, PHILIP, DAVID GORDON, and RED GROOM

GUARE, JOHN

Carroll, D. "Not-Quite Mainstream Male Playwrights: Guare, Durang, and Rabe," 41–61 in B. King, ed. *Contemporary American Theatre*

Cattaneo, A. "John Guare: The Art of Theatre IX," *Paris Review* 34(125):68–103, Wntr. 1992

Collins, G. "Damages Are Denied Again in 'Six Degrees' Lawsuit." *New York Times* 142:B4, 19 Jul. 1993

"Conversation with John Guare," *Dramatists Guild Quarterly* 28(4):6, Wntr. 1992

Grimes, W. "Court Ruling in 'Six Degrees' Suit," *New York Times* 141:B5, 30 Apr. 1992

Gussow, M. "John Guare Loves New York, One Step at a Time," *New York Times* 142:B6, 20 May 1993

Kasindorf, J. "Six Degrees of Impersonation," *New York* 24(12):40, 25 Mar. 1991

Kroll, J. "Broadway Unbound," *Newsweek* 119(7):60, 17 Feb. 1992

Reif, R. "To Fake It Well on the Set, It Pays to Be Genuine," *New York Times* 142:H26, 16 May 1993

Short, R. "John Guare Reveals His Sources," *Mirabella* 3(1):52, 1 Jun. 1991

Steinberg, J. "Jury Acquits Man of One Count in the Harassment of Playwright," *New York Times* 142:B3, 2 Oct. 1992

Story, R. D. "Six Degrees of Preparation," *New York* 26(23):38, 7 Jun. 1993

Four Baboons Adoring the Sun, 1991
>   Brustein, R. *New Republic* 206(19):32, 11 May 1992
>   Disch, T. M. *Nation* 254(15):535–536, 20 Apr. 1992
>   Friend, T. "The Guare Facts," *Vogue* 182(3):326–30, Mar. 1992
>   Gerard, J. *Variety* 346(10):112, 23 Mar. 1992
>   Guare, J. "Four Baboons Adoring the Sun," *Antaeus* 66:115–40, Sprg. 1991
>   Hornby, R. *Hudson Review* 45:296–8, Summ. 1992
>   Kanfer, S. *New Leader* 75(4):21, 23 Mar. 1992
>   Kroll, J. *Newsweek* 119(13):65, 30 Mar. 1992
>   Oliver, E. *New Yorker* 68(6):69, 30 Mar. 1992
>   Raymond, G. "Peter Hall's *Baboons*: The British Director Stages John Guare's New Play," *TheaterWeek* 5(31):32–34, 9 Mar. 1992

Riedel, M. *TheaterWeek* 4(48):6, 8 Jul. 1991
Simon, J. *New York* 25(13):87, 30 Mar. 1992
Weales, G. *Commonweal* 119(9):21, 8 May 1992

Six Degrees of Separation, 1990
Campbell, J. *TLS* (4656):19, 26 Jun. 1992
Gussow, M. *"Six Degrees, Rogers* Win Critics Awards," *New York Times* 140:B3, 14 May 1991
Lavender, A. *New Statesman & Society* 5(208):32, 26 Jun. 1992
Terry, P. S. *Shared Comedic Elements of Three Plays in Modern American Theater: Six Degrees of Separation, I'm Not Rappaport, and Broadway Bound.* M.A. Thesis; U of Nevada, Las Vegas, 1992
Weales, G. *Commonweal* 118(1):17, 11 Jan. 1991

GUNN, BILL

Diawara, M., and P. R. Klotman. "Ganja and Hess: Vampires, Sex, and Addictions," *Black American Literature Forum* 25(2):299, Summ. 1991
Williams, J. "Bill Gunn (1929–1989): A Checklist of His Films, Dramatic Works and Novels," *Black American Literature Forum* 25(4):781, Wntr. 1991

GURNEY, A. R.

Gurney, A. R. "The Problem," *Antaeus* 66:141–52, Sprg. 1991
Raymond, G. "Born to Cause Trouble: A. R. Gurney, the Paradox," *Performing Arts* 26(3):15, 1 Mar. 1992
Richards, D. "Good Breeding Can Be the Death of You," *New York Times* 142:H5, 30 May 1993
"Theater: A. R. Gurney's Males Are Out of Step in *The Snow Ball*," *Time* 138(16):93, 21 Oct. 1991
Williams, A. "Gurney Cuts Loose—Sort Of," *American Theatre* 10(10):12–14, Oct. 1993

The Cocktail Hour, 1988
Backalenick, I. "Letter from the Berkshires," *TheaterWeek* 6(4):32, 31 Aug. 1992

The Fourth Wall, 1992
Filichia, P. *TheaterWeek* 6(9):11, 5 Oct. 1992
Lazare, L. *Variety* 350(13):75, 26 Apr. 1993
Taylor, M. *Variety* 348(5):69, 24 Aug. 1992

Later Life, 1993
Barbour, D. *TCI* 27(9):11, Nov. 1993
Evans, G. "Closings Crowd Off B'Way," *Variety* 353(6):83–84, 13 Dec. 1993
Gerard, J. *Variety* 351(5):50, 7 Jun. 1993
Greene, A. *TheaterWeek* 6(46):35, 21 Jun. 1993
Henry, W. A., III. *Time* 141(24):75, 14 Jun. 1993

Horwitz, S. "A. R. Gurney's Later Life," *TheaterWeek* 7(2):18–22, 16 Aug. 1993
Kanfer, S. *New Leader* 76(11):23, 6 Sep. 1993
Kirkpatrick, M. *Wall Street Journal* A8(E), 28 May 1993
Oliver, E. *New Yorker* 69(17):98, 14 Jun. 1993
Rich, F. *New York Times* 142:C11(L), 24 May 1993
———. *New York Times* 142:C16(L), 13 Sep. 1993
Richards, D. "Good Breeding Can Be the Death of You," *New York Times* 142:H5(N), 30 May 1993
Simon, J. *New York* 26(23):62, 7 Jun.1993

HABER, ROBERT. *SEE* WRANGLER, JACK, HAL HACKADY, and ROBERT HABER

HACKADY, HAL. *SEE* WRANGLER, JACK, HAL HACKADY, and ROBERT HABER

HAGEDORN, JESSICA

Evangelista, S. "Jessica Hagedorn and Manila Magic," *Melus* 18(4):41, Wntr. 1993

HAILEY, OLIVER

Faison, S. "Oliver Hailey, 60, Author of Plays and Scripts," [obituary] *New York Times* 142:34, 23 Jan. 1993

HALL, ADRIAN

Woods, J. M. *Theatre to Change Men's Souls: The Artistry of Adrian Hall*

HAMILTON, WILLIAM

Interior Decoration, 1992
    Marowitz, C. *TheaterWeek* 6(4):29–30, 31 Aug. 1992
    Time 140(5):75, 8 Aug. 1992

HAMLISCH, MARVIN

"Sequel," *People Weekly* 38(15):89, 12 Oct. 1992

SEE ALSO SIMON, NEIL, MARVIN HAMLISCH, and DAVID ZIPPEL

HAMMERSTEIN, OSCAR, II

Hamburger, P. "Cameo: Happy Talk," *New Yorker* 69(15):76, 31 May 1993

HAMMERSTEIN, OSCAR, II, BENJAMIN F. GLAZER, and RICHARD RODGERS

Carousel (musical version of F. Molnar's *Liliom*), 1945
Brustein, R. *New Republic* 208(9):26, 1 Mar. 1993
Lahr, J. *New Yorker* 68(48):100, 18 Jan. 1993
Levy, P. *Wall Street Journal* A9(W), 28 Dec. 1992
Mordden, E. "A *Carousel* for All Seasons," *New York Times* 142:H5, 12 Sep. 1993
Pitman, J. "*Carousel* Spins to Life," *Variety* 348(3):61, 10 Aug. 1992
Rich, F. *New York Times* 142:B1, 17 Dec. 1992
Traubner, R. *American Record Guide* 56(2):25, Mar/Apr. 1993
———. *Opera News* 57(12):40, 27 Feb. 1993
Weber, B. "Looking for the Brass Ring," *New York Times* 142:B4, 25 Dec. 1992
———. "Royal Encounters, on the Stage and in Real Life," *New York Times* 143:C17, 7 Oct. 1993
Wolf, M. *Variety* 349(8):54, 14 Dec. 1992

HAMMERSTEIN, OSCAR, II, and JEROME KERN

Show Boat (musical version of E. Ferber's novel), 1927
Murray, K. "Cries of Racism Flood *Show Boat* Opening," *Variety* 352(10):61, 18 Oct. 1993

HAMMERSTEIN, OSCAR, II, JOSHUA LOGAN, and RICHARD RODGERS

South Pacific (musical version of J. A. Michener's *Tales of the South Pacific*), 1949
Beidler, P. D. "*South Pacific* and American Remembering; or, 'Josh, We're Going to Buy This Son of a Bitch!' " *Journal of American Studies* 27(2):207–22, Aug. 1993

HAMMERSTEIN, OSCAR, II, and RICHARD RODGERS

Fields, A., and L. M. Fields. *From the Bowery to Broadway: Lew Fields and the Roots of American Popular Theater.* 102, 119+
Fox, M. "Oh, What a Beautiful Anni," *Variety* 350(9):93, 29 Mar. 1993
Holden, S. "Their Songs Were America's Happy Talk," *New York Times* 142:H1, 24 Jan. 1993
Kellow, B. "Growing Up with Rodgers and Hammerstein," *Opera News* 58(1):20, Jul. 1993

Flower Drum Song
Tynan, K. "Critics' Round Table," *New Yorker* 69(15):118, 31 May 1993

Oklahoma! (musical version of L. Rigg's play *Green Grow the Lilacs*), 1943
Evans, L. J. "Rodgers and Hammerstein's 'Oklahoma!': The Development of the 'Integrated' Musical," (#DA9033934; U of California, Los Angeles) *DAI* 51(8):2567A, Feb. 1991
Hunt, G. W. "Of Many Things," *America* 168(8):2, 6 Mar. 1993

Pipe Dream
   Filichia, P. "A Lopsided Bust," *TheaterWeek* 5(13):13, 4 Nov. 1991

HAMPTON, CHRISTOPHER

Les Liasons Dangereuses, 1991
   Bethune, R. W. *Theatre Journal* 43:524–5, Dec. 1991
   Carson, K. "*Les Liasons Dangereuses* on Stage and Film," *Literature/Film Quarterly* 19(1):41–50, 1991
   Hall, C. "Valmont Redux: The Fortunes and Filmed Adaptations of *Les Liasons Dangereuses* by Cholderlos de Lacios," *Literature/Film Quarterly* 19(1):41–50, 1991

Tales from Hollywood, 1982
   Gussow, M. *New York Times* 142:C14(L), 18 Jan. 1993
   Simon, J. *New York* 26(4):70, 25 Jan. 1993
   Ungaro, J. *TheaterWeek* 6(26):27, 1 Feb. 1993

HANDLER, EVAN

Collins, G. "Actor's Recovery Inspires Comedy and Tragedy," *New York Times* 142:B3(N), 12 May 1993

Time on Fire, 1993
   Evans, G. *Variety* 351(5):50–51, 7 Jun. 1993
   Greene, A. *TheaterWeek* 6(45):37–38, 14 Jun. 1993
   Gussow, M. *New York Times* 142:C3(L), 14 May 1993

HANSBERRY, LORRAINE

Giovanni, N. "Sisters, Too: Great Women in African-American History," *Black Collegian* 22(3):60, Jan/Feb. 1992
McKelly, J. C. "Hymns of Sedition: Portraits of the Artist in Contemporary African-American Drama," *Arizona Quarterly* 48(1):87–107, Sprg. 1992
Shannon, S. G. "From Lorraine Hansberry to August Wilson: An Interview with Lloyd Richards," *Callaloo* 14(1):124–35, Wntr. 1991
Shatzky, J. "Lorraine Hansberry and the American Theater," *Jewish Currents* 46(6):26, 1 Jun. 1992
Shinn, T. J. "Living the Answer: The Emergence of African American Feminist Drama," *Studies in the Humanities* 17(2):149–59, Dec. 1990
Smith, J. C. *Epic Lives: One Hundred Black Women Who Made a Difference*
Stubbs, M. F. "Lorraine Hansberry and Lillian Hellman: A Comparison of Social and Political Issues in Their Plays and Screen Adaptations," (#DA9109762; Indiana U) *DAI* 51(11):3759A, May 1991

Les Blancs, 1970
   Gruesser, J. "Lies That Kill: Lorraine Hansberry's Answer to *Heart of Darkness* in *Les Blancs*," *American Drama* 1(2):1–14 Sprg. 1992

A Raisin in the Sun, 1959
    Cooper, D. D. "Hansberry's *A Raisin in the Sun*," *Explicator* 52(1):59, Fall 1993
    Lewis, K. *The Search for Personal Dignity in Three Modern American Dramas*. M.A. Thesis; Florida State U, 1991
    Tynan, K. "Critics' Round Table," *New Yorker* 69(15):118, 31 May 1993

HARNICK, SHELDON

Charlotte, S. *Creativity: Conversations with 28 Who Excel*

HARNICK, SHELDON, and JOE RAPOSO

It's a Wonderful Life (adaptation of Frank Capra's work), 1991
    Filichia, P. *TheaterWeek* 5(24):9, 20 Jan. 1992
    Harris, P. *Variety* 345(13):74, 13 Jan. 1992

SEE ALSO MASTEROFF, JOE, SHELDON HARNICK, and JERRY BOCK

SEE ALSO STEIN, JOSEPH, JERRY BOCK, and SHELDON HARNICK

HARPS, SAMUEL B.

Don't Explain, 1991
    Bell, J. *TheaterWeek* 4(23):33, 14 Jan. 1991

HARRIGAN, EDWARD

Dormon, J. H. "Ethnic Cultures of the Mind: The Harrigan-Hart Mosaic," *American Studies* 33(2):21–40, Fall 1992
Flynn, J. "Sites and Sights: The Iconology of the Subterranean in Late Nineteenth-Century Irish-American Drama," *MELUS* 18(1):5, Sprg. 1993
Koger, A. "An Edward Harrigan Bibliography," *Nineteenth Century Theatre* 19(1):29–44, Summ. 1991
    ———. "An Edward Harrigan Bibliography, Part II," *Nineteenth Century Theatre* 19(2):105, Wntr. 1991

HARRIS, WALTER MICHAEL

Hibiscus (a musical biography of George Harris III), 1992
    Bell, J. *TheaterWeek* 5(41):16, 18 May 1992

HARRISON, TONY

Square Rounds, 1992
    Lapenta, D. *Theatre Journal* 45:380–1, Oct. 1993

Lavender, A. *New Statesman & Society* 5(223):30–31, 9 Oct. 1992
Schulman, G. *Nation* 256(1):29, 4 Jan. 1993

The Trackers of Oxyrhynchus, 1991
  Chansky, D. *Theatre Journal* 43:523–4, Dec. 1991

HARWOOD, RONALD

Poison Pen, 1993
  Lindop, G. *TLS* (4705):19, 4 Jun. 1993

Reflected Glory, 1992
  Pitman, J. *Variety* 350(3):91, 15 Feb. 1993 "Stage Struck," *Plays and Players* (457):24, 1 Apr. 1992

HEELAN, KEVIN

Distant Fires, 1986
  Freedman, S. G. "Racial Clashes Push *Distant Fires* Closer to Home," *New York Times* 141:H5, 26 Jul. 1992
  Gussow, M. *New York Times* 141:C2(L), 28 Aug. 1992
  Heelan, K. "*Distant Fires*," in J. Beard, ed. *The Best Men's Stage Monologues of 1993*
  Osborn, M. E. "Culture Clash," *TheaterWeek* 6(2):19–22, 17 Aug. 1992
  Simon, J. *New York* 25(35):53, 7 Sep. 1992
  Simonson, R. *TheaterWeek* 5(13):40, 4 Nov. 1991

The Hope Zone, 1993
  "Help Yourself," *American Theatre* 9(10):10, Feb. 1993
  Marx, B. "Letter from New England," *TheaterWeek* 6(36):30–31, 12 Apr. 1993
  Taylor, M. *Variety* 350(3):91, 15 Feb. 1993

HEIFNER, JACK

Bargains, 1993
  Braunagel, D. *Variety* 347(1):53, 20 Apr. 1992
  Evans, G. *Variety* 350(4):231, 22 Feb. 1993
  Greene, A. *TheaterWeek* 6(31):35, 8 Mar. 1993
  Gussow, M. *New York Times* 142:C10(L), 19 Feb. 1993
  Richards, D. *New York Times* 142:H24(N), 21 Feb. 1993

HELLMAN, LILLIAN

Bailey, L. M. "Sex-Marked Language Differences: A Linquistic Analysis of Lexicon and Syntax in the Female and Male Dialogue in the Eight Original Plays of Lillian Hellman," (#DA9133271; Ball State U) *DAI* 52(6):2124A, Dec. 1991
Brown, L. G. "Toward a More Cohesive Self: Women in the Works of Lillian

Hellman and Marsha Norman,'' (#DA9201625; Ohio State U.) *DAI* 52(8):2919A, Feb. 1992

Diedrich, M. ''Shaken Out of the Magnolias—Lillian Hellman's Kriegsdramen,'' *Zeitschrift fur Anglistik und Amerikanistik* 39(2):134–48, 1991

Hartigan, P. ''Intruding on Lillian,'' *American Theatre* 10(7–8):10, Jul/Aug. 1993

Stubbs, M. F. ''Lorraine Hansberry and Lillian Hellman: A Comparison of Social and Political Issues in Their Plays and Screen Adaptations,'' (#DA9109762; Indiana U) *DAI* 51(11):3759A, May 1991

Titus, M. ''Murdering the Lesbian: Lillian Hellman's *The Children's Hour*,'' *Tulsa Studies in Women's Literature* 10(2):215, Fall 1991

Waites-Lamm, K. A. ''Lillian Hellman's *Maybe*: Autobiographical Revisioning,'' *Cea Critic* 55(1):39, Fall 1992

Westbrook, B. E. ''Lillian Hellman: Dramatist in Society,'' (#DA9137184; U of California, Davis) *DAI* 52(7):2558A, Jan. 1992

The Little Foxes, 1939
> Lenker, L. T. ''The Foxes in Hellman's Family Forest,'' 241–53 in S. M. Deats and L. T. Lenker, eds. *The Aching Hearth: Family Violence in Life and Literature*

HENLEY, BETH

Berkowitz, G. M. *American Drama of the Twentieth Century*. 198+

Kachur, B. ''Women Playwrights on Broadway: Henley, Howe, Norman, and Wasserstein,'' 15–40 in B. King, ed. *Contemporary American Theatre*

Kullman, C. H. ''Beth Henley's Marginalized Heroines,'' *Studies in American Drama 1945–Present*, 8(1):21–28, 1993

Shepard, A. C. ''Aborted Rage in Beth Henley's Women,'' *Modern Drama* 36(1):96–108, 1 Mar. 1993

Abundance, 1989
> Mason, W. ''The Wild West Meets the Wild East,'' *American Theatre* 10(10):122–24, Oct. 1993

Crimes of the Heart, 1979
> Haedicke, J. V. '' 'A Population [and Theater] at Risk': Battered Women in Henley's *Crimes of the Heart* and Shepard's *A Lie of the Mind*,'' *Modern Drama* 36(1):83, 1 Mar. 1993
>
> Lee, H. ''Female Bonding Through Recognition and Transformation: Beth Henley's *Crimes of the Heart*,'' *Journal of English Language and Literature* 37(3):719–36, Autm. 1991
>
> Thompson, L. ''Feeding the Hungry Heart: Food in Beth Henley's *Crimes of the Heart*,'' *Southern Quarterly* 30(2/3):99, Wntr. 1992

HERMAN, JERRY

''Inside Herman's Head,'' *Advocate* (632):82, 29 Jun. 1993

Provenzano, T. ''Hello, Jerry!'' *TheaterWeek* 6(47):14–18, 28 Jun. 1993

HIGHWAY, TOMSON

Dry Lips Oughta Move to Kapuskasing, 1989
> Honegger, G. "Native Playwright: Tomson Highway," *Theater* 23(1):88–92, Wntr. 1992

HILL, ABRAM

On Strivers Row, 1938
> "Abram Hill," 353–446 in L. Hamalian and J. V. Hatch, eds. *The Roots of African American Drama*

HIPKINS, ROBERT. *SEE* FRANDSEN, ERIK, MICHAEL GARIN, ROBERT HIPKINS, and PAULA LOCKHEART

HIRSON, DAVID

La Bête: A Comedy of Manners, 1990
> Brustein, R. "On Theater: In the Belly of *La Bête*," *New Republic* 204(11):33, 18 Mar. 1991
> Flatow, S. "*La Bête*: British Designer Richard Hudson Invades Broadway . . . ," *Theatre Crafts* 25(4):46–51, Apr. 1991
> Gerard, J. *Variety* 342(1):117, 14 Jan. 1991
> Gottfried, M. "Bête-r Than Thou," *TheaterWeek* 4(30):20–23, 4 Mar. 1991
> Holland, P. *TLS* (4637):21, 14 Feb. 1992
> Hornby, R. *Hudson Review* 44(2):291, Summ. 1991
> Kanfer, S. *New Leader* 74(3):23, 11 Feb. 1991
> "*La Bête*," *American Theatre* 8(3):32, 1 Jun. 1991
> Leslie, G. *TheaterWeek* 4(29):33, 25 Feb. 1991
> Pitman, J. *Variety* 346(6):259, 24 Feb. 1992
> Raymond, G. "(Bête)ing on Tom McGowan," *TheaterWeek* 4(28):16–20, 18 Feb. 1991
> Simon, J. *New York* 24(8):119, 25 Feb. 1991
> *Variety* 342(5):116, 11 Feb. 1991
> Weales, G. *Commonweal* 118(11):374, 1 Jun. 1991

HIXSON, LIN

Apple, J. "The Life and Times of Lin Hixson," *TDR* 35(4):27–45, Wntr. 1991
Jaremba, T. "Lin Hixson: An Interview," *TDR* 35(4):46–49, Wntr. 1991

HOFFMAN, WILLIAM M.

Loney, G. "Playwrights at the Met," *New Theatre Quarterly* 9(36):392, Nov. 1993
Mass, L. D. "John Corigliano and William M. Hoffman," *Opera Monthly* 4(7):5, 1 Nov. 1991
Ungaro, J. "Cino Days," *TheaterWeek* 5(13):12, 4 Nov. 1991

Van Ness, G. "Something Very Much Like Courage: The Agrarian Tradition and William Hoffman's *The Land That Drank the Rain*," *Shenandoah* 41(2):91, Summ. 1991

Wilson, L. "Ghost Writer," *Opera News* 56(8):16, 4 Jan. 1992

As Is, 1985
    Gross, G. D. "Coming Up for Air: Three AIDS Plays," *Journal of American Culture* 15(2):63, Summ. 1992
    Shatzky, J. "AIDS Enters the American Theater: *As Is* and *The Normal Heart*," 131–39 in E. S. Nelson, ed. *AIDS: The Literary Response*

HOLDEN, JOAN

Elstob, K. "Joan Holden and the San Francisco Mime Troupe Celebrate Radical Resistance to the Official Story," *CEA Critic* 55(1):59, Fall 1992

HOLLAND, ENDESHA IDA MAE

Horwitz, S. "From Prostitute to Playwright: The Life and Times of Dr. Endesha Ida Mae Holland," *TheaterWeek* 5(32):24–28, 16 Mar. 1992

McCourtie, C. "Reasoning with Dr. Endesha Ida Mae Holland, Playwright from the Mississippi Delta," *Crisis* 99(2):10, Feb. 1992

"Stage," *People Weekly* 36(21):201, 2 Dec. 1991

Whitaker, C. "Endesha Ida Mae Holland: From Prostitute to Playwright," *Ebony* 47(8):124, 1 Jun. 1992

Wilson, M. "Southern Rights," *TLS* (4007):S12, 16 Apr. 1993

From the Mississippi Delta, 1987
    Henry, W. A., III. *Time* 138(21):92, 25 Nov. 1991
    Spillane, M. *Nation* 253(1):29–30, 1 Jul. 1991
    Ungaro, J. *TheaterWeek* 5(18):34, 9 Dec. 1991
    Wilson, M. *TLS* (4007):12, 16 Apr. 1993

HOLLANDER, NICOLE, ARNOLD APRILL, TOM MULA, STEVE RASHID, and CHERI COONS

Sylvia's Real Good Advice (based on Hollander's *Sylvia*) 1991
    Chase, T. *TheaterWeek* 5(1):38, 12 Aug. 1991

HOLLINGSWORTH, MARGARET

"Collaborators," *Canadian Theatre Review* (69):15, Wntr. 1991

Knowles, R. P. "The Dramaturgy of the Perverse," *Theatre Research International* 17(3):226, Autm. 1992

HOLLOWAY, JONATHAN

Death in Venice, 1993
    Annan, G. *TLS* (4721):18, 24 Sep. 1993

HOLMES, RUPERT

The Mystery of Edwin Drood (title later changed to *Drood: The Musical Hall Mystery*; musical based on a novel by Charles Dickens), 1985
    Miller, E. *"The Mystery of Edwin Drood*: The Deconstructionist Musical of Rupert Holmes,'' *CLUES* 13(2):47–59, Fall/Wntr. 1992

Solitary Confinement, 1992
    Gerard, J. *Variety* 349(4):70, 16 Nov. 1992
    Gussow, M. *New York Times* 142:B1(N), 9 Nov. 1992
    Kanfer, S. *New Leader* 75(14):23, 2 Nov. 1992
    Oliver, E. *New Yorker* 68(40):130, 23 Nov. 1992
    Richards, D. *New York Times* 142:H5(N), 15 Nov. 1992
    Simon, J. *New York* 25(46):83, 23 Nov. 1992
    Simonson, R. *TheaterWeek* 6(18):34, 7 Dec. 1992
    Wilson, E. *Wall Street Journal* A12(W), 13 Nov. 1992

HOPKINS, PAULINE ELIZABETH

Peculiar Sam, or The Underground Railroad, 1879
    "Pauline Elizabeth Hopkins," 96–123 in L. Hamalian and J. V. Hatch, eds. *The Roots of African American Drama*

HOROVITZ, ISRAEL

Berkrot, P. "Israel Horovitz," *American Theatre* 9(6):39, Oct. 1992
Lazar, K. "Close-Up: Center Stage," *Runner's World* 27(11):40, 1 Nov. 1992
Taylor, M. "Horovitz Plight Prompts Policy," *Variety* 352(4):45, 6 Sep. 1993
———. "Playwright Denies Sex Harassment Claims," *Variety* 352(3):27, 30 Aug. 1993

Park Your Car in Harvard Yard, 1991
    Disch, T. M. *Nation* 254(2):66–68, 20 Jan. 1992
    Gerard, J. *Variety* 344(13):203, 7 Oct. 1991
    ———. *Variety* 345(5):58, 11 Nov. 1991
    Kanfer, S. *New Leader* 74(14):34, 30 Dec. 1991
    Oliver, E. *New Yorker* 67(39):126, 18 Nov. 1991

HOUSTON, DIANNE

The Fishermen, 1992
    "Jomandi Productions," *American Visions* 7(6):14, Dec/Jan. 1992

HOUSTON-JONES, ISHMAEL. *SEE* COOPER, DENNIS, ISHMAEL HOUSTON-JONES, and PETER BROSIUS

HOWE, TINA

Elder, S. "Who's Afraid of Tina Howe?" *Vogue* 183(2):106, 1 Feb. 1993
Horwitz, S. "The Playwright as Woman," *TheaterWeek* 5(3):22, 26 Aug. 1991

Johnston, K. E. "Tina Howe's Feminine Discourse," *American Drama* 1(2):15–25, Sprg. 1992
Kachur, B. "Women Playwrights on Broadway: Henley, Howe, Norman and Wasserstein," 15–40 in B. King, ed. *Contemporary American Theatre*
Lamont, R. C. "After Ionesco: The Surrealist Comedy of Tina Howe," *Theater-Week* 6(39):19–20, 3 May 1993
———. "Tina Howe's Secret Surrealism: Walking a Tightrope," *Modern Drama* 36(1):27–37, 1 Mar. 1993

Approaching Zanzibar, 1989
    Barlow, J. E. "The Road to Zanzibar," *TheaterWeek* 5(25):23–25, 27 Jan. 1992

Birth and Afterbirth
    Lamont, R. C., ed. *Women on the Verge: 7 Avant-Garde American Plays*

One Shoe Off, 1993
    Blaney, R. "Gone to Seed," *American Theatre* 10(5/6):8–9, May/Jun. 1993
    Gerard, J. *Variety* 350(12):53, 19 Apr. 1993
    Greene, A. *TheaterWeek* 6(39):27–28, 3 May 1993
    Oliver, E. *New Yorker* 69(11):99, 3 May 1993
    Rich, F. *New York Times* 142:B1, 16 Apr. 1993
    Simon, J. *New York* 26(18):82, 3 May 1993
    Time 141(17):71, 26 Apr. 1993

HUGHES, DUSTY

A Slip of the Tongue, 1992
    Lavender, A. *New Statesman & Society* 5(203):34, 22 May 1992
    Lazare, L. *Variety* 346(5):78, 17 Feb. 1992

HUGHES, HOLLY

Bowman, J. "Holly Hughes Turns Trash into Treasure," *New Mexico Magazine* 71(5):34, 1 May 1993
Carr, C. "No Trace of the Bland: An Interview with Holly Hughes," *Theater* 24(2):67, 1993
de Grazia, E. "Indecency Exposed," *Nation* 255(1):4, 6 Jul. 1992
Heins, M. "Portrait of a Much Abused Lady," *Index on Censorship* 22(1):9–10, Jan. 1993
Licata, E. "Let Us Now Praise Infamous Women," *Humanist* 51(3):15, 1 May 1991

Dress Suits to Hire, 1987
    Patraka, V. M. "Binary Terror and Feminist Performance: Reading Both Ways," *Discourse: Journal for Theoretical Studies in Media and Culture* 14(2):163–85, Sprg. 1992
    Raymond, G. *TheaterWeek* 5(6):41, 16 Sep. 1991

No Trace of the Blonde, 1993
   Walen, D. A. *Theatre Journal* 45(4):548, Dec. 1993

HUGHES, LANGSTON

Sanders, L. C. "Also Own the Theatre: Representation in the Comedies of Langston Hughes," *Langston Hughes Review* 11(1):6, Sprg. 1992
————. "I've Wrestled with Them All My Life: Langston Hughes's *Tambourines to Glory*," *Black American Literature Forum* 25(1):63, Sprg. 1991
"Zora Neale Hurston and Langston Hughes," *U.S. News & World Report* 110(7):18, 25 Feb. 1991

Mulatto, 1935
   Bienvenu, G. J. "Intracaste Prejudice in Langston Hughes's *Mulatto*," *African American Review* 26(2):341–53, Summ. 1992
   Saz, Sara M. "Cultura ajena y subversion: El 'Mulato' de Sastre," *Ojancano: Revista de Literatura Espanola* 6:3–18, Apr. 1992

SEE ALSO HURSTON, ZORA NEALE, LANGSTON HUGHES, and TAJ MAHAL

HUNT, MAME

Mackey, Heather. "He Said, She Said," *American Theatre* 10(3):10–11, Mar. 1993

HURLIN, DAN

Quintland (The Musical) (based on the story of the Dionne Quintuplets), 1992
   Bell, J. *TheaterWeek* 6(24):10, 18 Jan. 1993
   Gussow, M. *New York Times* 142:13(N), 19 Dec. 1992

HURSTON, ZORA NEALE

Carson, W. J. "Hurston as Dramatist: The Florida Connection," 121–29 in S. Glassman and K. L. Seidel, eds., *Zora in Florida*
O'Conor, M. "Zora Neale Hurston and Talking Between Cultures," *Canadian Review of American Studies*, 1:141, 1992
Smith, J. C. *Epic Lives: One Hundred Black Women Who Made a Difference*
Thomas, M. A. "Reflections on the Sanctified Church as Portrayed by Zora Neale Hurston," *Black American Literature Forum* 25(1):35, Sprg. 1991

The First One, 1927
   "Zora Neale Hurston," 186–201 in L. Hamalian and J. V. Hatch, eds. *The Roots of African American Drama*
   "Zora Neale Hurston and Langston Hughes," *U.S. News & World Report* 110(7):18, 25 Feb. 1991

HURSTON, ZORA NEALE, LANGSTON HUGHES, and TAJ MAHAL

Mule Bone (written by Hurston and Hughes in 1931, based on her short story "The Bone of Contention." Premièred in January 1991 with score by Taj Mahal), 1991

Finigan, K. "*Mule Bone*-Down-Home Blues Hit Broadway," *Down Beat* 58(2)22, Feb. 1991

Kanfer, S. *New Leader* 74(3)22–23, 11 Feb. 1991

Simpson, J. C. "Bone of Contention," *TheaterWeek* 4(28):21–25, 18 Feb. 1991

Weales, G. *Commonweal* 118(11):373, 1 Jun. 1991

HWANG, DAVID HENRY

Adult Learning Satellite Service, PBS. *Emanuel Azenberg; David Henry Hwang; Larry Gelbert; Robert Whitehead.* Videocassette

Deeney, J. J. "Of Monkeys and Butterflies: Transformation in M. H. Kingston's *Tripmaster Monkey* and D. H. Hwang's *M. Butterfly*," *Melus* 18(4):21, 1993

Du, W. "From *M. Butterfly* to *Madame Butterfly*; A Retrospective View of the Chinese Presence on Broadway," (#DA9305262; Washington U) *DAI* 53(9):3201A, Mar. 1993

Kors, S. "The Voyage," *Opera Monthly*, 5(7):5, 1 Nov. 1992

Loney, G. "Playwrights at the Met," *New Theatre Quarterly* 9(36):392–94, Nov. 1993

Martin, R. K. "Gender, Race, and the Colonial Body: Carson McCullers's *Filipino Boy* and David Henry Hwang's *Chinese Woman*," *Canadian Review of American Studies* 23(1):95 Fall 1992

Mitchell, K. S. "Intrinsic Intertextuality: A Methodology for Analyzing the Seamless Intertext," (#DA9123222; Louisiana State U) *DAI* 52(3):919A, Sep. 1991

Neely, K. "Intimacy or Cruel Love: Displacing the Other by Self Assertion," *Journal of Dramatic Theory and Criticism* 5(2):167–73, Sprg. 1991

Rabkin, G. "The Sound of a Voice: David Hwang," 97–114 in B. King, ed. *Contemporary American Theatre*

Weber, B. "Whither Hwang," *New York Times* 142:B8, 22 Jan. 1993

Wilson, E., interviewer. *David Henry Hwang, Playwright.* Videocassette

Bondage, 1992

Osborn, M. E. "Letter from Louisville," *TheaterWeek* 5(38):30, 27 Apr. 1992

Face Value, 1992

Evans, G. "Big Apple Loses 'Face,' " *Variety* 350(8):55, 22 Mar. 1993

Filichia, P. *TheaterWeek* 6(35):9, 5 Apr. 1993

Hsiao, A. *American Theatre* 10(4):46, Apr. 1993

Riedel, M. *TheaterWeek* 6(31):34, 8 Mar. 1993

Smith, D. "Face Values," *New York* 26(2):40, 11 Jan. 1993

Taylor, M. *Variety* 350(4):230, 22 Feb. 1993

Weber, B. "New from Hwang," *New York Times* 142:B7, 23 Oct. 1992

———. "Speak No Evil," *New York Times* 142:B9, 19 Mar. 1993

M. Butterfly, 1988

Daly, M. *Variety* 351(4):59, 24 May 1993

Haedicke, J. V. "David Henry Hwang's *M. Butterfly*: The Eye on the Wing," *Journal of Dramatic Theory and Criticism* 7(1):27–44, Fall 1992

Lochte, D. *Los Angeles Magazine* 36(8):202, Aug. 1991

Ma, S. "David Henry Hwang's *M. Butterfly*: From Puccini to East/Western Androgyn," *Tamkang Review* 21(3):287, Sprg. 1991

Marowitz, C. *TheaterWeek* 5(1):40–41, 12 Aug. 1991

Pao, A. "The Critic and the Butterfly: Socio-cultural Contexts and the Reception of David Henry Hwang's *M. Butterfly*," *Amerasia Journal* 18(3):1, 1992

Shimakawa, K. " 'Who's to Say?' or, Making Space for Gender and Ethnicity in *M. Butterfly*," *Theatre Journal* 45(3):349–62, Oct. 1993

Soo Hoo, M. C. *David Henry Hwang's M. Butterfly: Subversive Text or 'Orientalia for Intelligentsia'?* M.A. Thesis; UCLA, 1992

SEE ALSO GLASS, PHILIP, and DAVID HENRY HWANG

INGE, WILLIAM MOTTER

Berkowitz, G. M. *American Drama of the Twentieth Century*. 99 +

Courant, J. "The Drama of William Inge: A Critical Reassessment," (#DA9103667; U of California, Berkeley) *DAI* 51(9):2928A, Mar. 1991

———. "Social and Cultural Prophecy in the Works of William Inge," *Studies in American Drama, 1945–Present* 6(2):135–51, 1991

Eadie, J. *Strength in What Remains: What Ever Happened to William Inge?* M.A. Thesis; Bibliotheque Nationale du Canada: U of Alberta, 1993

Inge, L. C. *Travels in Search of the Past*

Jones, T. A. "An Individual Peace: The Work and Life of William Inge," (#DA9117053; U of Colorado) *DAI* 52(1):162A, Jul. 1991

Lai, Y. *William Inge: The Voice of Small-Town America*. M.A. Thesis; California State U, Fullerton, 1991

McClure, A. F. *A Bibliographical Guide to the Works of William Inge (1913–1973)*

Shuman, R. B. "Review: A Valuable Service," *College English* 53(3):349, Mar. 1991

Bus Stop, 1955

Meyer, W. E. H., Jr. "*Bus Stop*: American Eye Versus Small-Town Ear," *Modern Drama* 35(3):444–50, Sep. 1992

Wolcott, B. K. *William Inge's Bus Stop*. M.F.A. Thesis. U of South Dakota, 1992

The Disposal (never before produced), 1992

Ungaro, J. *TheaterWeek* 6(3):41, 24 Aug. 1992

INNAURATO, ALBERT

Innaurato, A. "A Matter of Voice," *Opera News* 58(3):12, 1 Sep. 1993

———. "A Taste for Caviar," *Opera News* 57(13):10, 13 Mar. 1993

———. "Those Demonic Divas," *Opera News* 57(4):20, 1 Oct. 1992

IRWIN, BILL

Hiss, T. "Really Rosie: Storyboard by Maurice Sendak," *New Yorker* 68(48):70, 18 Jan. 1993
Weber, B. "Just Clowning Around with Intellect," *New York Times* 142:B1, 3 Mar. 1993

IRWIN, BILL, and DAVID SHINER

Fool Moon, 1993
  Evans, G. "At Last, Tony Approves Oddball Entries," *Variety* 352(11):145, 25 Oct. 1993
  ————. "Test of a Salesman for Two Tough Shows," *Variety* 350(7): 69, 15 Mar. 1993
  Gerard, J. *Variety* 350(5):64, 1 Mar. 1993
  Greene, A. *TheaterWeek* 6(32):41, 15 Mar. 1993
  Kanfer, S. *New Leader* 76(4):22, 8 Mar. 1993
  Newman, B. "Another Opening, Another Show," *Dancing Times* 83(994):980, 1 Jul. 1993
  Oliver, E. *New Yorker* 69(3):101, 8 Mar. 1993
  Rich, F. *New York Times* 142:B1, 26 Feb. 1993
  Richards, D. *New York Times* 142:H5, 7 Mar. 1993
  Rosen, C. "Clown with an Edge," *TheaterWeek* 6(45):22–27, 14 Jun. 1993
  Shapiro, L. *Newsweek* 121(11):82, 15 Mar. 1993
  Simon, J. *New York* 26(10):86, 8 Mar. 1993
  "Stage," *People Weekly* 39(13):93, 5 Apr. 1993
  Time 141(10):73, 8 Mar. 1993
  Vaughan, D. "The Silent Treatment, in This Case, Speaks Volumes," *New York Times* 142:H5(N), 21 Feb. 1993
  Weales, G. *Commonweal* 120(7):24, 9 Apr. 1993
  Weber, B. "Falling into Place," *New York Times* 142:B2, 6 Nov. 1992
  Wilson, E. *Wall Street Journal* A14(W), 9 Mar. 1993

JEFFREYS, STEPHEN

A Going Concern, 1993
  Walker, J. K. L. *TLS* (4720):18, 17 Sep. 1993

JENKIN, LEN

Castagno, P. C. "Desultory Structures: Language as Presence in the Works of Overmyer, Wellman, and Jenkin," *Text & Presentation* 11:1–7, 1991
————. "Varieties of Monologic Strategy: The Dramaturgy of Len Jenkin and Mac Wellman," *New Theater Quarterly* 9(34):134–46, May 1993

JESURUN, JOHN

Bilderback, W., et al. "Shoestring Virtuosos," *American Theatre* 10(10):42, Oct. 1993

Point of Debarkation, 1992
    Bell, J. *TheaterWeek* 6(24):9–10, 18 Jan. 1993
    Gussow, M. *New York Times* 142:C19(L), 3 Feb. 1993

Iron Lung, 1992
    Bell, J. *TheaterWeek* 5(28):10–11, 17 Feb. 1992

JOHNSON, CINDY LOU

The Years, 1993
    Gerard, J. *Variety* 350(1):105, 1 Feb. 1993
    Gussow, M. *New York Times* 142:B3, 25 Jan. 1993
    Richards, D. *New York Times* 142:H5, 7 Feb. 1993
    Simon, J. *New York* 26(6):67, 8 Feb. 1993
    Time 141(6):83, 8 Feb. 1993
    Torrens, J. S. *America* 168(7):16, 27 Feb. 1993
    Ungaro, J. *TheaterWeek* 6(29):31–32, 22 Feb. 1993
    Weber, B. "Casting Troubles for *The Years*," *New York Times* 142:B8, 22
        Jan. 1993

JOHNSON, GEORGIA DOUGLAS

Hutchinson, G. B. "Jean Toomer and the 'New Negroes' of Washington," *American Literature* 63(4):683–92, Dec. 1991
Miller, J. A. "Georgia Douglas Johnson and May Miller: Forgotten Playwrights of the New Negro Renaissance," *College Language Association Journal* 33(4):349–66, Jun. 1990

JOHNSTON, JENNIFER

How Many Miles to Babylon, 1993
    Jeffery, K. *TLS* (4722):18, 1 Oct. 1993

JONES, FELICITY. *SEE* EPP, STEVEN, FELICITY JONES, and DOMINIQUE SERRAND

JONES, JESSIE. *SEE* BOTTRELL, DAVID, and JESSIE JONES

JONES, LeROI. *SEE* BARAKA, IMAMU AMIRI

JONES, PRESTON

The Oldest Living Graduate (the third play of *A Texas Trilogy* (the first is *Lu Ann Hampton Laverty Oberlander*; the second is *The Last Meeting of the Knights of the White Magnolias*), 1974
    Schlatter, J. F. "Some Kind of a Future: The War for Inheritance in the Work

of Three American Playwrights of the 1970s,'' *South Central Review* 7(1):59–75, Sprg. 1990

JONES, RHODESSA

Big Butt Girls, Hard-Headed Women, 1992
    Chansky, D. *TheaterWeek* 6(19):33, 14 Dec. 1992

JONES, TOM, and HARVEY SCHMIDT

The Fantasticks, 1960
    Farber, D. C., and R. Viagas. *The Amazing Story of The Fantasticks: America's Longest-Running Play*

SEE ALSO NASH, RICHARD N., TOM JONES, and HARVEY SCHMIDT

JORDAN, BRUCE. *SEE* ABRAMS, MARILYN, and BRUCE JORDAN

JORDAN, LOUIS. *SEE* PETERS, CLARKE, and LOUIS JORDAN

JUA, CHAKULA CHA

Jua, C. C. ''The Ladder: A One-Act Allegorical Play About Drugs,'' *African American Review* 27(1):61–66, Sprg. 1993

KALMAR, BERT. *SEE* KAUFMAN, GEORGE S., MORRIE RYSKIND, BERT KALMAR, and HARRY RUBY

KANDER, JOHN, and FRED EBB

Botto, L. ''The Sound of Kander and Ebb,'' *Playbill* 9(6):36, 31 Mar. 1991
Gregson, S. I. ''Musical for Our Times,'' *Plays International* 9(3):10, 1 Nov. 1993

Chicago, 1992
    Marowitz, C. *TheaterWeek* 5(47):33–34, 29 Jun. 1992

The World Goes 'Round, 1991
    Evans, G. ''Off B'Way Thumbs Ride Along a Rocky Road,'' *Variety* 348(12):191–92, 12 Oct. 1992
    Holden, S. *New York Times* 140:C3(L), 6 Sep. 1991
    Lochte, D. *Los Angeles Magazine* 37(11):159, Nov. 1992
    Simon J. *New York* 24(13):65, 1 Apr. 1991
    Taylor, M. *Variety* 348(7):57, 7 Sep. 1992

SEE ALSO McNALLY, TERRENCE, JOHN KANDER, and FRED EBB

KANIECKI, MICHAEL

Love Songs for the S.S., 1991
   Bell, J. *TheaterWeek* 4(41):35, 20 May 1991

KANIN, MICHAEL

Collins, G. "Michael Kanin, 83, Film Writer for Hepburn and Tracy, Is Dead,"
   New York Times 142:A16, 16 Mar. 1993
"Kanin, Michael: Obituary," *Facts on File* 53(2729):196, 18 Mar. 1993

KAUFMAN, GEORGE S.

Frederic-Nuzo, C. *The Social Philosophy of George S. Kaufman and Moss Hart
   as Revealed by Recurring Themes and Devices within Their Plays.* Diss.; Florida State U, 1993
James, C. "At Wit's End: Algonquinities in Hollywood," *New York Times*
   142:B1, 8 Jan. 1993
Leff, R. A. *George S. Kaufman and the American Myth of Success.* Diss.; U of
   Kansas, 1992

KAUFMAN, GEORGE S., and RING LARDNER

June Moon, 1929
   Hirschhorn, C. *TheaterWeek* 6(17):28, 30 Nov. 1992

KAUFMAN, GEORGE S., MORRIE RYSKIND, GEORGE GERSHWIN, and
IRA GERSHWIN

Of Thee I Sing, 1931
   Davis, R. "Wintergreen for Precedent," *American Theatre* 9(7):12, Nov.
   1992
   Henry, W. A., III. *Time* 140(15):84, 12 Oct. 1992
   Rich, F. *New York Times* 142:B1, 29 Sep. 1992

KAUFMAN, GEORGE S., MORRIE RYSKIND, BERT KALMAR, and HARRY
RUBY

Animal Crackers, 1928
   Holden, S. *New York Times* 142:A17, 4 Nov. 1992
   Taylor, M. *Variety* 349(4):72–73, 16 Nov. 1992

KAYE, HEREWARD. *SEE* LONGDEN, ROBERT, and HEREWARD KAYE

KEARNS, MICHAEL

intimacies/more intimacies, 1989–90
   Kearns, M. "intimacies," 237–269 in T. Helbing, ed. *Gay and Lesbian Plays
   Today*

KEATLEY, CHARLOTTE

My Mother Said I Never Should, 1993
    Krasner, D. *Theatre Journal* 45(3):384–5, Oct. 1993
    Taylor, M. *Variety* 350(2):82, 8 Feb. 1993

KELLEY, SAMUEL

Pin Hill, 1993
    King, R. L. *North American Review* 278:45, Mar/Apr. 1993

KELLOGG, PETER, and DANIEL LEVINE

Anna Karenina (adapted from Leo Tolstoy's *Anna Karenina*), 1992
    Gerard, J. *Variety* 348(6):63–64, 31 Aug. 1992
    Gillen, M. A. *Billboard* 104(37):43, 12 Sep. 1992
    Gussow, M. *New York Times* 141:B3(N), 27 Aug. 1992
    Henry, W. A., III. *Time* 140(10):66, 7 Sep. 1992
    Kanfer, S. *New Leader* 75(12):21, 21 Sep. 1992
    Mandelbaum, K. *TheaterWeek* 6(6):32–33, 14 Sep. 1992
    Simon, J. *New York* 25(35):52–53, 7 Sep. 1992
    Stephens, L. "Ann Crumb Meets Anna Karenina," *TheaterWeek* 6(6):14–17, 14 Sep. 1992

KELLY, JOHN

Acocella, J. "Maybe It's Cold Outside-Review," *Art America* 79:53+, Jun. 1991
Wald, J. "John Kelly: Poet on a Flying Trapeze," *American Theatre* 10(11):50, Nov. 1993

Akin, 1992
    Bell, J. *TheaterWeek* 5(35):14, 6 Apr. 1992

Light Shall Lift Them, 1993
    Holden, S. *New York Times* 143:B11, 12 Nov. 1993
    Tobias, T. *New York* 26(47):76, 29 Nov. 1993

KEMPLINSKI, TOM

Sex Please, We're Italian, 1991
    Williams, H. *TLS* (4607):17, 19 Jul. 1991

KENDALL, ROY

Body and Soul, 1991
    Bruckner, D. J. R. *New York Times* 140:C18, 10 Jul. 1991
    Hebblethwaite, P. *TLS* (4654):18, 12 Jun. 1992
    Variety 344(2):60, 22 Jul. 1991

KENNEDY, ADRIENNE

Bryant-Jackson, P. K., and L. M. Overbeck. *Intersecting Boundaries: The Theatre of Adrienne Kennedy*

Cummings, S. T. "Adrienne Kennedy," *American Theatre* 9(3):32, Jun. 1992

Diamond, E. "Rethinking Identification: Kennedy, Freud, Brecht," *Kenyon Review* 15(2):86–99, Sprg. 1993

Elwood, W. R. "Mankind and Sun: German-American Expressionism," *Text & Presentation* 11:9–12, 1991

Kennedy, A. "She Talks to Beethoven," *Antaeus* 66:248–58, Sprg. 1991

Kintz, L. *The Subject's Tragedy: Political Poetics, Feminist Theory, and Drama*

Kolin, P. C. "The Adrienne Kennedy Festival at the Great Lakes Theater Festival: A Photo Essay," *Studies in American Drama, 1945–Present* 8(1):85–94, 1993

Martin, H. *Adrienne Kennedy: An Annotated Secondary Bibliography and Essay*. M.A. Thesis; U of South Carolina, 1993

Shinn, T. J. "Living the Answer: The Emergence of African American Feminist Drama," *Studies in the Humanities* 17(2):149–59, Dec. 1990

An Evening with Dead Essex, 1973
> Zinman, T. S. " 'In the Presence of Mine Enemies': Adrienne Kennedy's *An Evening with Dead Essex*," *Studies in American Drama, 1945–Present* 6(1):3–13, 1991

Funnyhouse of a Negro, 1964
> Lee, K. B. *Bludgeoning Father's Head: The Politics of Marginality and Oppression in Funnyhouse of a Negro by Adrienne Kennedy*. M.A. Thesis; U of Florida, 1992
>
> Sollors, W. "Owls and Rats in the American Funnyhouse: Adrienne Kennedy's Drama," *American Literature* 63(3):507–34, 1 Sep. 1991

A Movie Star Has to Star in Black and White, 1992
> Kintz, L. "The Sanitized Spectacle: What's Birth Got to Do with It?" *Theatre Journal* 44(1):67–86, 1 Mar. 1992

KERN, JEROME

Smart, J. H. "The Internal Development of the Princess Theatre Musical Shows," (#DA9209987; U of Missouri, Columbia) *DAI* 52(10):3479A, Apr. 1992

SEE ALSO HAMMERSTEIN, OSCAR, II, and JEROME KERN

KERR, JEAN

Mary, Mary, 1961
> *Spree* 17(3):15, Fall 1992

KETRON, LARRY

Laureen's Whereabouts, 1993
> Evans, G. *Variety* 350(11):80, 12 Apr. 1993

Greene, A. *TheaterWeek* 6(38):29, 26 Apr. 1993
Gussow, M. *New York Times* 142:C18(L), 13 Apr. 1993

KIMBRELL, MARKETA

Blues in Rags, 1991
Bell, J. *TheaterWeek* 4(37):15, 22 Apr. 1991
Holden, S. *New York Times* 140:B4, 10 Apr. 1991
TheaterWeek 4(39):33, 6 May 1991

KING, LARRY L.

Smith, S. A. "Humor as Rhetoric and Cultural Argument," *Journal of American Culture* 16(2):51–64, Summ. 1993

KING, LARRY L., and BEN Z. GRANT

The Kingfish, 1991
King, L. L., and B. Z. Grant. *The Kingfish*
Simon, J. *New York* 24(14):95, 8 Apr. 1991
Sneerwell, R. *TheaterWeek* 4(36):38, 15 Apr. 1991
Variety 342(11):75, 1 Apr. 1991

KINOY, ERNEST, and WALTER MARKS

Bajour, 1964
Driscoll, T. "Forgotten Musicals: *Bajour*," *TheaterWeek* 4(49):23–27, 15 Jul. 1991

KLEIN, JON

Southern Cross, 1989
Bruckner, D. J. R. *New York Times* 142:C21, 29 Apr. 1993

KLEINMANN, KURT

Weeks, J. "In Living Black and White," *TheaterWeek* 4(26):30- 31, 4 Feb. 1991

KLING, KEVIN

Home and Away, 1990
Holbrook, C. "Kling's Fling," *TheaterWeek* 5(1):36, 12 Aug. 1991
Holden, S. *New York Times* 140:C16, 24 Jul. 1991
Simon, J. *New York* 24(31):67, 12 Aug. 1991

KNEE, ALLEN

Shmulnik's Waltz, 1992
    Evans, G. *Variety* 347(3):298, 4 May 1992
    Filichia, P. "The Great Waltz," *TheaterWeek* 5(35):9, 6 Apr. 1992

KOCIOLEK, TED, and JAMES RACHEFF

Abyssinia, 1991
    Mandelbaum, K. "Season Preview: The Musicals," *TheaterWeek* 5(1):20, 12
    Aug. 1991

KOFMAN, GIL

One of Us, 1991
    Holbrook, C. *TheaterWeek* 5(6):40, 16 Sep. 1991

KONDOLEON, HARRY

Kondoleon, H. "Linda Her," *Antaeus*, 66:259–66, Sprg. 1991

Fat Men in Skirts, 1991
    Harvey, D. *Variety* 345(11):49, 23 Dec. 1991
    Richards, D. "Life's Underside Often Gives You the Woolies," *New York
    Times* 140:H5, 11 Aug. 1991

Love Diatribe, 1990
    Resnikova, E. *National Review* 43(4):65, 18 Mar. 1991
    Simon, J. *New York* 24(2):56, 14 Jan. 1991
    Ungaro, J. *TheaterWeek* 4(22):30, 7 Jan. 1991
    Weales, G. *Commonweal* 118(2):56, 25 Jan. 1991

KOPIT, ARTHUR

Kopit, A. "Success," *Antaeus* 66:267–71, Sprg. 1991

Road to Nirvana (formerly titled *Bone-the-Fish*), 1990
    Lochte, D. *Los Angeles Magazine* 37(4):130–31, Apr. 1992
    Variety 342(9):70, 11 Mar. 1991
    Weales, G. *Commonweal* 118(8):261, 19 Apr. 1991

Wings, 1978
    Albert, W. *American Theatre* 10(3):8–9, Mar. 1993
    Brustein, R. *New Republic* 208(17):29, 26 Apr. 1993
    Gerard, J. *Variety* 350(7):70–71, 15 Mar. 1993
    Henning, J. *Wall Street Journal* A12(W), 23 Nov. 1992
    Kelley, M. A. "Order Within Fragmentation: Postmodernism and the Stroke
    Victim's World," *Modern Drama* 34(3):383–91, Sep. 1991

Lazare, L. *Variety* 349(8):56, 14 Dec. 1992
Oliver, E. *New Yorker* 69(7):97, 5 Apr. 1993
Rich, F. *New York Times* 142:B1, 10 Mar. 1993
Richards, D. *New York Times* 142:H5, 22 Nov. 1992
Simon J. *New York* 26(12):83, 22 Mar. 1993
Time 141(12):79, 22 Mar. 1993
Weales, G. *Commonweal* 120(7):24, 9 Apr. 1993
Weber, B. "Almost Literally Reborn, A Director Finds His Play," *New York Times* 142:H5, 7 Mar. 1993

KOPIT, ARTHUR, and MAURY YESTON

Phantom (based on the novel by Gaston Leroux), 1992
Filichia, P. "Phantomtasmagoria," *TheaterWeek* 6(14):11, 9 Nov. 1992
Horwitz, S. "The Other Phantom," *TheaterWeek* 6(46):19–23, 21 Jun. 1993
Mandelbaum, K. "Another Masked Musical," *TheaterWeek* 6(8):31–33, 28 Sep. 1992
Richards, D. *New York Times* 142:H3(N), 4 Jul. 1993

KORDER, HOWARD

"Behind the Scene: Secret Garden; Howard Korder," *Dramatist's Guild Quarterly* 29(1):55, Sprg. 1992

Search and Destroy, 1990
Gerard, J. *Variety* 346(7):62, 2 Mar. 1992
Henry, W. A., III. *Time* 139(11):66, 16 Mar. 1992
King, R. L. *Massachusetts Review* 32(1):157, Sprg. 1991
Oliver, E. *New Yorker* 68(3):81, 9 Mar. 1992
Riedel, M. "In Search of Howard Korder: The Playwright Unmasks American Ambition," *TheaterWeek* 5(34):25–27, 30 Mar. 1992
Ungaro, J. *TheaterWeek* 5(36):35, 13 Apr. 1992

KORNBLUTH, JOSH

Red Diaper Baby, 1991
Evans, G. *Variety* 346(13):72, 13 Apr. 1992
Richards, D. *New York Times* 141:H5(N), 12 Jul. 1992
Time 140(2):81, 13 Jul. 1992
Ungaro, J. *TheaterWeek* 5(38):37, 27 Apr. 1992

KOSTICK, GAVIN

The Ash Fire, 1993
Cheyette, B. *TLS* (4688):17, 5 Feb. 1993

KOUTOUKAS, H. M.

Awful People Are Coming Over . . . , 1991
Hammond, J. *TheaterWeek* 4(28):37, 18 Feb. 1991

Only a Countess May Dance When She's Crazy, 1991
      Hammond, J. *TheaterWeek* 4(28):37, 18 Feb. 1991

KRAMER, LARRY

Ben-Levi, J. "Kramer's Proposals," *Minnesota Review* (40):126, Sprg. 1993
Bergman, D. "Larry Kramer and the Rhetoric of AIDS," 175–86 in E. S. Nelson, ed. *AIDS: The Literary Response*
Evans, G. "Top-Line Playwrights Write Off Broadway," *Variety* 348(6):63, 31 Aug. 1992
Gilbey, L. "Being What We Are," *Plays International* 9(2):14, 1 Oct. 1993
"Interview: Larry Kramer," *Advocate* (618):42, 15 Dec. 1992
Kramer, L. "Little Murders," *Advocate* (631):80, 15 Jun. 1993
Lear, F. "Frances Lear Meets with Playwright Larry Kramer," *Lear's* 6(3):13–17, May 1993
Leo, J. "The AIDS Activist with Blurry Vision," *U.S. News & World Report* 109(2):16, 9 Jul. 1990
"Playboy Interview: Larry Kramer," *Playboy* 40(9):61, 1 Sep. 1993
Shnayerson, M. "Kramer vs. Kramer: Larry Kramer," *Vanity Fair* 55(10):228, 1 Oct. 1992
Zonana, V. "Larry Kramer vs. the World," *Advocate* (617):40, 1 Dec. 1992
———. "Larry Kramer vs. the World," (part 2), *Advocate* (618):42, 15 Dec. 1992
———. "Larry Kramer Interview," *Outrage* (117):16, 1 Feb. 1992
———. "Larry Kramer Interview, Part II," *Outrage* (118):28, 1 Mar. 1993

The Destiny of Me, 1992
      Gilbey, L. "Being What We Are," *Plays International* 9(2):14, 1 Oct. 1993
      Henry, W. A., III. *Time* 140(18):69, 2 Nov. 1992
      Kanfer, S. *New Leader* 76(1):20–21, 11 Jan. 1993
      Klinghoffer, D. *National Review* 44(24):55, 14 Dec. 1992
      Kramer, L. "*Destiny of Me*," in J. Beard, ed. *The Best Men's Stage Monologues of 1993*
      Kroll, J. *Newsweek* 120(18):104, 2 Nov. 1992
      "Larry Kramer Play Wins Lortel Award," *New York Times* 142:B4, 9 Apr. 1993
      Simon, J. *New York* 25(43):101, 2 Nov. 1992
      Simonson, R. "Hat Trick," *TheaterWeek* 6(17):13–17, 30 Nov. 1992
      ———. *TheaterWeek* 6(15):46–48, 16 Nov. 1992
      Weber, B. "All in the Viewpoint," *New York Times* 142:B2, 1 Jan. 1993

The Normal Heart, 1985
      Bradley, R. "The Abnormal Affair of *The Normal Heart*," *Text and Performance Quarterly* 12(4):362–71, Oct. 1992
      Cox, J. R. "Performing Memory/Speech: Aesthetic Boundaries and 'the Other' in *Ghetto* and *The Normal Heart*," *Text and Performance Quarterly* 12(4):383–90, Oct. 1992
      Gross, G. D. "Coming Up for Air: Three AIDS Plays," *Journal of American Culture* 15(2):63–67, Summ. 1992

Roach, J. "Normal Heartlands," *Text and Performance Quarterly* 12(4):377–84, Oct. 1992

Shatzky, J. "AIDS Enters the American Theater: *As Is* and *The Normal Heart*," 131–39 in E. S. Nelson, ed. *AIDS: The Literary Response*

Strine, M. S. "Art, Activism, and the Performance (Con)Text: A Response," *Text and Performance Quarterly* 12(4):391–94, Oct. 1992

KRAUSNICK, DENNIS

The Inner House (adapted from the writings of Edith Wharton), 1992
Backalenick, I. "Letter from the Berkshires," *TheaterWeek* 6(4):32, 31 Aug. 1992

Maisie (adaptation of a Henry James novel), 1992
Backalenick, I. "Letter from the Berkshires," *TheaterWeek* 6(4):32, 31 Aug. 1992

KRAUSS, KEN

There's a War Going On, 1993
Horwitz, S. "Gays in the Military," *TheaterWeek* 6(37):23–26, 19 Apr. 1993

KREISEL, HENRY

Van Herk, A. "Henry Kreisel: 1922–1991," *Canadian Literature* 131:261–63, Wntr. 1991

KUSHNER, TONY

Kushner, T. "Intimacy. Sex Is Still Worth It," *Esquire* 120(4):158, 1 Oct. 1993

Lubow, A. "Paradise Lost: Tony Kushner Examines Love in the Time of AIDS," *New Yorker* 68(41):59, 30 Nov. 1992

"Man and Woman of the Year," *Advocate* (645):45, 28 Dec. 1993

Szentgyorgyi, T. "Look Back—and Forward—in Anger," *TheaterWeek* 4(23):15–19, 14 Jan. 1991

Tucker, S. "A Storm Blowing from Paradise," *Humanist* 53:32–35, 1993

Angels in America: Millennium Approaches, 1991
"Angels in America Parts I & II: Mark Fleming at RNT Cottesloe," *Plays and Players* (477):14, 1 Dec. 1993
"Angels in America: Part Two," *Mirabella* 5(7):50, 1 Dec. 1993
Borreca, A. *Theatre Journal* 45:235–8, May 1993
Brustein, R. "On Theater: *Angels in America*," *New Republic* 208(21):29, 24 May 1993
"Cultural Elite," *Vanity Fair* 56(3):72, 1 Mar. 1993
Evans, G. "Angels on Broadway: Fall's Big Openings," *Variety* 353(5):43, 6 Dec. 1993
———. " 'Angels' Pulitzer Proves a Box Office Blessing," *Variety* 350(12):51, 19 Apr. 1993

Greene, A. *TheaterWeek* 6(41):28, 17 May 1993
Hay, D. "Angels in Sydney," *Outrage* (117):54, 1 Feb. 1993
Henry, W. A., III. "The Gay White Way," *Time* 141(20):62, 17 May 1993
Hornby, R. *Hudson Review* 46(1):189–91, Sprg. 1993
———. *Hudson Review* 46:531, Autm. 1993
Kroll, J. "A Broadway Godsend: *Angels in America*, an Epic of AIDS and
    Homosexuality, Is a Big Ticket," *Newsweek* 121(19):56, 10 May 1993
Kurzweil, E. "A Visit to the Theatre," *Partisan Review* 60(3):341, Summ.
    1993
Marowitz, C. *TheaterWeek* 6(20):30–32, 21 Dec. 1992
Raymond, G. "Tony Kushner's *Angels* at the National," *TheaterWeek*
    5(28):30–31, 17 Feb. 1992
Richards, D. "Visions of Heaven—and of Hell," *New York Times* 142:H1,
    16 May 1993
Roe, A. *TheaterWeek* 4(49):40–41, 15 Jul. 1991
Rogoff, G. "*Angels in America*, Devils in the Wings," *Theater* 24(2):21,
    1993
Schmaltz, J. "Will Angels Fly?" *Advocate* (616):82, 17 Nov. 1992
Simon, J. "*Angels in America II* Is No Worse, and No Better Than Part I,"
    New York 26(48):130, 6 Dec. 1993
Simonson, R. "Goodnight, Roy," *TheaterWeek* 6(40):20–23, 10 May 1993
"Theater: Gays at Center Stage," *Time* 141(20):62, 17 May 1993

A Bright Room Called Day, 1991
    Disch, T. M. *Nation* 252(10):352, 18 Mar. 1991
    Leslie, G. *TheaterWeek* 4(24):39, 21 Jan. 1991
    Sneerwell, R. *TheaterWeek* 4(24):38, 21 Jan. 1991
    Variety 342(1):118, 14 Jan. 1991
    Weales, G. *Commonweal* 118(4):132, 22 Feb. 1991

Perestroika (the second part of *Angels in America*), 1993
    Brustein, R. *New Republic* 209(26):25–27, 27 Dec. 1993
    Economist 329(7840):92–93, 4 Dec. 1993
    Frascella, L. *Advocate* (645):73–75, 28 Dec. 1993
    Gerard, J. *Variety* 353(5):33–34, 6 Dec. 1993
    Henry, W. A., III. *Time* 142(24):75–76, 6 Dec. 1993
    Kroll, J. *Newsweek* 122(23):83, 6 Dec. 1993
    Lahr, J. *New Yorker* 69(42):129–33, 13 Dec. 1993
    Lavender, A. *New Statesman & Society* 6(280):35–36, 26 Nov. 1993
    Raymond, G. "Season Preview: The Plays," *TheaterWeek* 7(5):14, 6 Sep.
        1993
    Rich, F. *New York Times* 143:B1(N), 24 Nov. 1993
    Simon, J. *New York* 26(48):130–31, 6 Dec. 1993
    Wilson, E. *Wall Street Journal* A12(W), 2 Dec. 1993
    Wolf, M. *Variety* 353(5):33B, 6 Dec. 1993

Widows (adaptation of Ariel Dorfman's 1983 novel), 1991
    Berman, M. *Variety* 344(5):49, 12 Aug. 1991
    Lochte, D. *Los Angeles Magazine* 36(9):154–56, Sep. 1991
    Marowitz, C. *TheaterWeek* 5(4):40–41, 2 Sep. 1991

LaCHUISA, MICHAEL JOHN. *SEE* ESSMAN, JEFFREY, and MICHAEL JOHN LaCHUISA

LAHR, JOHN

Carmody, D. "John Lahr Is Appointed *New Yorker* Drama Critic," *New York Times* 141:B2, 16 Sep. 1992
Nakayama, R. S. "Domesticating Mr. Orton," *Theatre Journal* 45:185–95, May 1993

The Manchurian Candidate, 1991
    Brogan, H. *TLS* (4609):16, 2 Aug. 1991

LAMONT, ALONZO D., JR.

Vivisections from the Blown Mind, 1993
    Schroeder, P. R. *Theatre Journal* 45:258–9, May 1993

LANGELLA, FRANK

Not Like Me at All, 1991
    Marowitz, C. *TheaterWeek* 4(51):41, 29 Jul. 1991

LAPINE, JAMES

Gerard, J. "Lapine Signs on as New Shubert Ally," *Variety* 352(3):27–28, 30 Aug. 1993

Luck, Pluck, and Virtue, 1993
    Braunagel, D. *Variety* 352(1):40, 16 Aug. 1993
    Morris, R. "Nice Guys Finish (Last)(First)," *American Theatre* 10(7/8):13, Jul/Aug. 1993
    Welsh, A. M. *TCI* 27(8):7, Oct. 1993

LAPINE, JAMES, and WILLIAM FINN

Falsettos (the pairing of *March of the Falsettos* and *Falsettoland*), 1992
    Collins, G. "The Many Faces and Facets of Keeping *Falsettos* Afloat," *New York Times* 142:C13(L), 26 Nov. 1992
    Disch, T. M. *Nation* 254(22):796–97, 8 Jun. 1992
    Gerard, J. *Variety* 347(3):298, 4 May 1992
    ———. *Variety* 350(5):64, 1 Mar. 1993
    Harris, J. "*Falsettos* vs. Cagelles," *Christopher Street* 14(13):9–10, 6 Jan. 1992
    Haynes, K. "The Finn Men," *New York* 25(17):21, 27 Apr. 1992
    Helbing, T. "Truth and *Falsettos*," *Advocate* (602):70, 5 May 1992
    Henry, W. A. III. "The Gay White Way," *Time* 141(20):62, 17 May 1993
    ———. "The Quirky William Finn," *Time* 139(19):57, 11 May 1992

Kanfer, S. *New Leader* 75(7):30–31, 1 Jun. 1992
Kramer, M. *New Yorker* 68(12):79, 11 May 1992
Mandelbaum, K. *TheaterWeek* 5(41):33–34, 18 May 1992
Rich, F. "Discovering Family Values at *Falsettos*," *New York Times* 141:H1(N), 12 Jul. 1992
————. *New York Times* 141:B1(N), 30 Apr. 1992
Richards, D. "An Ode to Joy on Broadway," *New York Times* 141:H1(N), 10 May 1992
Riedel, M. "James Lapine Welcomes You to Falsettos," *TheaterWeek* 5(41):18–23, 18 May 1992
Sandla, R. *Dance Magazine* 66(8):53–54, Aug. 1992
Scher, H. "William Finn," *American Theatre* 10(3):27–28, Mar. 1993
Simon, J. *New York* 25(21):81–82, 25 May 1992
Taylor, M. *Variety* 349(12):83, 18 Jan. 1993
Torrens, J. S. *America* 166(20):516, 6 Jun. 1992
Weales, G. *Commonweal* 119(17):22–23, 9 Oct. 1992
Witchel, A. "Find the Ginger: It's Anxiety Time for an Original," *New York Times* 141:H8(N), 26 Apr. 1992

Falsettoland (third play of *Marvin's Trilogy*; the first is *In Trousers* by Finn; the second is *March of the Falsettos* by Finn, which see), 1990
Evans, G. "Family Ad Campaign True to *Falsettos*," *Variety* 348(5):67–68, 24 Aug. 1992
Kramer, M. *New Yorker* 68(12):79, 11 May 1992
Mandelbaum, K. *TheaterWeek* 5(13):38–39, 4 Nov. 1991
Michaud, C. "Time Marches On, and So Do *Falsettos*: William Finn Has a Hit in *Falsettoland*," *Advocate* (568):61, 15 Jan. 1991

LAPINE, JAMES, and STEPHEN SONDHEIM

Into the Woods, 1986
Filichia, P. *TheaterWeek* 6(27):13, 8 Feb. 1993
Lapine, J., director, *Into the Woods*. Videocassettes.
Lauris, A. C. *The Role of the Witch in "Into the Woods"*. M.F.A. Thesis; Mankato State U, 1992
Marowitz, C. *TheaterWeek* 6(41):29, 17 May 1993
Orme, M. T. *The Role of Jack in Into the Woods*. M.F.A. Thesis; Mankato State U, 1992
Sudduth, A. C. *Process and Performance: Recreating the Role of the Baker's Wife in Into the Woods*. M.F.A. Thesis; San Diego State U, 1992

LARDNER, RING. *SEE* KAUFMAN, GEORGE S., and RING LARDNER

LAURENTS, ARTHUR, CHARLES STROUSE, and RICHARD MALTBY, JR.

Nick and Nora (musical based on characters created by D. Hammett), 1991
Ames, K. *Newsweek* 118(25):73, 16 Dec. 1991
Evans, G. "Asta Muzzled Again; Crix Bark," *Variety* 345(5):57–58, 11 Nov. 1991

———. "Investigating N and N's Untimely Demise," *Variety* 345(10):63–64, 16 Dec. 1991

"Eye on . . . Opening Nights," *Harper's Bazaar* (3357):186, 1 Sep. 1991

Filichia, P. "Stagestruck," *TheaterWeek* 5(6):11–12, 16 Sep. 1991

Finn, W. "He's Brought Street Gangs, a Monster Mother, and Now Singing Detectives to Broadway," *Vogue* 181(11):156–58, Nov. 1991

Gerard, J. *Variety* 345(9):80, 9 Dec. 1991

Harris, J. *Christopher Street* 14(14):10–12, 20 Jan. 1992

Henry, W. A., III. *Time* 138(24):67, 16 Dec. 1991

Kanfer, S. *New Leader* 74(14):34, 30 Dec. 1991

Mandelbaum, K. "Season Preview: The Musicals," *TheaterWeek* 5(1):18, 12 Aug. 1991

———. *TheaterWeek* 5(20):22, 23 Dec. 1991

Oliver, E. *New Yorker* 67(44):94, 23 Dec. 1991

Richards, D. "The New Nora in Joanna Gleason's World," *New York Times* 140:H9, 8 Sep. 1991

Riedel, M. "Linda and Leida vs. *Nick and Nora*," *TheaterWeek* 5(16):8, 25 Nov. 1991

———. "*Nick and Nora*: Postponed Again," *TheaterWeek* 5(15):8, 18 Nov. 1991

Ruling, K. G. "On the Go with *Nick and Nora*: Using Computer Technology to Make Scenery Move," *Theater Crafts* 26(2):68–70, Feb. 1992

Simon J. *New York* 25(1):60, 6 Jan. 1992

Smith, S. E. "The Nine Lives of *Nick and Nora*," *TheaterWeek* 5(7):20–23, 23 Sep. 1991

Story, R. D. "Theater," *New York* 24(37):46, 23 Sep. 1991

Wolf, W. *Playbill* 10(2):10, 30 Nov. 1991

LAURO, SHIRLEY

"Behind the Scenes: Alice's Fourth Floor; Shirley Lauro; Plays for Children," *Dramatists Guild Quarterly* 28(4):41, Wntr. 1992

A Piece of My Heart (based on oral histories in K. Walker's book), 1989
Chansky, D. *TheaterWeek* 5(18):37, 9 Dec. 1991
Gerard, J. *Variety* 345(4):66, 4 Nov. 1991
Gussow, M. *New York Times* 140:B1, 10 Apr. 1991
Kramer, M. *New Yorker* 67(39):126–27, 18 Nov. 1991
Liston, W. T. *Theatre Journal* 43(4):526–30, Dec. 1991
Torrens, J. S. *America* 166(2):40, 18 Jan. 1992

LAWRENCE, JEREMY

Uncommon Ground, 1991
Abarbanel, J. *TheaterWeek* 4(30):34, 4 Mar. 1991

LAWRENCE, JEROME

Garfield, K. "Jerome Lawrence's Broadway: The Playwright Reflects on a Long Career Defending the Freedom to Be Different," *Advocate* (569):58–59, 29 Jan. 1991

LAWRENCE, JEROME, and ROBERT E. LEE

Couch, N. "An Interview with Jerome Lawrence and Robert E. Lee," *Studies in American Drama, 1945–Present* 7(1):3–18, 1992
Lawrence, J., and R. E. Lee, "The Angels Weep," *Studies in American Drama, 1945–Present* 7(1):19, 1992
————. "The Dynamic of Duos," *Writer's Digest* 72(6):6–8, Jun. 1992
Winchester, M. D. "Jerome Lawrence and Robert E. Lee: A Classified Bibliography," *Studies in American Drama, 1945–Present* 7(1):88–160, 1992

Inherit the Wind, 1955
 Filichia, P. *TheaterWeek* 5(25):10, 27 Jan. 1992
 Taylor, M. *Variety* 344(5):49, 12 Aug. 1991

LAWSON, JOHN HOWARD

Mishra, K. *American Leftist Playwrights of the 1930's: A Study of Ideology and Technique in the Plays of Odets, Lawson, and Sherwood*

LEBOW, BARBARA

Parmet, H. L. "An Approach Toward the Inclusion of Women Writers . . ." *Feminist Teacher* 7(3):41–48, Fall 1993

LeCOMPTE, ELIZABETH

Arratia, E. "Island Hopping: Rehearsing the Wooster Group's *Brace Up*," *TDR* 36(4):121–42, Wntr. 1992
Cole, S. L. *Directors in Rehearsal: A Hidden World*
Coleman, B. "Just Mask: Beth Coleman Talks with Elizabeth LeCompte and Kate Valk," *Artforum* 31(9):83–86, 1 May 1993
Greene, A. "Elizabeth LeCompte and the Wooster Group," 117–34 in B. King, ed. *Contemporary American Theatre*
Schmidt, P. "The Sounds of *Brace Up*: Translating the Music of Chekov," *TDR* 36(4):154–57, Wntr. 1992

A Shayna Maidel, 1985
 Lochte, D. *Los Angeles Magazine* 36(1):125, Jan. 1991

LeCOMPTE, ELIZABETH, and OTHERS

Rumstick Road (Part two of of *Three Places in Rhode Island*), 1977
 King, W. D. "Dramaturgical Text and Historical Record in the New Theatre: The Case of *Rumstick Road*," *Journal of Dramatic Theory and Criticism* 7(1):71–87, Fall 1992

LEE, CAROLYN. *SEE* COMDEN, BETTY, ADOLPH GREEN, MOOSE CHARLAP, and CAROLYN LEE

LEE, LESLIE

Black Eagles, 1990
   Erstein, H. "The Eagles Who Touched the Sky," *Insight* 7(9):53, 4 Mar.
   1991
   Rich, F. *New York Times* 140:B5, 22 Apr. 1991
   Ungaro, J. *TheaterWeek* 4(39):31, 6 May 1991
   Wilbekin, E. *New York Times* 140:H10, 21 Apr. 1991

LEE, ROBERT E. *SEE* LAWRENCE, JEROME, and ROBERT E. LEE

LEGUIZAMO, JOHN

Connors, C. "Leguizamo," *Seventeen* 52(7):68–69, Jul. 1993
Cordero, C. K. "John Leguizamo," *Premiere* 5(12):49 Aug. 1992
Garcia, G. "Mocking the Ethnic Beast," *Time* 138(17):85, 28 Oct. 1991
"John Leguizamo," *Playboy* 39(5):126–129, May 1992
Leguizamo, J. "New Voices from Latinolandia Whisper in America's Ear," *New York Times* 140:H5, 14 Jul. 1991
Marin, R. "Loco Hero," *TV Guide* 41(20):34–35, 15 May 1993

Mambo Mouth, 1990
   Botto, L. "Mambo Mouth Speaks," *Playbill* 9(11):36, 31 Aug. 1991
   Gussow, M. *New York Times* 140:C3, 14 Jun. 1991
   "John Leguizamo Goes for the Jugular," *People Weekly* 36(18):148, 11 Nov.
   1991
   Kanfer, S. *New Leader* 74(4):23, 11 Mar. 1991
   Rivera, L. "Mambo King of Comedy," *Hispanic* P. 11, 1 Mar. 1992
   Smith, C. "Mambo King," *New York* 24(23):44–48, 10 Jun. 1991
   Treen, J., and T. Kahn. "A Man for All Faces," *People Weekly* 36(18):148–
   49, 11 Nov. 1991

Spic-O-Rama, 1992
   Bell, J. "Sheros," *TheaterWeek* 6(14):15, 2 Nov. 1992
   Brustein, R. *New Republic* 207(24):34, 7 Dec. 1992
   "By Popular Demand," *New York Times* 142:B6, 20 Nov. 1992
   Gerard, J. *Variety* 349(2):93–94, 2 Nov. 1992
   Greene, A. "No Such Thing as 'Normal,' " *TheaterWeek* 6(16):17–20, 23
   Nov. 1992
   Henry, W. A., III. *Time* 140(19):83–84, 9 Nov. 1992
   Kanfer, S. *New Leader* 75(14):22–23, 2 Nov. 1992
   Kirkpatrick, M. *Wall Street Journal* A12(W), 4 Nov. 1992
   Kroll, J. *Newsweek* 120(24):87, 14 Dec. 1992
   Lahr, J. *New Yorker* 68(38):142–43, 9 Nov. 1992
   Rich, F. *New York Times* 142:B1, 28 Oct. 1992
   Richards, D. *New York Times* 142:H5, 8 Nov. 1992
   Simon, J. *New York* 25(47):126, 30 Nov. 1992
   Weber, B. "Leguizamo and Friends," *New York Times* 142:B7, 23 Oct. 1992
   Weiss, P. "Going Solo," *Vogue* 183(4):242–44, Apr. 1993

LEICHT, JOHN

Moot, 1992
> Jones, C. "Atomic Circus," *American Theatre* 9(4):4–5, Jul/Aug. 1992
> ———. *Variety* 347(3):300, 4 May 1992

LEIGH, MITCH

Evans, G. "Do or Don't Quixote?" *Variety* 344(9):69–70, 9 Sep. 1991

SEE ALSO ADAMS, LEE, MITCH LEIGH, and THOMAS MEEHAN

LEPAGE, ROBERT

Ackerman, M. "Alanienouidet: Simultaneous Space and Action," *Canadian Theatre Review* 70:32–34, Sprg. 1992
Bell, K. "Robert Lepage Makes Opera Debut," *Performing Arts & Entertainment in Canada* 28(1):12, Sprg. 1993
Came, B. "Robert LePage," *Maclean's* 106(52):18–19, 27 Dec. 1993
"Canada Dream," *Plays and Players* (460):14, 1 Jul. 1992
Carson, C. "Collaboration, Translation, Interpretation," *New Theatre Quarterly* 9(33):31–36, 1 Feb. 1993
Croyden, M. "Letter from Montreal," *TheaterWeek* 6(52):38–40, 2 Aug. 1993
Horwitz, S. "Hot Director: Robert Lepage Breaks Barriers at BAM," *TheaterWeek* 6(27):14–17, 8 Feb. 1993
Jacobson, L. "Tectonic States," *American Theatre* 8(8):16, 1 Nov. 1991
Mackay, G. "The Dreamspinner: Robert Lepage Is a Wizard of the Stage," *Maclean's* 106(5):63, 1 Feb. 1993
"Opera: Robert Lepage," *Maclean's* 106(5):63, 1 Feb. 1993
Roy, I. *Le Théâtre Repère*
Salter, D. "Between Worlds: Lepage's Shakespeare Cycle," *Theater* 24(3):61–70, Summ/Fall 1993
———. "Borderlines: An Interview with Robert Lepage and le Theatre Repere," *Theater* 24(3):71–79, 1993
Sheehy, C. "A Critic in Every Port: O Brave New France," *American Theatre* 10(9):24–25, Sep. 1993
Swed, M. "Wizard of Id," *Opera News* 57(10):18–19, 30 Jan. 1993
Wolf, M. "Robert Lepage: Multicultural and Multifaceted," *New York Times* 142:H5, 6 Dec. 1992

Coriolan, 1993
> Morris, T. *TLS* (4732):17, 10 Dec. 1993

The Dragons' Trilogy, 1990
> Campbell, J. *TLS* (4624):20, 15 Nov. 1991
> Moy, J. S. *Theatre Journal* 42:499–501, Dec. 1990

Needles and Opium, 1992
> Bell, J. *TheaterWeek* 6(22):12, 4 Jan. 1993
> Gussow, M. *New York Times* 142:B3, 10 Dec. 1992

Lahr, J. *New Yorker* 68(45):190–92, 28 Dec. 1992
Levy, D. *New Statesman & Society* 5(201):28–29, 8 May 1992
Wolf, M. *Variety* 349(6):96, 30 Nov. 1992

LERNER, ALAN JAY

Phillips, L. "Humor," *Poet* 3(2):43, Fall 1991

LERNER, ALAN JAY, and FREDERICK LOEWE

Grode, E. "How to Handle a Revue," *TheaterWeek* 6(52):25–28, 2 Aug. 1993
Nachman, G. "Champagne for the Masses," *TheaterWeek* 5(14):22, 11 Nov. 1991
Portantiere, M. "Beyond Broadway," *TheaterWeek* 7(2):28, 16 Aug. 1993

My Fair Lady (musical version of G. B. Shaw's play *Pygmalion*), 1956
    Canby, V. *New York Times* 143:H5(N), 19 Dec. 1993
    Collins, G. "Anything but Loverly," *New York Times* 142:B9(N), 2 Jul. 1993
    Filichia, P. "Loverly," *TheaterWeek* 6(40):13–14, 10 May 1993
    Garebian, K. *The Making of My Fair Lady*
    Gerard, J. *Variety* 353(7):37, 20 Dec. 1993
    Handelmann, J. *Variety* 350(11):82, 12 Apr. 1993
    Harris, P. *Variety* 351(6):61, 14 Jun. 1993
    Jansen, W. *My Fair Lady: Die Deutsche Erstauffuhrung*
    Kanfer, S. *New Leader* 76(15):34–35, 27 Dec. 1993
    Kroll, J. *Newsweek* 122(25):123, 20 Dec. 1993
    "Loverly Memories of *My Fair Lady*," *New York Times* 143:H5, 5 Dec. 1993
    Richards, D. *New York Times* 143:B1, 10 Dec. 1993
    Stempel, L. "The Musical Play Expands," *American Music* 10(2):136–69, Summ. 1992
    Weber, B. "A Novice's Luverly *Fair Lady* Role," *New York Times* 142:9, 30 Jan. 1993
    ———. "Offstage Drama Tries to Define Eliza's Essence," *New York Times* 143: B1(N), 15 Dec. 1993

LEVIN, IRA

"Ira Levin," *Current Biography* 52(8):37–40, Aug. 1991

LEVIN, MEYER

Rubin, S. J. "The Ghetto and Beyond: First-Generation American-Jewish Autobiography and Cultural History," 178–206 in J. R. Payne, ed. *Multicultural Autobiography: American Lives*
Torres, T. *Les Maisons hantées de Meyer Levin*

LEVINE, DANIEL. *SEE* KELLOGG, PETER, and DANIEL LEVINE

LEVY, DEBORAH

Charitou, I. "Questions of Survival: Towards a Postmodern Feminist Theatre," *New Theatre Quarterly* 9(35):225–30, 1 Aug. 1993

————. "Three Plays by Deborah Levy," *New Theatre Quarterly* 9(35):230–2, 1 Aug. 1993

Levy, D. "Surreal Encounters: Some Alternatives to the Well-Behaved Costume Drama," *New Statesman & Society* 4(156):38, 21 Jun. 1991

LEWIS, IRA

Chinese Coffee, 1992
Gerard, J. *Variety* 347(11):69–70, 29 Jun. 1992
Gussow, M. *New York Times* 141:B3(N), 26 Jun. 1992
Henry, W. A., III. *Time* 140(1):70, 6 Jul. 1992
Kanfer, S. *New Leader* 75(9):22–23, 13 Jul. 1992
Leslie, G. *TheaterWeek* 5(51):33, 27 Jul. 1992
Simon, J. *New York* 25(27):66, 13 Jul. 1992

LEWISOHN, LUDWIG

Hutner, G. "The Dynamics of Erasure: Anti-Semitism and the Example of Ludwig Lewisohn," *Prospects* 16:391, 1991

LIEBERMAN, HAL

Kafka in Love, 1991
Skevington, O. R. *TLS* (4625):18, 22 Nov. 1991

LINNEY, ROMULUS

Linney, R. "Ambrosio," *Kenyon Review* 15(2):177–184, Sprg. 1993
————. "Can Can," *Antaeus* (66):283, Sprg. 1991
Schlatter, J. F. "Storyteller in the Wilderness: The American Imagination of Romulus Linney," *Southern Quarterly* 30(2):63, Wntr. 1992

Akhmatova, 1993
Mason, W. "The Wild West Meets the Wild East," *American Theatre* 10(10):122–24, Oct. 1993

The Sorrows of Frederick, 1991
Bell, J. "Frederick the Great," *TheaterWeek* 5(15):10, 18 Nov. 1991

Unchanging Love (adapted from Chekhov's short story "In the Hollow"), 1991
Disch, T. M. *Nation* 252(10):355, 18 Mar. 1991
Simonson, R. *TheaterWeek* 4(28):36, 18 Feb. 1991

LIPPA, LOUIS

Harry, L., and M. Ahearn. "The Face: Louis Lippa," *Philadelphia Magazine* 82(4):216, Apr. 1991

Sister Carrie (adaptation of Theodore Dreiser's novel), 1991
   Lingeman, R. *Nation* 252(20):711–12, 27 May 1991
   Simonson, R. *TheaterWeek* 4(43):40, 3 Jun. 1991

LOCKHEART, PAULA. *SEE* FRANDSEN, ERIC, MICHAEL GARIN, ROBERT
HIPKENS, and PAULA LOCKHEART

LOESSER, FRANK

Buckley, M. "Loesser-Mania," *TheaterWeek* 5(6):22–27, 16 Sep. 1991
Konas, G. "Frank Loesser's Hidden Class," *Biography* 16(3):264 Summ. 1993
Loesser, S. *A Most Remarkable Fella*
Sobran, J. "Adult Entertainment," *National Review* 44(10):46, 25 May 1992

The Most Happy Fella (musical version of *They Knew What They Wanted*, play by
   S. Howard), 1956
   Ansen, D. *Newsweek* 119(8):72, 24 Feb. 1992
   "Broadway Ballyhoo," *American Theatre* 254(11):392, 23 Mar. 1992
   Buckley, M. "Honey, I Shrunk the Musical," *TheaterWeek* 5(26):15–19, 3
      Feb. 1992
   ———. "The Most Happy Couple," *TheaterWeek* 6(2):23–25, 17 Aug.
      1992
   Corliss, R. "The Most Snappy Fella," *Time* 138(11):67–68, 16 Sep. 1991
   Dalva, N. "Crazy for *The Most Happy Fella*," *Dance Magazine* 66(5):60,
      May 1992
   Disch, T. M. *Nation* 254(11):392, 23 Mar. 1992
   Flood, P. *Vogue* 181(10):192, Oct. 1991
   ———. "Coward Meets Beckett," *Christopher Street* (175):7, 30 Mar. 1992
   Harris, J. *Christopher Street* 14(19):9, 6 Apr. 1992
   Holden, S. "That Two-Piano 'Fella,' " *New York Times* 141:H5, 2 Feb. 1992
   Kanfer, S. *New Leader* 75(3):22–23, 9 Mar. 1992
   Kozinn, A. "Spiro Malas, the Very Happy Star of Broadway's *Most Happy
      Fella*," *New York Times* 141:B3, 19 Feb. 1992
   Kramer, M. *New Yorker* 68(1):82–83, 24 Feb. 1992
   Mandelbaum, K. "Season Preview: The Musicals," *TheaterWeek* 5(1):18, 12
      Aug. 1991
   ———. *TheaterWeek* 5(7):34–35, 23 Sep. 1991
   ———. *TheaterWeek* 5(30):31, 2 Mar. 1992
   Osborne, C. L. "*Happy Fella* Yields Up Its Operatic Heart," *New York Times*
      140:H5, 1 Sep. 1991
   Rich, F. *New York Times* 140:B3, 30 May 1991
   ———. *New York Times* 141:B1, 14 Feb. 1992
   Richards, D. *New York Times* 140:H7, 2 Jun. 1991
   ———. *New York Times* 141:H5, 16 Feb. 1992
   Rothstein, E. *New York Times* 140:B8, 6 Sep. 1991
   Sobran, J. *National Review* 44(10):46, 25 May 1992
   Stempel, L. "The Musical Play Expands," *American Music* 10(2):136,
      Summ. 1992

"Suit Filed Over *Most Happy Fella* Music," *New York Times* 142:26, 23 Jan. 1993
Weales, G. *Commonweal* 119(10):13, 22 May 1992
Witchel, A. *New York Times* 140:B2, 12 Jul. 1991

SEE ALSO BURROWS, ABE, JO SWERLING, and FRANK LOESSER

SEE ALSO BURROWS, ABE, JACK WEINSTOCK, WILLIE GILBERT, and FRANK LOESSER

LOEWE, FREDERICK. *SEE* LERNER, ALAN JAY, and FREDERICK LOEWE

LOGAN, JOHN

Abarbanel, J. "John Logan: An Infatuation with History," *American Theatre* 9(5):40–41, Sep. 1992

Hauptmann, 1991
    Abarbanel, J. *TheaterWeek* 5(13):31, 4 Nov. 1991
    Disch, T. M. *Nation* 255(5):188, 17 Aug. 1992
    Evans, G. *Variety* 347(7):74, 1 Jun. 1992
    Gussow, M. *New York Times* 141:B7, 29 May 1992

Riverview: A Melodrama with Music, 1992
    Lazare, L. *Variety* 347(11):71, 29 Jun. 1992

LOGAN, JOSHUA. *SEE* HAMMERSTEIN, OSCAR, II, JOSHUA LOGAN, and RICHARD RODGERS

LONG, QUINCY

The Virgin Molly, 1992
    Bell, J. *TheaterWeek* 5(37):9–11, 20 Apr. 1992
    Evans, G. *Variety* 346(11):85, 30 Mar. 1992
    Gussow, M. *New York Times* 141:C3, 27 Mar. 1992

LONGDEN, ROBERT, and HEREWARD KAYE

Moby Dick (a rock version of Herman Melville's novel), 1992
    Filichia, P. "A Whale of a Tale," *TheaterWeek* 7(3):10–11, 23 Aug. 1993
    Hirschhorn, C. *TheaterWeek* 5(37):23–24, 20 Apr. 1992

LONSDALE, FREDERICK

On Approval, 1926
    Walker, J. K. L. *TLS* (4696):18, 2 Apr. 1993

LOPEZ, JOSEFINA

McFerran, V. D. "Chicana Voices in American Drama: Silviana Wood, Estela Portillo Trambley, Cherríe Moraga, Milcha Sanchez-Scott, Josefina Lopez," (#DA9119397; U of Minnesota) *DAI* 52(6):1946A, Dec. 1991

LUCAS, CRAIG

"Lucas, Craig," *Current Biography* 52(9):33–38, Sep. 1991
Lucas, C. *"Throwing Your Voice*: A New One-Act Commissioned by Naked Angels to Honor Amnesty International," *TheaterWeek* 5(23):22–28, 13 Jan. 1992

Orpheus in Love, 1992
 Coen, S. "See You in Hell," *American Theatre* 10(3):19–23, Mar. 1993
 Evans, G. *Variety* 349(9):68–69, 21 Dec. 1992
 Holland, B. "Busby: *Orpheus in Love*," *New York Times* 142:B3, 16 Dec. 1992
 Simon, J. *New York* 26(1):51, 4 Jan. 1993
 Simonson, R. *"Orpheus in Love* at Circle Repertory Theater," *Opera Monthly* 5(9):9, 1 Jan. 1993
 Weales, G. *Commonweal* 120(3):16–17, 12 Feb. 1993
 Weber, B. "A Clash of Performing Cultures," *New York Times* 142:B4, 25 Dec. 1992

Prelude to a Kiss, 1988
 Resnikova, E. "Prelude to a Movie," *National Review* 43(4):65, 18 Mar. 1991

LUCE, WILLIAM

Lucifer's Child, 1991
 Henry, W. A., III. *Time* 137(15):62, 15 Apr. 1991
 Kanfer, S. *New Leader* 74(5):21, 8 Apr. 1991
 Rich, F. *New York Times* 140:B2, 5 Apr. 1991
 Simon, J. *New York* 24(15):66, 15 Apr. 1991
 Simonson, R. *TheaterWeek* 4(38):34, 29 Apr. 1991

LUDLAM, CHARLES

Kennicott, P. "Outer Orbits: Explore the Ring's Lunatic Fringe—from Charles Ludlam to Melvin Gorham," *Opera News* 57(15):8, 10 Apr. 1993
Ludlam, C. "Charles Ludlam: In His Own Words," *TheaterWeek* 5(30):11–20, 2 Mar. 1992

Bluebeard (loosely based on *The Island of Lost Souls*, a sixty-year-old film), 1970
 Chansky, D. *TheaterWeek* 5(32):36, 16 Mar. 1992

Camille: A Tearjerker (adaptation of A. Dumas's *La Dame aux Camelias*), 1973
 Hornby, R. *Hudson Review* 44:109–12, Sprg. 1991
 O'Connor, P. *TLS* (4616):19, 20 Sep. 1991

LUDWIG, KEN

Lend Me a Tenor, 1991
>   Anderson, C. E. "From Harvard Law to Broadway; Attorney-Playwright Wins Critical Acclaim with *Lend Me a Tenor*," *ABA Journal* 77:36, Jan. 1991
>
>   Harvey, D. "Controversy Quakes San Francisco Theater," *Variety* 349(3):67–68, 9 Nov. 1992
>
>   Marowitz, C. *TheaterWeek* 5(27):38, 24 Feb. 1992
>
>   Riedel, M. "Carey Perloff to Ken Ludwig: 'Don't Lend *Us* a Tenor,' " *TheaterWeek* 6(8):22–23, 28 Sep. 1992

LUDWIG, KEN, GEORGE GERSHWIN, and IRA GERSHWIN

Crazy for You (revival of *Girl Crazy* with new book), 1991
>   Brustein, R. "Awards vs. Achievements," *New Republic* 207(2):28–29, 6 Jul. 1992
>
>   Clark, R. S. *Hudson Review* 45(4):629–36, Wntr. 1993
>
>   Disch, T. M. *Nation* 254(15):533–534, 20 Apr. 1992
>
>   Dunning, J. "Crazy for Dance, a Broadway Gypsy Creates Her Own," *New York Times* 141:H5, 16 Feb. 1992
>
>   Evans, G. "London Hit Filling 'Crazy' Coffers," *Variety* 350(13):73, 26 Apr. 1993
>
>   Filichia, P. "On the Leavel," *TheaterWeek* 5(32):11, 16 Mar. 1992
>
>   Flatow, S. *Playbill* 10(6):10, 31 Mar. 1992
>
>   Gerard, J. "Broadway Braces for Hot Tony Races," *Variety* 347(3):297–98, 4 May 1992
>
>   ———. *Variety* 345(11):48, 23 Dec. 1991
>
>   ———. *Variety* 346(6):256, 24 Feb. 1992
>
>   ———. *Variety* 349(12):83, 18 Jan. 1993
>
>   Gubernick, L. "Gershwin Crazy," *Forbes* 149(8):129, 13 Apr. 1992
>
>   Henry, W. A., III. "Tap Dancing into Yesterday," *Time* 139(9):56, 2 Mar. 1992
>
>   Herbert, I. *TCI* 27(5):13, May 1993
>
>   Horwitz, S. "Roger Horchow's Crazy," *TheaterWeek* 5(28):18–21, 17 Feb. 1992
>
>   Kanfer, S. *New Leader* 75(3):22, 9 Mar. 1992
>
>   Kroll, J. *Newsweek* 119(9):66, 2 Mar. 1992
>
>   Lochte, D. *Los Angeles Magazine* 38(7):94, Jul. 1993
>
>   Mandelbaum, K. "Season Preview: The Musicals," *TheaterWeek* 5(1):18, 12 Aug. 1991
>
>   ———. *TheaterWeek* 5(31):35–37, 9 Mar. 1992
>
>   Marowitz, C. *TheaterWeek* 7(3):38–39, 23 Aug. 1993
>
>   Moran, T. "Nice Work if You Can Get It," *TheaterWeek* 5(38):25–27, 27 Apr. 1992
>
>   Morley, S. "West End *Crazy* Rakes in Raves," *Variety* 350(6):67–68, 8 Mar, 1993
>
>   Oliver, E. *New Yorker* 68(2):68, 2 Mar. 1992

Ostlere, H. "Susan Stroman's Dream Season," *Dance Magazine* 66(5):36–39, May 1992

Rich, F. *New York Times* 141:B1, 20 Feb. 1992

———. *New York Times* 141:H13(N), 26 Apr. 1992

Shenton, M. *"Crazy for You,"* *Plays International* 8(6):10, 1 Jan. 1993

Simon, J. *New York* 25(9):56, 2 Mar. 1992

"Stage," *People Weekly* 37(11):96, 23 Mar. 1992

Torrens, J. S. *America* 168(5):120, 29 Aug. 1992

Weeks, J. *Variety* 351(4):53, 24 May 1993

Witchel, A. " 'If I Lost Every Single Penny, We Would Never Look Back,'" *New York Times* 141:H23, 16 Feb. 1992

Wolf, M. *Variety* 350(6):70, 8 Mar. 1993

LUNDEN, JEFFREY, and ARTHUR PERLMAN

Wings (a musical based on Arthur Kopit's play), 1993

Buckley, M. "The *Wings* of Words: A Q-and-A with Linda Stephens," *TheaterWeek* 6(32):26–31, 15 Mar. 1993

MacDONALD, ANN-MARIE

Goodnight Desdemona, (Good Morning Juliet), 1989

Coen, S. "Live Girls," *American Theatre* 9(8):10–11, Dec. 1992

Evans, G. *Variety* 349(1):75–76, 26 Oct. 1992

Gussow, M. *New York Times* 142:C26, 22 Oct. 1992

Powell, S. *"Goodnight Desdemona (Good Morning Juliet),"* *Shakespeare Bulletin*, 11(4):20, Fall 1993

Richards, D. *New York Times* 142:H5, 25 Oct. 1992

Weales, G. *Commonweal* 119(21):20, 4 Dec. 1992

MacLEAN, ROSS

Hyaena, 1992

Osborn, M. E. "Letter from Louisville," *TheaterWeek* 5(38):30, 27 Apr. 1992

Simons, T. *American Theatre* 9(2):52–53, May 1992

MacLEOD, WENDY

Barbecue in 29 Palms, 1992

Chase, A. "Reflections: A New Play Series at Geva," *TheaterWeek* 5(51):21–23, 27 Jul. 1992

The My House Play, 1993

Chansky, D. *TheaterWeek,* 4(30):37, 4 Mar. 1993

MADDOW, ELLEN

Brown Dog Is Dead, 1993

Bell, J. *TheaterWeek* 6(28):16, 15 Feb. 1993

SEE ALSO ZIMET, PAUL, and ELLEN MADDOW

MAGNUSON, ANN

You Could Be Home Now, 1992
   Bell, J. "Sheros," *TheaterWeek* 6(14):15, 2 Nov. 1992
   Chansky, D. "Ladies Not Ready to Lunch," *TheaterWeek* 6(14):30–31, 2
   Nov. 1992
   Greene, A. "Performance Power: An Interview with Ann Magnuson," *The-
   aterWeek* 6(12):28–29, 26 Oct. 1992

MAHAL, TAJ. *SEE* HURSTON, ZORA NEALE, LANGSTON HUGHES, and
TAJ MAHAL

MALECZECH, RUTH

Downey, R. "Hunkering Down with Mabou Mines," *American Theatre* 9(8):44–
   45, Dec. 1992

MALPEDE, KAREN

Kramer, R. E. "An Interview with Karen Malpede," *Studies in American Drama,
   1945-Present* 8(1):45–60, 1993

Better People: A Surreal Comedy About Genetic Engineering, 1990
   Mazer, S. *Theatre Journal* 42:369–70, Oct. 1990

Blue Heaven, 1992
   Bell, J. *TheaterWeek* 6(8):14, 28 Sep. 1992
   Lamont, R. C. *TheaterWeek* 6(13):33–34, 2 Nov. 1992

Kassandra (adaptation of Christa Wolf's novel), 1993
   Lamont, R. C. *TheaterWeek* 6(46):33–34, 21 Jun. 1993

Us, 1987
   Lamont, R. C., ed. *Women on the Verge: 7 Avant-Garde American Plays*

MALTBY, RICHARD, JR. *SEE* LAURENTS, ARTHUR, CHARLES STROUSE,
and RICHARD MALTBY, JR.

MAMET, DAVID

Blondell, J. D. "Myth and Antimyth in the Work of David Mamet,"
   (#DA9104489; U of California, Santa Barbara), *DAI* 52(2):348A, Aug. 1991
Caplan, B. "The Gender Benders," *New Statesman & Society* 6(259):34–35, 2
   Jul. 1993

Carroll, D. "The Recent Mamet Films: 'Business' versus Communion," 175–90 in L. Kane, ed. *David Mamet: A Casebook*

Chakravartee, M. "Open Theatre and 'Closed Society': Jean-Claude van Itallie and Mamet Reconsidered," *Literary Criterion* 26(3):48, 1991

Chi, W. *The Role of Language in the Plays of Mamet, Wilson, and Rabe*. Diss.; U of Iowa, 1991

Cohn, R. "How Are Things Made Round?" 109–21 in L. Kane, ed. *David Mamet: A Casebook*

Evans, G. "Top-Line Playwrights Write Off Broadway," *Variety* 348(6):63–64, 31 Aug. 1992

Gale, S. H. "David Mamet's *The Verdict*: The Opening Cons," 161–74 in L. Kane, ed. *David Mamet: A Casebook*

Goodman, W. "In Mamet's World, You Are How You Speak," *New York Times* 142:H24(N), 4 Oct. 1992

Hofrichter, T. G. *An Examination of David Mamet's World View*. M.A. Thesis; Marquette U, 1991

Hudgins, C. C. "Comedy and Humor in the Plays of David Mamet," 191–228 in L. Kane, ed. *David Mamet: A Casebook*

Joki, I. *Mamet, Baktin, and the Dramatic: The Demotic as a Variable of Addressivity*

Jones, N. W., and S. Dykes, eds. *File on Mamet*

Kane, L. "Interview with Gregory Mosher," 231–47 in L. Kane ed. *David Mamet: A Casebook*

———. "Interview with Joe Mantegna," 249–69 in L. Kane, ed. *David Mamet: A Casebook*

———. "Time Passages," *Pinter Review: Annual Essays* p. 30–49, 1990

Kane, L. and G. Brewer. "Bibliography," 271–310 in L. Kane, ed. *David Mamet: A Casebook*

Klaver, E. T. "Postmodernism and Metatextual Space in the Plays of Beckett, Ionesco, Albee, and Mamet," (#DA9034598; U of California, Riverside) *DAI* 51(7):2377A, Jan. 1991

Lopate, P. "With Pen in Hand, They Direct Movies," *New York Times* 141:H7(N), 16 Aug. 1992

Mamet, D. *The Cabin: Reminiscence and Diversions*

———. "Homespun Fop," *New York Times Magazine* 141:14, 21 Jun. 1992

———. "Hotel Atlantic," *Grand Street* 41:145–47, Wntr. 1991

———. "A Joe from Chicago," *Vogue* 181(4):308–11, Apr. 1991

———. "A Life with No Joy in It," *Antaeus* (66):291–296, Sprg. 1991

———. "Our Best Director: A Tribute to Gregory Mosher," *TheaterWeek* 5(37):29 +, 20 Apr. 1992

———. "The Rake: A Few Scenes from My Childhood," *Harper's Magazine* 284(1705):69–72, Jun. 1992

———. "Two Colors," *New Yorker* 69(38):80, 15 Nov. 1993

———. "The Waterworld," *Ploughshares* 19(1):187, Sprg. 1993

McDonough, C. J. "Every Fear Hides a Wish: Unstable Masculinity in Mamet's Drama," *Theatre Journal* 44(2):195–205, May 1992

———. "Staging Masculinity: The Search for Male Identity in Contemporary American Drama," (#DA9306664; U of Tennessee) *DAI* 53(11):3910A, May 1993

Nelson, J. A. "A Machine Out of Order: Indifferentiation in David Mamet's *The*

Disappearance of the Jews," *Journal of American Studies* 25: 461–72, Dec. 1991

Radavich, D. "Man Among Men: David Mamet's Homosocial Order," *American Drama* 1(1):46–60, Fall 1991

Richards, D. "Mamet's Women," *New York Times* 142:H1(N), 3 Jan. 1993

Savran, D. "New Realism: Mamet, Mann and Nelson," 63–80 in B. King, ed. *Contemporary American Theatre*

Story, R. D. "Mamet Plows Second Avenue," *New York* 25(36):58, 14 Sep. 1992

Taylor, M. "Mamet Fires Up Kinescope," *Variety* 347(1):49, 20 Apr. 1992

Wilentz, S. "Tales of Hoffa: A Movie's Shady Connections and Disconnections," *New Republic* 208(5):53, 1 Feb. 1993

Zinman, T. S. "Jewish Aporia: The Rhythm of Talking in Mamet," *Theatre Journal* 44(2):207–15, May 1992

American Buffalo, 1976

    King, T. L. "Talk and Dramatic Action in *American Buffalo,*" *Modern Drama* 34(4):538–48, Dec. 1991

    LaRosa, J. E. *On Directing Mamet's American Buffalo.* M.A. Thesis; Emerson College, 1993

    Zeifman, H. "Phallus in Wonderland: Machismo and Business in David Mamet's *American Buffalo* and *Glengarry Glen Ross,*" 123–35 in L. Kane, ed. *David Mamet: A Casebook*

Duck Variations, 1975

    Goist, P. D. "Ducks and Sex in David Mamet's Chicago," *Midamerica* 18:143–52, 1991

Glengarry Glen Ross, 1983

    Bernstein, R. "Despite Odds, *Glengarry* Becomes a Film," *New York Times* 140:B1(N), 15 Aug. 1991

    Kim, Y. "Degradation of the American Success Ethic: *Death of a Salesman, That Championship Season,* and *Glengarry Glen Ross,*" *Journal of English Language and Literature* 37(1):233–48, Sprg. 1991

    Woods, M. *David Mamet's Games in Glengarry Glen Ross, Homicide, and House of Games.* M.A. Thesis; Florida Atlantic U, 1993

Homicide

    Woods, M. *David Mamet's Games in Glengarry Glen Ross, Homicide, and House of Games.* M.A. Thesis; Florida Atlantic U, 1993

House of Games

    Woods, M. *David Mamet's Games in Glengarry Glen Ross, Homicide, and House of Games.* M.A. Thesis; Florida Atlantic U, 1993

A Life in the Theater, 1977

    Simonson, R. *TheaterWeek* 5(34):34, 30 Mar. 1992

Oleanna, 1992

    Evans, G. "Closings Crowd Off B'way," *Variety* 353(6):83–84, 13 Dec. 1993

Gerard, J. *Variety* 349(1):76, 26 Oct. 1992

Greene, A. *TheaterWeek* 6(17):30, 30 Nov. 1992

Henry, W. A., III. *Time* 140(18):69, 2 Nov. 1992

Holmberg, A. "The Language of Misunderstanding," *American Theatre* 9(6):94–95, Oct. 1992

Hornby, R. *Hudson Review* 46:193–4, Sprg. 1993

Kanfer, S. *New Leader* 75(16):26–27, 14 Dec. 1992

Kroll, J. *Newsweek* 120(19):65, 9 Nov. 1992

Lahr, J. *New Yorker* 68(39):121–25, 16 Nov. 1992

Mufson, D. *Theater* 24(1):111–13, Wntr. 1993

Resnikova, E. *National Review* 45(1):54–56, 18 Jan. 1993

Rich, F. *New York Times* 142:B1(N), 26 Oct. 1992

Richards, D. *New York Times* 142:H1(N), 8 Nov. 1992

Showalter, E. *TLS* (4675):16–17, 5 Nov. 1992

Silverthorne, J. "PC Playhouse," *Artforum* 31(7):10–11, Mar. 1993

Simon, J. *New York* 25(44):72, 9 Nov. 1992

Simpson, J. C. "Mamet Man: William H. Macy Battles the Sexes in *Oleanna*," *TheaterWeek* 6(14):21–23, 2 Nov. 1992

Story, R. D. "David Mamet Raises Outrage to an Artform in *Oleanna*," *New York* 25(36):58–59, 14 Sep. 1992

Taylor, M. *Variety* 347(4):127, 11 May 1992

Weales, G. *Commonweal* 119(21):15–16, 4 Dec. 1992

Weber, B. "Sex Battle, No Code," *New York Times* 142:B6(N), 30 Oct. 1992

Wolf, M. *American Theatre* 10(11):77–78, Nov. 1993

Sexual Perversity in Chicago, 1975

Goist, P. D. "Ducks and Sex in David Mamet's Chicago," *Midamerica: The Yearbook of the Society for the Study of Midwestern Literature* 18:143–52, 1991

Skeele, D. "The Devil and David Mamet: *Sexual Perversity in Chicago* as Homiletic Tragedy," *Modern Drama* 36(4):512–518, Dec. 1993

Speed-the-Plow, 1988

Gussow, M. *New York Times* 140:B3(N), 15 Aug. 1991

Hall, A. C. "Playing to Win: Sexual Politics in David Mamet's *House of Games* and *Speed-the-Plow*," 137–60 in L. Kane, ed., *David Mamet: A Casebook*

Stafford, T. J. "*Speed-the-Plow* and *Speed the Plough*: The Work of the Earth," *Modern Drama* 36(1):38–47, Mar. 1993

Squirrels, 1974

Hirschhorn, C. *TheaterWeek* 6(37):16, 19 Apr. 1993

Showalter, E. *TLS* (4695):18, 26 Mar. 1993

Wolf, M. *Variety* 350(10):185–86, 5 Apr. 1993

Three Sisters (adaptation of Chekov)

Simonson, R. *TheaterWeek* 4(40):33, 13 May 1991

The Water Engine

Hunter, J. C. *Two Designs for the Theatre*. M.F.A. Thesis; U of Texas at Austin, 1993

Westerman, K. M. *A Production of David Mamet's The Water Engine*. M.F.A. Thesis; U of Texas, Austin, 1993

MANN, EMILY

Mitchell, K. S. "Intrinsic Intertextuality: A Methodology for Analyzing the Seamless Intertext," (#DA9123222; Louisiana State U) *DAI* 52(3):919A, Sep. 1991
Savran, D. "New Realism: Mamet, Mann and Nelson," 63–80 in B. King, ed. *Contemporary American Theatre*

SEE ALSO SHANGE, NTOZAKE, EMILY MANN, and BAIKIDA CARROLL

MANTEGNA, JOE

Mamet, D. "A Joe from Chicago," *Vogue* 181(4):308–11, Apr. 1991
Seidenberg, R. "Joe Mantegna's Mountain of Work," *American Film* 16:47–8, Jan. 1991
Tanner, L. "Who's in Town," *Films in Review* 43(1/2)38–39, Jan/Feb. 1992

MARAINI, DACIA

Dialogue Between a Prostitute and Her Client
    Mitchell, T. " 'Scrittura Femminile': Writing the Female in the Plays of Dacia Maraini," *Theatre Journal*, Oct. 1990

MARGOLIN, DEBORAH

Gestation, 1991
    Richheimer, J. "High-Heeled and Pregnant," *TheaterWeek* 5(9):23–25, 7 Oct. 1991

Lesbians Who Kill, 1992
    Hart, L. *Theatre Journal* 44(4):515–18, Dec. 1992
    Raymond, G. "Lesbians Who Kill: Peggy Shaw and Lois Weaver and the Men That Made Them Do It," *TheaterWeek* 5(47):22–26, 29 Jun. 1992

MARGOLIN, DEBORAH, and PEGGY SHAW

Little Women: the Tragedy (based on the life and work of Louisa May Alcott), 1992
Margolin, D., and P. Shaw, *Little Women: the Tragedy* (excerpt), *Kenyon Review* 15(2):14–26, Sprg. 1993
Patraka, V. M. "Split Britches in *Little Women: the Tragedy*: Staging, Censorship, Nostalgia, and Desire," *Kenyon Review* 15(2):6–13, Sprg. 1993

MARGOLIN, DEB, and RAE C. WRIGHT

The Breaks, 1992
Ungaro, J. *TheaterWeek* 6(9):37, 5 Oct. 1992

MARGULIES, DONALD

Margulies, D. "A Playwright's Search for the Spiritual Father," *New York Times* 141:H5(N), 21 Jun. 1992
―――. "Sight Unseen," *American Theatre* 9(7):1A, Nov. 1992

The Loman Family Picnic, 1989
Brantley, B. *New York Times* 143:B1(N), 19 Nov. 1993
Evans, G. *Variety* 353(4):32–33, 39 Nov. 1993
Henry, W. A., III. *Time* 142(23):73, 29 Nov. 1993
Simon, J. *New York* 26(48):131, 6 Dec. 1993

Sight Unseen, 1992
Disch, T. M. *Nation* 254(8):282, 2 Mar. 1992
Dubner, S. J. "In the Paint," *New York* 25(10):48–52, 9 Mar. 1992
Haus, M. "Masterpiece Theater," *ARTnews* 91(6):20–21, Summ. 1992
Hornby, R. *Hudson Review* 45(3):452–58, Autm. 1992
Kanfer, S. *New Leader* 75(9):23, 13 Jul. 1992 Kramer, M. *New Yorker* 67(50):70–71, 3 Feb. 1992
Schlueter, J. "Ways of Seeing in Donald Margulies' *Sight Unseen*," *Studies in American Drama, 1945-Present* 8(1):3, 1993
Simon, J. *New York* 25(5):53–54, 3 Feb. 1992
―――. *New York* 25(30):51, 3 Aug. 1992
Simonson, R. *TheaterWeek* 5(27):35, 24 Feb. 1992
Torrens, J. S. *America* 166(18):463–64, 23 May 1992

MARKS, WALTER. *SEE* KINOY, ERNEST, and WALTER MARKS

MARLEY, DONOVAN. *SEE* SERGEL, CHRISTOPHER, GAYLE SERGEL, and DONOVAN MARLEY

MAROWITZ, CHARLES

Burnt Bridges, 1991
Tallmer, J. *TheaterWeek* 4(23):36–39, 14 Jan. 1991

MARREN, HOWARD. *SEE* SWEET, JEFFREY, SUSAN BIRKENHEAD, and HOWARD MARREN

MARSHALL, GARRY, and LOWELL GANZ

Caputi, J. "Sleeping with the Enemy as Pretty Woman, Part II? or What Happened After the Princess Woke Up," *Journal of Popular Film and Television* 19:2–8, Sprg. 1991

Greenberg, H. R. "Rescrewed: Pretty Woman's Co-opted Feminism," *Journal of Popular Film and Television* 19:9–13, Sprg. 1991

Wrong Turn at Lungfish, 1993
    Everett, T. *Variety* 347(7):74, 1 Jun. 1992
    Gerard, J. *Variety* 350(5):64–65, 1 Mar. 1993
    Greene, A. *TheaterWeek* 6(31):35, 8 Mar. 1993
    Henry, W. A., III. *Time* 141(9):64, 1 Mar. 1993
    Kanfer, S. *New Leader* 76(4):23, 8 Mar. 1993
    Oliver, E. *New Yorker* 69(3):101, 8 Mar. 1993
    Rich, F. *New York Times* 12:B1(N), 22 Feb. 1993
    Richards, D. *New York Times* 142:H5(N), 28 Feb. 1993
    Simon, J. *New York* 26(10):85–86, 8 Mar. 1993

MARTIN, JANE

Gussow, M. "Plays by Women, Mostly About Violence," *New York Times* 142:B1(N), 24 Mar. 1993

Keely and Du, 1993
    King, R. L. *North American Review* 278:44–45, Mar/Apr. 1993
    Pearce, M. "Is Forgiveness Possible?" *American Theatre* 19(11):8–9, Nov. 1993

MASON, TIMOTHY

Babylon Gardens, 1991
    Disch, T. M. *Nation* 253(18):682–83, 25 Nov. 1991
    Ungaro, J. *TheaterWeek* 5(12):40–41, 28 Oct. 1991

MASTEROFF, JOE, SHELDON HARNICK, and JERRY BOCK

Corman, A. "Curtain Call for the 'Ice Cream' Team," *New York Times* 143:H5(N), 3 Oct. 1993

She Loves Me, 1963
    Buckley, M. "We Love Her: Sally Mayes on Broadway in *She Loves Me*," *TheaterWeek* 6(45):18–21, 14 Jun. 1993
    Gerard, J. *Variety* 351(7):45–47, 21 Jun. 1993
    ———. *Variety* 352(10):53, 18 Oct. 1993
    Harris, W. "This Actor's Director Has Been There Himself," *New York Times* 142:H5(N), 6 Jun. 1993
    Henry, W. A., III. *Time* 141(25):68, 21 Jun. 1993
    Kanfer, S. *New Leader* 76(9):21–22, 12 Jul. 1993
    Mandelbaum, K. *TheaterWeek* 6(47):37–38, 28 Jun. 1993
    Oliver, E. *New Yorker* 69(19):95, 28 Jun. 1993
    Rich, F. *New York Times* 142:B1(N), 11 Jun. 1993
    ———. *New York Times* 143:C20(L), 8 Oct. 1993

Richards, D. *New York Times* 142:H5(N), 20 Jun. 1993
———. *New York Times* 143:H5(N), 24 Oct. 1993
Simon, J. *New York* 26(27):58–59, 12 Jul. 1993
———. *New York* 26(42):100, 25 Oct. 1993

MATTEI, PETER

Tiny Dimes, 1992
Simonson, R. *TheaterWeek* 6(52):36–37, 2 Aug. 1992

MAY, ELAINE

Mr. Gogol and Mr. Preen, 1991
Gussow, M. *New York Times* 140:B3(N), 10 Jun. 1991
Ungaro, J. *TheaterWeek* 4(49):42, 15 Jul. 1991

McCABE, PATRICK 1955

Frank Pig Says Hello, 1993
O'Neill, J. *TLS* (4696):19, 2 Apr. 1993

McCAULEY, ROBBIE

Outlaw, M. D. "New Tracks on Tobacco Road," *American Theatre* 10(10):100–02, Summ. 1993
Patraka, V. "Robbie McCauley: Obsessing in Public," *TDR* 37(2):25–55, Summ. 1993
Solomon, A. "A New York Diary, 1992," *Theater* 24(1):7–18, Wntr. 1993

Mississippi Freedom: South and North, 1993
McCauley, R. *Theater* 24(2):88–97, Sprg. 1993

Sally's Rape, 1992
Solomon, A. "A New York Diary, 1992," *Theater* 24(1):7–18, Wntr. 1993

SEE ALSO CARLOS, LAURIE, and ROBBIE McCAULEY

McCLINTON, MARION ISAAC

Police Boys, 1992
Giuliano, M. *Variety* 347(2):101, 27 Apr. 1992
Nesmith, N. G. "Marion Isaac McClinton: Listening for the Music," *American Theatre* 10(5/6): 41, May/Jun. 1993

McCUTCHEN, HEATHER

A Walk on Lake Erie, 1991
Bell, J. *TheaterWeek* 4(32):40, 18 Mar. 1991

McDONALD, HEATHER

Dream of a Common Language, 1992
    Gussow, M. *New York Times* 141:B3(N), 26 May 1992
    Harvey, D. *Variety* 347(3):300, 4 May 1992

McGHEE-ANDERSON, KATHLEEN

Mothers, 1993
    Ungaro, J. *TheaterWeek* 6(36):28, 12 Apr. 1993

McGUINNESS, FRANK

Someone Who'll Watch Over Me, 1992
    Kanfer, S. *New Leader* 75(15):22–23, 30 Nov. 1992
    King, R. L. *North American Review* 278(2):41–42, Mar/Apr. 1993
    Oliver, E. *New Yorker* 68(42):154, 7 Dec. 1992
    Pilarz, S. *America* 168(11):17, 3 Apr. 1993
    Rich, F. *New York Times/NYTIA* 142:B1(N), 24 Nov. 1992
    Simon, J. *New York* 25(48):68–69, 7 Dec. 1992
    Skipitares, T. *New York Times* 142:H5(N), 6 Dec. 1992
    Weales, G. *Commonweal* 120(5):15–16, 12 Mar. 1993
    Weber, B. "Reason for a Playwright to Relax," *New York Times* 142:B4(N),
        26 Feb. 1993

McHUGH, JIMMY. *SEE* ALLEN, RALPH, JIMMY McHUGH, and MICHAEL
VALENTI

McINTYRE, DENNIS

Modigliani, 1978
    Gussow, M. *New York Times* 140:C15(L), 1 May 1991

McKAY, W. COLIN

Nagasaki Dust, 1992
    Mazer, C. M. *American Theatre* 9(5):11, Sep. 1992

McLARTY, RON

The Dropper, 1991
    Ungaro, J. *TheaterWeek* 5(20):38, 23 Dec. 1991

McNALLY, TERRENCE

Corliss, R. "Success Is His Best Revenge," *Time* 142(8):73, 23 Aug. 1993
McNally, T. "Prelude and Liebestod," *Antaeus* (66):309–319, Sprg. 1991

Richards, D. "A Working Playwright Edges into Fame," *New York Times* 142:H1(N), 29 Aug. 1993

Lips Together, Teeth Apart, 1991
Filichia, P. "Let's Go on with the Show," *TheaterWeek* 5(35):11, 6 Apr. 1992
Henry, W. A., III. *Time* 138(3):65, 22 Jul. 1991
Janowitz, B. "More Hits from the Right," *American Theatre* 10(10):95–96, 23 May 1992
Leslie, G. *TheaterWeek* 4(50):42, 22 Jul. 1991
Montgomery, B. "*Lips Together, Teeth Apart*: Another Version of Pastoral," *Modern Drama* 36(4):547–555, Dec. 1993
Oliver, E. *New Yorker* 67(20):78, 8 Jul. 1991
Resnikova, E. *National Review* 43(14):55, 12 Aug. 1991
Rich, F. *New York Times* 140:B3(N), 26 Jun. 1991
Richards, D. *New York Times* 140:H5(N), 14 Jul. 1991
Rothstein, M. *New York Times* 140:C11(L), 3 Jul. 1991
Tallmer, J. "Lobster Quadrille," *TheaterWeek* 4(48):29–31, 8 Jul. 1991
Torrens, J. S. *America* 166(18):463, 23 May 1992
Witchel, A. "Home Cooking on Stage in *Lips*," *New York Times* 140:B2(N), 28 Jun. 1991

The Lisbon Traviata, 1985 (later revised)
Roman, D. " 'It's My Party and I'll Die if I Want to': Gay Men, AIDS, and the Circulation of Camp in U.S. Theatre," *Theatre Journal* 44(3):305–27, Oct. 1992

A Perfect Ganesh, 1993
Brustein, R. *New Republic* 209(8/9):32–33, 23 Aug. 1993
Gerard, J. *Variety* 351(9):58, 12 Jul. 1993
Henry, W. A., III. *Time* 142(2):60, 12 Jul. 1993
Kanfer, S. *New Leader* 76(10):23, 9 Aug. 1993
Oliver, E. *New Yorker* 69(21):95, 12 Jul. 1993
Rich, F. *New York Times* 142:B1(N), 28 Jun. 1993
Simon, J. *New York* 26(30):57, 2 Aug. 1993
Torrens, J. S. *America* 169(4):22, 14 Aug. 1993
Weales, G. *Commonweal* 120(16):20, 24 Sep. 1993

McNALLY, TERRENCE, JOHN KANDOR, and FRED EBB

Kiss of the Spider Woman (musical version of novel by M. Puig), 1990
Chase, A. "Terrence McNally's *Kiss*," *TheaterWeek* 6(41):16–19, 17 May 1993
Evans, G. "'92 Carry-Overs Count in Rocky Season Tally," *Variety* 351(2):243–44, 10 May 1993
Fricker, K. "*Kiss of the Spider Woman* Is Part of Harold Prince's Web," *New York Times* 142:H7(N), 2 May 1993
Gerard, J. *Variety* 351(2):244, 10 May 1993
Henry, W. A., III. "Along Comes the Spider," *Time* 141(18):70–71, 3 May 1993

————. "The Gay White Way," *Time* 141(20):62–63, 17 May 1993
————. *Time/TYMEA* 140(22):77, 30 Nov. 1992
Hirschhorn, C. "Spider Woman," *TheaterWeek* 6(17):27, 30 Nov. 1992
Johnson, B. D. "Kiss of Stardom," *Maclean's* 106(23):58, 7 Jun. 1993
Kanfer, S. *New Leader* 76(8):23, 14 Jun. 1993
Kroll, J. *Newsweek* 121(20):70, 17 May. 1993
Mandelbaum, K. *TheaterWeek* 6(42):27–29, 24 May 1993
Morley, S. "Will *Spider Woman* Weave West End Web?" *Variety* 349(1):73–74, 26 Oct. 1992
Murray, K. *Variety* 347(10):50, 22 Jun. 1992
Oliver, E. *New Yorker* 69(14):104, 24 May 1993
Peyser, M. N. *Newsweek* 121(21):63, 24 May 1993
Raymond, G. "Meet Chita!" *TheaterWeek* 6(22):14–18, 4 Jan. 1993
Rich, F. *New York Times* 142:B1(N), 4 May 1993
Richards, D. "Visions of Heaven—and of Hell," *New York Times* 142:H1(N), 16 May 1993
Sandla, R. "*Kiss of the Spider Woman*: Jerome Sirlin Creates a Shadowy World of Dreams and Despair," *TCI* 27(5):36, May 1993
Simon, J. *New York* 26(20):103, 17 May 1993
"A Starlight Spider's Web," *Americas* 44(2):3 +, Mar/Apr. 1992
"Tony Awards Presented," *Facts on File* 53(2742):454, 17 Jun. 1993
Torrens, J. S. *America* 169(16):21, 20 Nov. 1993
Wallach, A. "Designing Spider Woman," *TheaterWeek* 6(39):14–18, 3 May 1993
Weber, B. "*Kiss of the Spider Woman* and *Tommy* Dominate the Predictions," *New York Times* 142:B8(N), 4 Jun. 1993
Wilson, E. *Wall Street Journal* A18, 5 May 1993
Wolf, M. *Variety* 349(1):73–74, 26 Oct. 1992

McPHERSON, SCOTT

Anderson, P. "Fabulous Invalids," *TheaterWeek* 5(18):34, 9 Dec. 1991
Lambert, B. "Scott W. McPherson, 33, Actor and Author of a Hit Stage Play," *New York Times* 142:C11(N), 9 Nov. 1992

Marvin's Room, 1991
Disch, T. M. *Nation* 254(15):534, 20 Apr. 1992
Harris, J. "PWA's—Playwrights with AIDS," *Christopher Street* 14(20):5–7, 13 Apr. 1992
Ickes, B. "Lying Down on the Job," *New York* 25(20):19, 18 May 1992
King, R. L. *Massachusetts Review* 32(1):158–59, Sprg. 1991
Simonson, R. *TheaterWeek* 5(21):28, 30 Dec. 1991
"Winning Writers," *American Theatre* 8(10):62–63, Jan. 1992
Weales, G. *Commonweal* 119(2):27, 31 Jan. 1992

MEDLEY, CASSANDRA

Medley, C. "Waking Women," *Antaeus* 334–340, Sprg. 1991

MEDOFF, MARK

Gladstein, M. "An Interview with Mark Medoff," *Studies in American Drama, 1945-Present* 8(1):61–83, 1993

MEE, CHARLES L., JR.

Mee, C. L., Jr. *Orestes, Performing Arts Journal* (45):29–79, Sep. 1993

Another Person Is a Foreign Country, 1991
  Chansky, D. *TheaterWeek* 5(8):37, 30 Sep. 1991
  Holden, S. *New York Times* 140:B1(N), 10 Sep. 1991

MEEHAN, CHARLOTTE

voices of women and other girls, 1991
  Holbrook, C. *TheaterWeek* 5(6):40, 16 Sep. 1991

MEEHAN, THOMAS, MARTIN CHARNIN, and CHARLES STROUSE

Annie Warbucks, 1992
  Brantley, B. *New York Times* 142:B1(N), 10 Aug. 1993
  Buckley, M. "Donna McKechnie: But You Go On," *TheaterWeek* 6(52): 17–23, 2 Aug. 1993
  Collins, G. "Another Postponement for *Annie* Sequel," *New York Times* 142:8(N), 20 Feb. 1993
  Evans, G. " 'Warbucks' Big Bucks Blur Barriers," *Variety* 351(12):1–2, 2 Aug. 1993
  Gerard, J. "Slimmed-Down *Annie* Heads Downtown," *Variety* 351(4):1–2, 24 May 1993
  ———. "Warbucks to No Bucks: *Annie* Orphaned Again," *Variety* 350(4):229–30, 22 Feb. 1993
  ———. *Variety* 352(2):21–22, 23 Aug. 1993
  Grimes, W. "Will Tomorrow Come for *Annie Warbucks*?" *New York Times* 142:H8(N), 7 Mar. 1993
  ———. "Tomorrow Isn't Just Another Day," *New York Times* 142:H5(N), 8 Aug. 1993
  Harris, J. *Christopher Street* (207):4–5, Nov. 1993
  Henry, W. A., III. *Time* 142(8):69, 23 Aug. 1993
  Lazare, L. "In Chicago, B'Way Bound and Unbound," *Variety* 347(8):57–58, 8 Jun. 1992
  Mandelbaum, K. *TheaterWeek* 7(4):30–31, 30 Aug. 1993
  McGee, C. "When Annie Talks, People Listen," *New York Times* 142:H8(N), 29 Aug. 1993
  Oliver, E. *New Yorker* 69(27):162, 23 Aug. 1993
  Peyser, M. *Newsweek* 122(6):58, 9 Aug. 1993
  Richards, D. *New York Times* 142:H5(N), 15 Aug. 1993
  Riedel, M. "Two Strikes; Bases Loaded," *TheaterWeek* 6(52):11- 16, 2 Aug. 1993
  ———. "Wonderful Town," *TheaterWeek* 6(31):33–34, 8 Mar. 1993
  Sandla, R. "*Annie Warbucks* at Last," *Dance Magazine* 67(12):86, Dec. 1993
  Simon, J. *New York* 26(33):52, 23 Aug. 1993
  Smith, S. *TheaterWeek* 5(27):33, 24 Feb. 1992

SEE ALSO ADAMS, LEE, MITCH LEIGH, and THOMAS MEEHAN

MELVILLE, HERMAN

Kubiak, A. "Modern Theatre and Melville's *Moby-Dick*: Writing and Sounding the Whale," *Modern Drama* 34(1):107–17, Mar. 1991

MENKEN, ALAN, ALAN BENNERT, and DAVID SPENCER

Weird Romance, 1992
    Helbing, T. *TheaterWeek* 5(51):35, 27 Jul. 1992

MERRIAM, EVE

"Merriam, Eve." *Facts on File* 52(2682):279, 16 Apr. 1992
Lambert, B. "Eve Merriam, 75, Poet and Author Who Wrote for Children, Is Dead," *New York Times* 141:B5(N), 13 Apr. 1992
Minnich, E. K. "An Appreciation of Eve Merriam," *Ms. Magazine* 3(3):62, Nov/ Dec. 1992

MERZER, GLEN

Stopping the Desert, 1991
    Marowitz, C. *TheaterWeek* 4(38):38–39, 29 Apr. 1991

MEYER, MARLANE

"Blackburn Award Winner," *New York Times* 142:B2(N), 25 Feb. 1993

Etta Jenks, 1988
    Dolan, J. "Gender, Sexuality and 'My Life' in the Theater," *Kenyon Review* 15(2):185–200, Sprg. 1993

MILLER, ARTHUR

Adam, J. *Versions of Heroism in Modern American Drama: Redefinitions by Miller, O'Neill and Anderson*
Adler, T. P. "The Embrace of Silence: Pinter, Miller, and the Response to Power," *Pinter Review: Annual Essays* 4–9, 1991
Amin, S. "Migrants and Migration in the Plays of Arthur Miller," in N. Zaman, ed. *Migration, Migrants and the United States*
Babcock, G. *Rewriting the Masculine: The National Subject in Modern American Drama*. Diss.; Louisiana State U, 1993
Balakian, J. N. "The Evolution of Arthur Miller's Dramaturgy: 1944 to the Present," (#DA9204009; Cornell U) *DAI* 52(8):2922A, Feb. 1992
——. "An Interview with Arthur Miller," *Studies in American Drama, 1945-Present* 6(1):29–47, 1991

Banner, B. Ex. Producer. *A Tribute to Arthur Miller.* Videocassette

Berkowitz, G. M. *American Drama of the Twentieth Century.* 77, 156, 169

Billah, Q. M. *Arthur Miller: Theatre of Moral Quest.* M.A. Thesis; U of Texas, Dallas, 1992

Campo, C. A. *The Role of Friendship in Arthur Miller: A Study of Friendship in His Major Dramatic and Non-Dramatic Writing.* Diss.; U of Nevada, Las Vegas, 1993

Centola, S. R. *Arthur Miller in Conversation*

————. " 'Just Looking for a Home': A Conversation with Arthur Miller," *American Drama* 1(1):85–94, Fall 1991

Cohn, L. "Salutes to Vet Writers Highlight Guild Fete," *Variety* 350(9):16, 29 Mar. 1993

Cook, K. K. *"These Goddamned Women Have Injured Me": The Child-Narcissist in Arthur Miller's American Men.* M.A. Thesis; Millersville U, Pennsylvania, 1992

Davis, N. D., "The Playwright Who Planted Trees," *American Forests* 97 (3/4):56–59, Mar/Apr. 1991

Egri, P. "Dramatic Exposition and Resolution in O'Neill, Williams, Miller and Albee," *Neohelicon: Acta Comparationis Litterarum Universarum* 19(1):175–84, 1992

Evans, G. "Top-Line Playwrights Write Off Broadway," *Variety* 348(6):63, 31 Aug. 1992

Gintsburg, A., ed. *Naftule zeman: otobiyografyah*

Harris, J. "Decline and Fallacy," *Christopher Street* (199):4–5, Mar. 1993

Kallenberg-Schroder, A. *Autobiographisches in Arthur Millers familienzentrierten Dramen*

Kane, L. "Dreamers and Drunks: Moral and Social Consciousness in Arthur Miller and Sam Shepard," *American Drama* 1(1):27–45, Fall, 1991

Leshem-Ezra, D. *Artur Miler, Moto shel sokhen*

Miller, A. "After the Canonization," in M. E. Biggs, *In the Vernacular: Interviews at Yale with Sculptors of Culture*

————. *"The Last Yankee,"* *Antaeus* (66):341–8 Sprg. 1991

————. "Lost Horizon," *American Theatre* 9(4):68, Jul/Aug. 1992

————. "Way Back When," *Index on Censorship* 21(2):3, Feb. 1992

————. "We're Probably in an Art That Is—Not Dying," *New York Times* 142:H5(N), 17 Jan. 1993

Nourse, J. T. *Artur Miler Tsayad ha-mekhashefot*

Savran, D. *Communists, Cowboys, and Queers: The Politics of Masculinity in the Work of Arthur Miller and Tennessee Williams*

Wang, Qun. "On the Dramatization of the Illusory World in Tennessee Williams, Arthur Miller, and Edward Albee's Major Plays," (#DA9101987; U of Oregon) *DAI* 51(8):2569A, Feb. 1991

Zeineddine, N. *Because It Is My Name: Problems of Identity Experienced by Women, Artists, and Breadwinners in the Plays of Henrik Ibsen, Tennessee Williams, and Arthur Miller*

All My Sons, 1947

Boston Conservatory Recording. *Senior Directing Scene Workshops*

Townsend, P. D. *The Consequences of an Ambiguous Idealism: An Alternate View of Arthur Miller's All My Sons.* M.A. Thesis; West Chester U, 1993

The Crucible, 1953

Baker, I. L. *Brodie's Notes on Arthur Miller's The Crucible*

Fox, L. P. "A Comparative Analysis of Arthur Miller's *The Crucible* and Robert Ward's *The Crucible*," Chapter IV in *A Comparative Analysis of Selected Dramatic Works and Their Twentieth Century Operatic Adaptations*. Diss.; U of South Carolina, 1992

Garnett, E. H. *The Trials of Creativity: A Rhetorical Analysis of A View from the Bridge and The Crucible by Arthur Miller*. M.A. Thesis; California State U, San Bernardino, 1993

Hendrickson, G. P. "The Last Analogy: Arthur Miller's Witches and America's Domestic Communists," *Midwest Quarterly* 33(4):447–55, Summ. 1992

Hornby, R. *Hudson Review* 45:111–13, Sprg. 1992

Horton, L. M. *The Conflict of Conscience in Arthur Miller's The Crucible and A View from the Bridge*. M.A. Thesis; U of South Carolina, 1992

Mancini, A. *Focus on The Crucible by Arthur Miller*

Martine, J. J. *The Crucible: Politics, Property, and Pretense*

Pearson, M. "John Proctor and the Crucible of Individuation on Arthur Miller's *The Crucible*," *Studies in American Drama, 1945-Present* 6(1):15–27, 1991

Pinder, B. *Arthur Miller, Death of a Salesman, The Crucible, A Workshop Approach*

Death of a Salesman, 1949

Babcock, G. " 'What's the Secret?': Willy Loman as Desiring Machine," *American Drama* 2(1):59–83, Fall 1992

Centola, S. R. "Family Values in *Death of a Salesman*," *College Language Association Journal* 37(1):29–41, Sep. 1992

Cline, G. S. "The Psychodrama of the 'Dysfunctional' Family: Desire Subjectivity, and Regression in Twentieth-Century American Drama," (#DA9130458; Ohio State U) *DAI* 52(5):1742–43A, Nov. 1991

Diamond, C. *Theatre Journal* 45(1):108–10, Mar. 1993

Hart, J. "The Promised End: The Conclusion of Hoffman's *Death of a Salesman*," *Literature-Film Quarterly* 19(1):60–5, 1991

Kim, Y. "Degradation of the American Success Ethic: *Death of a Salesman, That Championship Season*, and *Glengarry Glen Ross*," *Journal of English Language and Literature* 37(1):233–48, Sprg. 1991

Lewis, K. *The Search for Personal Dignity in Three Modern American Dramas*. M.A. Thesis; Florida State U, 1991

Pinder, B. *Arthur Miller, Death of a Salesman, The Crucible, A Workshop Approach*

Stummer, A. *Kafka's Gregor Samsa and Miller's Willy Loman: A Comparison*. M.A. Thesis; U of Notre Dame, 1992

Tyson, L. "The Psychological Politics of the American Dream: *Death of a Salesman* and the Case for an Existential Dialectics," *Essays in Literature* 19(2):260–78, Fall 1992

Vogel, D. "From Milkman to Salesman: Glimpses of the Galut," *Studies in American Jewish Literature* 10(2):172–78, Fall 1991

Wang, Qun. "On the Dramatization of the Illusory World in Tennessee Williams, Arthur Miller and Edward Albee's Major Plays,'' (#DA9101987; U of Oregon) *DAI* 51(8):2569A, Feb. 1991

Zorn, T. E. "Willy Loman's Lesson: Teaching Identity Management with *Death of a Salesman*," *Communication Education* 40(2):219–24, Apr. 1991

The Last Yankee, 1992

Corliss, R. *Time* 141(6):72, 8 Feb. 1993

Gerard, J. *Variety* 349(13):140, 25 Jan. 1993

Greene, A. *TheaterWeek* 6(27):28, 8 Feb. 1993

Gussow, M. *New York Times* 140:C12(L), 19 Jun. 1991

———. *New York Times* 142:B5(N), 22 Jan. 1993

McNeil, H. *TLS* (4688):17, 5 Feb. 1993

Oliver, E. *New Yorker* 68(50):102, 1 Feb. 1993

Richards, D. *New York Times* 142:H8(N), 31 Jan. 1993

Simon, J. *New York* 26(5):61–62, 1 Feb. 1993

Simonson, R. "Values, Old and New," *TheaterWeek* 6(24):13–18, 18 Jan. 1993

Torrens, J. S. *America* 168(7):16–17, 27 Feb. 1993

Wolf, M. *Variety* 350(3):91, 15 Feb. 1993

Playing for Time (adaptation of his 1980 television drama), 1985

Pell, S. K. *A Feminist Analysis of Arthur Miller's Play Playing for Time*. M.A. Thesis; U of North Carolina, Chapel Hill, 1992

The Price, 1968

Gerard, J. *Variety* 347(9):62, 15 Jun. 1992

Gussow, M. *New York Times* 141:B3(N), 11 Jun. 1992

Hornby, R. *Hudson Review* 45(3):456–7, Autm. 1992

Murphy, K. C. *The Problematics of the Family in Buero Vallejo's El Tragaluz and Arthur Miller's The Price*. M.A. Thesis; U of North Carolina, Chapel Hill, 1993

Oliver, E. *New Yorker* 68(18):84, 22 Jun. 1992

Richards, D. *New York Times* 141:H5(N), 28 Jun. 1992

Simon, J. *New York* 25(27):66, 13 Jul. 1992

Simonson, R. *TheaterWeek* 5(51):30–31, 27 Jul. 1992

The Ride Down Mount Morgan, 1991

Raymond, G. "Letter from London," *TheaterWeek* 5(17):26, 2 Dec. 1991

Williams, H. *TLS* (4623):29, 8 Nov. 1991

Wolf, M. "Miller and Hare in Less than Top Form," *American Theatre* 8(10):50–53, Jan. 1992

A View from the Bridge, 1955 (revised 1956)

Costello, D. P. "Arthur Miller's Circles of Responsibility: *A View from the Bridge* and Beyond," *Modern Drama* 36(3):443–53, Sep. 1993

Garnett, E. H. *The Trials of Creativity: A Rhetorical Analysis of A View from the Bridge and The Crucible by Arthur Miller*. M.A. Thesis; California State U, San Bernardino, 1993

Horton, L. M. *The Conflict of Conscience in Arthur Miller's The Crucible and A View from the Bridge.* M.A. Thesis; U of South Carolina, 1992

McGurn, R. W. *Directing A View from the Bridge.* M.F.A. Thesis; U of Virginia, 1991

MILLER, JASON

That Championship Season, 1972

Kim, Y. "Degradation of the American Success Ethic: *Death of a Salesman, That Championship Season,* and *Glengarry Glen Ross,*" *Journal of English Language and Literature* 37(1):233–48, Sprg. 1991

MILLER, MAY

Miller, J. A. "Georgia Douglas Johnson and May Miller: Forgotten Playwrights of the New Negro Renaissance," *College Language Association Journal* 33(4):349–66, Jun. 1990

Nails and Thorns, 1933

"May Miller," 307–327 in L. Hamalian and J. V. Hatch, eds. *The Roots of African American Drama*

MILLER, TIM

Durland, S. "An Anarchic, Subversive, Erotic Soul: An Interview with Tim Miller," *TDR* 35:171–77, Fall, 1991

Miller, T. "Stretch Marks," *TDR* 35:143–70, Fall 1991

My Queer Body, 1992

Anderson, J. "Portraits of Gay Men, with No Apologies," *New York Times* 142:H6(N), 10 Jan. 1993

de Grazia, E. "Indecency Exposed," *Nation* 255(1):4–5, 6 Jul. 1992

Goodman, L. "Death and Dancing in the Live Arts: Performance, Politics and Sexuality in the Age of AIDS," *Critical Quarterly* 35:99–116, Summ. 1993

Gussow, M. *New York Times* 142:C14(L), 11 Dec. 1992

Phelan, P. "Tim Miller's *My Queer Body*: An Anatomy in Six Sections," *Theater* 24(2):30–34, Sprg. 1993

MITCHELL, JOSEPH S.

Help Wanted, 1929

"Joseph S. Mitchell," 204–30 in L. Hamalian and J. V. Hatch, eds. *The Roots of African American Drama*

MONK, MEREDITH

Anderson, J. "A Pair of Post-Modernists Look to Their Roots," *New York Times* 140:H6(N), 2 Jun. 1991

Mazo, J. H. "*Dance Magazine* Presents Its 1992 Awards for Distinguished Careers in Dance," *Dance Magazine* 66(4):16–17, Apr. 1992

Solomons, G., Jr. "Meredith Monk: Danspace Project at St. Mark's," *Dance Magazine* 65(8):66–67, Aug. 1991

Vanden Heuvel, M. "Complementary Spaces: Realism, Performance and a New Dialogics of Theatre," *Theatre Journal* 44(1):47–58, Mar. 1992

Atlas, 1991
  Baker, R. "Material Worlds," *PARABOLA* 16(3):88–92, Fall 1991
  Jowitt, D. "Ice Demons, Clicks and Whispers: Ever the Pioneer, Meredith Monk Is Still Pushing the Limits of Her Stagecraft," *New York Times Magazine* 140:18, 30 Jun. 1991
  Kozinn, A. "Keeping Up with Meredith Monk," *New York Times* 141:C19(L), 14 May, 1992
  Sandla, R. "Dream Weaver," *Opera News* 55(11):8–11, 16 Feb. 1991

MONTANO, LINDA

Something About Fear and Desire, 1990
  Cronacher, K. *Theatre Journal* 42:367–8, Oct. 1990

MORAGA, CHERRÍE

Lewis, A. "The Next Stage: She's Looking for a Bold New Theater of Color," *Mother Jones* 16(1):15, Jan/Feb. 1991

McFerran, V. D. "Chicana Voices in American Drama: Silviana Wood, Estela Portillo Trambley, Cherríe Moraga, Milcha Sanchez-Scott, Josefina Lopez," (#DA9119397; U of Minnesota) *DAI* 52(6):1946A, Dec. 1991

Moraga, C. "Art in America, Con Acento," *Frontiers* 12(3):154–160, Wntr. 1992

Romero, L. " 'When Something Goes Queer': Familiarity, Formalism, and Minority Intellectuals in the 1980's," *Yale Journal of Criticism* 6(1):121–41, Sprg. 1993

Rosenberg, L. "The House of Difference: Gender, Culture, and the Subject-in-Process on the American Stage," *Journal of Homosexuality* 26(2/3):97–110, Aug/Sep. 1993

MORRIS, MARK

Dalva, N. "Monnaie Dance Group/Mark Morris," *Dance Magazine* 65(2):110–11, Feb. 1991

Dunning, J. "Mark Morris Dance Group," *New York Times* 141:B3(N), 13 Jul. 1992

Morris, M. "Misha and Mark: Out on a Limb," *Dance Magazine* 65(1): 38–43, Jan. 1991

The Hard Nut (adaptation of Tchaikovsky's *Nutcracker*), 1991
  Acocella, J. *Vogue* 182(12):264–69, Dec. 1992
  Banks, D. "A New *Nutcracker*," *TheaterWeek* 6(18):24–25, 7 Dec. 1992

Croce, A. *New Yorker* 68(45):193–95, 28 Dec. 1992
Deresiewicz, B. *Dance Magazine* 67(3):92–93, Mar. 1993
Duffy, M. *Time* 140(26):67, 28 Dec. 1992
Dunning, J. "Mark Morris Gives *The Nutcracker* a Twist," *New York Times* 142:H1(L), 6 Dec. 1992
———. *New York Times* 143:C14(L), 16 Dec. 1993
Horn, M. "A *Nutcracker* Grows in Brooklyn," *U.S. News & World Report* 118(23):20, 14 Dec. 1992
Kisselgoff, A. *New York Times* 142:B1(N), 14 Dec. 1992
"Mark Morris Likes the Holidays, Really," *New Yorker* 69(43):56–57, 20 Dec. 1993
Moffet, L. *Dance Magazine* 65(4):87, Apr. 1991
O'Connor, J. J. *New York Times* 142:B5(N), 16 Dec. 1992
Ostlere, H. *Dance Magazine* 66(12):56–59, Dec. 1992
Shapiro, L. *Newsweek* 120(25):62–63, 21 Dec. 1992
Stanley, A. "Giving an Edge to *The Nutcracker*," *New York Times* 142:B1(L), 25 Dec. 1992
Tobias, T. *New York* 26(1):53, 4 Jan. 1993

MORRIS, PETER, and BRAD ELLIS

The Remarkable Ruth Fields, 1991
Filichia, P. *TheaterWeek* 5(9):13, 7 Oct. 1991

MORSE, CARL

Annunciation, 1991
Morse, C. *Annunciation*, 273–280 in T. Helbing, ed. *Gay and Lesbian Plays Today*

MORTON, CARLOS

Morton, C. "Rewriting Southwestern History: A Playwright's Perspective," *Mexican Studies-Estudios Mexicanos* 9(2):225–39, Summ. 1993

MOYER, JUDITH

It Had to Be Done, So I Did It, 1990
Pepe, F. L. *Oral History Review* 18:138–42, Fall 1990

MUELLER, LAVONNE

Violent Peace
Miles, J., ed. *Playwriting Women: 7 Plays from the Women's Project*

MULA, TOM. *SEE* HOLLANDER, NICOLE, ARNOLD APRILL, TOM MULA, STEVE RASHID, and CHERI COONS

NABOKOV, VLADIMIR

Boyd, B. "From Vladimir Nabokov, The American Years," *Scripsi* 7(1):35, 1991
Centerwall, B. S. "Vladimir Nabokov: A Case Study in Pedophilia," *Psychoanalysis and Contemporary Thought* 15(2):199, 1992

NARITA, JUDE

Coming into Passion/Song for a Sensei, 1991
    Burk, J. T. *Theatre Journal* 43(1):114–15, Mar. 1991
    Morris, R. "Jude Narita: No Exotic Flower," *American Theatre* 10(4):28, Apr. 1993

NASH, N. RICHARD, TOM JONES, and HARVEY SCHMIDT

110 in the Shade (musical version of Nash's play *The Rainmaker*), 1963
    Collins, G. "When Homeliness Is in the Eye of the Beholder," *New York Times* 141:C13(L), 30 Jul. 1992
    Davis, P. G. *New York* 25(30):54, 3 Aug. 1992
    Gerard, J. *Variety* 348(2):44, 3 Aug. 1992
    Griffiths, P. *New Yorker* 68(26):73, 17 Aug. 1992
    Jones, T. "The Making of *110 in the Shade*: Or, How We Learned to Work with David Merrick," *TheaterWeek* 5(50):14–21, 20 Jul. 1992
    Richards, D. *New York Times* 141:H5(N), 2 Aug. 1992
    Rothstein, E. *New York Times* 141:B3(N), 21 Jul. 1992
    Simon, J. *New York* 25(30):50–51, 3 Aug. 1992
    Traubner, R. *American Record Guide* 55(6):56–58, Nov/Dec. 1992

NAVE, BILL

Necktie Breakfast, 1991
    Chansky, D. *TheaterWeek* 5(16):39 + , 25 Nov. 1991

NEIPRIS, JANET

Neipris, J. "Brussels Sprouts," *Kenyon Review* 13(2):163–68, Sprg. 1991

NELSON, RICHARD

Savran, D. "New Realism: Mamet, Mann and Nelson," 63–80 in B. King, ed. *Contemporary American Theatre*

Between East and West, 1988
    Gussow, M. *New York Times* 142:B4(N), 12 Nov. 1992
    Scasserra, M. P. "Jack Hofsiss Directs Richard Nelson's New Play," *TheaterWeek* 6(13):30–32, 2 Nov. 1992

Columbus and the Discovery of Japan, 1992
    "Columbus," *Economist* 324(7771):78, 8 Aug. 1992
    Martin, M. "Discovering *Columbus*," *Plays International* 7(12):11, 1 Jul.
    1992
    Pitman, J. *Variety* 347(12):47, 13 Jul. 1992
    Reynolds, O. *TLS* (4661):18, 31 Jul. 1992

Misha's Party, 1993
    Wolf, M. *Variety* 352(4):28, 6 Sep. 1993
    Zinik, Z. *TLS* (4714):17, 6 Aug. 1993

Two Shakespearean Actors, 1991
    Alleman, R. *Vogue* 182(3):230, Mar. 1992
    Gerard, J. *Variety* 346(1):146, 20 Jan. 1992
    Henry, W. A., III. *Time* 139(4):67, 27 Jan. 1992
    Horwitz, S. "Tackling *Two Shakespearean Actors*," *TheaterWeek* 5(24):30–
    36, 20 Jan. 1992
    Kanfer, S. *New Leader* 75(2):22, 10 Feb. 1992
    Kramer, M. *New Yorker* 67(49):58–59, 27 Jan. 1992
    Lemon, B. "A Dry Wit's Season," *Connoisseur* 221(958):38–43, Nov. 1991
    Sandla, R. "*Two Shakespearean Actors*: Recalling the Grandeur of 19th-
    Century Theatre," *Theatre Crafts* 26(4):40–44, Apr. 1992
    Simon, J. *New York* 25(4):56–57, 27 Jan. 1992
    Simonson, R. *TheaterWeek* 5(28):37, 17 Feb. 1992

NELSON, RICHARD, TIM RICE, BENNY ANDERSSON, and BJÖRN
ULVAEUS

Chess, 1986 (Nelson did the book for this musical for the 1988 New York produc-
    tion; Des McAnuff and Robert Coe did further revisions in 1990)
    Evans, G. *Variety* 346(4):88–89, 10 Feb. 1992
    Gussow, M. *New York Times* 141:C19(L), 5 Feb. 1992
    Mandelbaum, K. *TheaterWeek* 5(27):28–32, 24 Feb. 1992
    Simon, J. *New York* 25(8):132, 24 Feb. 1992
    Wontorek, P. "*Chess*: the Rematch," *TheaterWeek* 5(28):22–23, 17 Feb.
    1991

NEMEROV, HOWARD

Potts, D. L. "Howard Nemerov: An Annotated Bibliography of Secondary
    Sources," *Bulletin of Bibliography* 50(4):63, 1 Dec. 1993
Rubin, L. D. "Obituary," *Sewanee Review* 99:673–8, Fall 1991

NEU, JIM

Situation Room, 1991
    Simonson, R. *TheaterWeek* 4(48):38, 8 Jul. 1991

NICHOLS, ANNE

Abie's Irish Rose, 1922
   Israel, L. "The Hit They Loved to Hate," *TheaterWeek* 4(52):25–27, 5 Aug.
      1991
   "Reversal of Fortune," *Opera News* 57(12):18, 27 Feb. 1993

NICHOLSON, WILLIAM

Shadowlands, 1991
   Disch, T. M. *Nation* 252(1):27–28, 7 Jan. 1991
   "Nigel Hawthorne: King of Heartbreak," *People Weekly* 35(5):57, 11 Feb.
      1991
   Hornby, R. "Performing the Classics," *Hudson Review* 44(1):105–12, Sprg.
      1991
   Torrens, J. S. *America* 164(14):421, 13 Apr. 1991
   Weales, G. *Commonweal* 118(3):99–100, 8 Feb. 1991

NOONAN, JOHN FORD

Music from Down the Hill, 1993
   Brantley, B. *New York Times* 143:B11(N), 31 Dec. 1993

The Rez Sisters, 1992
   Preston, J. "Weesageechak Begins to Dance: Native Earth Performing Arts
      Inc.," *TDR* 36(1):135–59, Sprg. 1992

Talking Things Over with Chekhov, staged reading in 1985
   Evans, G. *Variety* 350(9):88, 29 Mar. 1993

NORMAN, MARSHA

Berkowitz, G. M. *American Drama of the Twentieth Century*. 198 +
Brown, L. G. "Toward a More Cohesive Self: Women in the Works of Lillian
   Hellman and Marsha Norman," (#DA9201625; Ohio State U) *DAI*
   52(8):2919A, Feb. 1992
Chen, L. *Violence in the Spotlight: Exploring the Violent and Violated Female
   Characters in Selected Plays of Marsha Norman and Maria Irene Fornes*. M.A.
   Thesis; Northern Illinois U, 1993
Coen, S. "Marsha Norman's Triple Play," *American Theatre* 8(12):22–26, Mar.
   1992
Horwitz, S. "The Playwright as Woman," *TheaterWeek* 5(3):22, 26 Aug. 1991
Kachur, B. "Women Playwrights on Broadway: Henley, Howe, Norman, and Was-
   serstein," 15–40 in B. King, ed. *Contemporary American Theatre*
Kentucky Center for the Arts. *Marsha Norman*. Cassette
Workman, J. A. *Marsha Norman's Ghosts: The Embodiment of the Past on Stage*.
   M.A. Thesis; Indiana State U, 1993

Getting Out, 1977

    Britain, M. M. *Directing a Production of Marsha Norman's Getting Out.*
    M.F.A. Thesis; U of Massachusetts, Amherst, 1992

    Cline, G. S. "The Psychodrama of the 'Dysfunctional' Family: Desire, Sub-
    jectivity, and Regression in Twentieth-Century American Drama,"
    (#DA9130458; Ohio State U) *DAI* 52(5):1742–43A, Nov. 1991

Loving Daniel Boone, 1992

    Osborn, M. E. "Letter from Louisville," *TheaterWeek* 5(38):32, 27 Apr.
    1992

    Taylor, M. "Norman Play May Prove a Boone for Stamford," *Variety*
    348(8):55–56, 14 Sep. 1992

'night, Mother, 1983

    Demastes, W. W. "Jessie and Thelma Revisited: Marsha Norman's Concep-
    tual Challenge in *'Night Mother*," *Modern Drama* 36:109–19, Mar. 1993

    Smith, R. H. " *'night Mother* and *True West*: Mirror Images of Violence and
    Gender," 277–90 in J. Redmond, ed. *Violence in Drama*

NORMAN, MARSHA, and LUCY SIMON

Sarah and Abraham, 1992

    Daniels, R. L. *Variety* 346(5):78, 17 Feb. 1992

    Simonson, R. *TheaterWeek* 5(36):38, 13 Apr. 1992

    Weales, G. *Commonweal* 119(7):18–19, 10 Apr. 1992

The Secret Garden (musical version of novel by F. H. Burnett), 1989

    Anderson, P. "John Cameron Mitchell: The Deepest Secret in Broadway's
    Garden," *TheaterWeek* 5(37):33–35, 20 Apr. 1992

    Barbour, D. "*The Secret Garden*; Music and Mystery in a Haunted Doll's
    House," *Theatre Crafts* 25(8):42–47, Oct. 1991

    Buckley, M. "A Kinder, Gentler Uncle Archibald," *TheaterWeek* 5(20):14–
    15, 23 Dec. 1991

    ———. "The Secret Gardner," *TheaterWeek* 4(49):28–31, 15 Jul. 1991

    Evans, G. "Success of Garden Is No Promo Secret," *Variety* 343(12):39–40,
    1 Jul. 1991

    Gerard, J. *Variety* 348(10):86–87, 28 Sep. 1992

    Horwitz, S. "Inside the *Secret Garden*," *TheaterWeek* 5(27):22–27, 10 Feb.
    1992

    Huntington, J. "Making the *Secret Garden* Grow," *Theatre Crafts* 25(8):64–
    66, Oct. 1991

    Kanfer, S. *New Leader* 74(6):22–23, 6 May 1991

    Kennedy, L. "YPT Presents *The Secret Garden*," *Performing Arts & Enter-
    tainment in Canada* 27(1):9, Wntr. 1991

    Kramer, M. *New Yorker* 67(12):84–85, 13 May 1991

    Kroll, J. *Newsweek* 117(18):69, 6 May 1991

    Lassell, M. *Dance Magazine* 65(8):52, Aug. 1991

    McGee, C. "Gambling on a *Garden*," *New York* 24(16):64–68, 22 Apr. 1991

    Mandelbaum, K. *TheaterWeek* 4(40):38–39, 13 May 1991

    Pollack, J. *Variety* 347(6):60, 25 May 1992

Resnikova, E. *National Review* 43(14):56, 12 Aug. 1991
Stanley, A. "Marsha Norman Finds Her Lost Key to Broadway," *New York Times* 140:H5(N), 21 Apr. 1991
Weales, G. *Commonweal* 118(12):405–06, 14 Jun. 1991

NORMAN, MARSHA, and JULE STYNE

The Red Shoes, 1993
Mandelbaum, K. *TheaterWeek* 7(3):17, 23 Aug. 1993
"Marsha Norman: A Pulitzer-Winning Playwright Kicks Up Her Heels with *The Red Shoes*," *Mirabella* 5(7):60, 1 Dec. 1993
Tobias, T. "From Film to Stage, *The Red Shoes* Once Again Dances the Dance of Obsession," *New York* 26(36):80–81, 13 Sept. 1993

OATES, JOYCE CAROL

Grobel, L. "Playboy Interview," *Playboy* 40(11):63–73, Nov. 1993
Oates, J. C. "The Anatomy Lesson (excerpt from *The Secret Mirror*)," *Kenyon Review* 14(4):100–04, Fall 1992
———. "I've Got Something for You (excerpt from *The Secret Mirror*)," *Kenyon Review* 14(4):105–11, Fall 1992
———. "A Novelist Finds the Bare Bones of a Play," *Modern Drama* 34(1):1–3, Mar. 1991
———. "The Sacrifice," *American Poetry Review* 22:35–40, May/Jun. 1993
———. "Tone Clusters," *Antaeus* (66):349–368, Sprg. 1991
Todd, D. Y. "An Interview with Joyce Carol Oates," *Gettysburg Review* 6(2):291–99, Sprg. 1993

I Stand Before You Naked, 1990
Coon, B., Director. Videocassette
Disch, T. M. *Nation* 252(1):27–28, 7 Jan. 1991
Oates, J. C. *I Stand Before You Naked*. New York: S. French, 1991

Procedure, 1992
Osborn, M. E. "Letter from Louisville," *TheaterWeek* 5(38):32, 27 Apr. 1992

ODETS, CLIFFORD

Cantor, H. "Anderson and Odets and the Group Theater," 27–39 in N. J. D. Hazelton and K. Krauss, eds. *Maxell Anderson and the New York Stage*
Demastes, W. W. *Clifford Odets: A Research and Production Sourcebook*
Idleman, S. A. *Clifford Odets: The Family Plays*. M.A. Thesis; Drew U, 1992
Jones, B. S. R. *The Jewish Heritage in Four Plays of Clifford Odets*. M.A. Thesis; Angelo State U, 1992
Mishra, K. *American Leftist Playwrights of the 1930's: A Study of Ideology and Technique in the Plays of Odets, Lawson, and Sherwood*

Awake and Sing!, 1935
> King, R. L. *North American Review* 278:44–5, Mar/Apr. 1993
> Lahr, J. *New Yorker* 68(36):119–22, 26 Oct. 1992
> Nielsen, H. R. "Articulating Protest: The Personal and Political Rhetorics of Clifford Odets and Mari Sandoz in the 1930s," (#DA9129566; U of Nebraska, Lincoln) *DAI* 52(5):1535A, Nov. 1991

Golden Boy, 1937
> McCarten, J. "Cameo: The *Golden Boy*," *New Yorker* 69(15):68–70, 31 May 1993

Waiting for Lefty, 1935
> Bray, B. "Against All Odds: The Progressive Arts Club's Production of *Waiting for Lefty*," *Journal of Canadian Studies* 25:106–22, Fall 1990
> Krutch, J. W. "*Waiting for Lefty* and *Till the Day I Die*," in G. Miller, ed. *Critical Essays on Clifford Odets*

OLIENSIS, ADAM

Cowboy in His Underwear, 1992
> Simonson, R. *TheaterWeek* 5(34):33, 30 Mar. 1992

OLIVE, JOHN

Evelyn and the Polka King, 1992
> Olive, J. "*Evelyn and the Polka King*"
> Osborn, M. E. "Letter from Louisville," *TheaterWeek* 5(38):32, 27 Apr. 1992
> Rawson, C. *Variety* 350(10):186, 5 Apr. 1993

ONDAATJE, MICHAEL

Angelou, M., and H. Hertzberg, moderators. *Michael Ondaatje*. Videocassette.
Barbour, D. *Michael Ondaatje*
Bok, C. "Destructive Creation: The Politicization of Violence in the Works of Michael Ondaatje," *Canadian Literature* 132:109–24, Sprg. 1992
Bowen, D. "The Well-Lit Road and the Darkened Theatre: Photography in Biographies by Michael Ignatieff and Michael Ondaatje," *World Literature Written in English* 31(1):43, Sprg. 1991
Clavel, A. "Writers Without Borders," *World Press Review* 40(12):49, Dec. 1993
Garvie, M. "Listening to Michael Ondaatje," *Queen's Quarterly* 99(4):928, Wntr. 1992
Ray, S. "Memory, Identity, Patriarchy: Projecting a Past in the Memories of Sara Suleri and Michael Ondaatje," *Modern Fiction Studies* 39(1):37, Sprg. 1993
Siemerling, W. "Discoveries of the Other: Alterity in the Work of Leonard Cohen, Hubert Aquin, Michael Ondaatje, and Nicole Brossard," (#DANN69174; U of Toronto) *DAI* 53(8):2820A, Feb. 1993

The Collected Works of Billy the Kid, 1975
> Grace, D. M. "Ondaatje & Charleton Comics' *Billy the Kid,"* *Canadian Literature* 133:199–203, Summ 1992

O'NEAL, JOHN

DeRose, D. J. "John O'Neal: Do Start Him Talking," *Theater* 23(1):66–70, Wntr. 1992

Hammer, K. "John O'Neal, Actor and Activist: The Praxis of Storytelling," *TDR* 36(4):12, Wntr. 1992

O'NEILL, EUGENE

Adam, J. *Versions of Heroism in Modern American Drama: Redefinitions by Miller, Williams, O'Neill and Anderson*

Alexander, D. *Eugene O'Neill's Creative Struggle: The Decisive Decade, 1924–1933*

Babcock, G. *Rewriting the Masculine: The National Subject in Modern American Drama.* Diss.; Louisiana State U, 1993

Berkowitz, G. M. *American Drama of the Twentieth Century.* 16, 30, 66, 105,

Berlin, N. "O'Neill the 'Novelist,' " *Modern Drama* 34(1):49–58, Mar. 1991

Black, S. A. *File on O'Neill*

Bogard, T., ed. *The Eugene O'Neill Songbook*

———. *From the Silence of Tao House: Essays about Eugene & Carlotta O'Neill and the Tao House Plays*

Bower, M. G. *Eugene O'Neill's Unfinished Threnody and Process of Invention in Four Cycle Plays*

Cahill, G. "Mothers and Whores: The Process of Integration in the Plays of Eugene O'Neill," *Eugene O'Neill Review* 16(1):5–23, Sprg. 1992

Campana-Garcia, A. X. *A Woman's Quest for Happiness: O'Neill's "Private Myth".* M.A. Thesis; Eastern Illinois U, 1992

Ciancio, R. A. "Richard Wright, Eugene O'Neill, and the Beast in the Skull," *Modern Language Studies* 23(3):45, Summ. 1993

Cooper, B. L. "Some Problems in Adapting O'Neill for Film," 73–86 in R. F. Moorton, Jr., ed. *Eugene O'Neill's Century: Centennial Views on America's Foremost Tragic Dramatist*

Costello, D. P. "Forgiveness in O'Neill," *Modern Drama* 34(4):499–512, Dec. 1991

Cummingham, F. R. "Eugene O'Neill in Our Time: Overcoming Student Resistance," *Eugene O'Neill Review* 16(2):45, Fall 1992

Durling, E. A. *A Study of the Unrealized Projects and Related Ideas of Eugene O'Neill.* Theses Canadiennes. Ottawa: Bibliotheque nationale du Canada, 1991

Egri, P. "Dramatic Exposition and Resolution in O'Neill, Williams, Miller and Albee," *Neohelicon: Acta Comparationis Litterarum Universarum* 19(1):175–84, 1992

Flynn, J. "Sites and Sights: The Iconology of the Subterranean in Late Nineteenth-Century Irish-American Drama," *MELUS* 18(1):5 +, Sprg. 1993

Friesen, L., ed. *Theatre and Religion*

Hall, A. C. *A Kind of Alaska: Women in the Plays of O'Neill, Pinter, and Shepard*

Hammerman, H. J. "On Collecting O'Neill," *Eugene O'Neill Review* 15(1):93–96, Sprg. 1991

Harris, J. "Quintero Directs O'Neill," *TheaterWeek* 5(14):10, 11 Nov. 1991

Herr, L. "Theater and the Critics," 207–11 in R. F. Moorton, Jr., ed. *Eugene O'Neill's Century: Centennial Views on America's Foremost Tragic Dramatist*

Hoover, M. L. "Three O'Neill Plays in 1920s Productions by Tairov's Kamerny Theater," *Theater History Studies* 11:123–27, 1991

Houchin, J. H. *The Critical Response to Eugene O'Neill*

Khare, R. R. *Eugene O'Neill & His Visionary Quest*

Koreneva, M. "Eugene O'Neill and the Ways of American Drama," 100–25 in S. Chakovsky and M. T. Inge, eds. *Russian Eyes on American Literature*

Krutch, J. W., ed. *Nine Plays by Eugene O'Neill*

Lal, D. K. *Myth and Mythical Concept in O'Neill's Plays*

Mann, B. J. "An FBI Memorandum on O'Neill," *Eugene O'Neill Review* 15(1):58–63, Sprg. 1991

Maufort, M. "The Playwright as Lord of Touraine," *English Studies* 71:501–8, Dec. 1990

McDonough, E. J. *Quintero Directs O'Neill*

McGuire, L. A. *William Shakespeare and Eugene O'Neill: An Analysis of Power*. M.A. Thesis; California State U, Long Beach, 1993

Miller, G. "The Visionary Moment in the Plays of Eugene O'Neill," *Annals of Scholarship* 9(3):293, 1992

Moorton, R. F., Jr. "Eugene O'Neill's American Eumenides," 105–18 in R. F. Moorton, Jr., ed. *Eugene O'Neill's Century: Centennial Views on America's Foremost Tragic Dramatist*

Muller, K. *Inszenierte Wirklichkeiten: die Erfahrung der Moderne im Leben und Werk Eugene O'Neills*

Murphy, B. "Fetishizing the Dynamo: Henry Adams and Eugene O'Neill," *Eugene O'Neill Review* 16(1):85–90, Sprg. 1992

Nelson, L. *The Offstage Women in Selected Plays by Eugene O'Neill*. M.A. Thesis; California State U, Northridge, 1993

Noren, L. *Och ge oss skuggorna*

O'Neill, E. " 'Greed of the Meek': The Scenario for Act One of the First Play of His Eight Play Cycle, Edited and Introduced by Donald Gallup," *Eugene O'Neill Review* 16(2):5, Fall 1992

Pfefferkorn, K. "Searching for Home in O'Neill's America," 119–43 in R. F. Moorton, Jr., ed. *Eugene O'Neill's Century: Centennial Views on America's Foremost Tragic Dramatist*

Popovich, H. H., and J. R. Keller. "Desire and Strife: The Violent Families of Eugene O'Neill," in S. Munson Deats and L. Tallent, eds. *The Aching Hearth: Family Violence in Life and Literature*

Prasad, S. *Tradition and Experiment in the Plays of Eugene O'Neill*

Price, J. *The Portrayal of Women in Two Plays by Eugene O'Neill*. M.A. Thesis; Radford U, 1993

Ranald, M. L. "When They Weren't Playing O'Neill: The Antithetical Career of Carlotta Monterey," *Theatre History Studies* 11:81–106, 1991

Sands, J. E. "O'Neill's Stage Direction and the Actor," 191–205 in R. F. Moorton, Jr., ed. *Eugene O'Neill's Century: Centennial Views on America's Foremost Tragic Dramatist*

Schvey, H. I. "The Master and His Double: Eugene O'Neill and Sam Shepard," *Journal of Dramatic Theory and Criticism* 1991 5(2):49–60, Sprg. 1991

Shaughnessy, E. L. "Ella, James, and Jamie O'Neill: 'My Name Is Might-Have-Been,' " *Eugene O'Neill Review* 15(2):5–92, Fall 1991

Simon, M. "Eugene O'Neill's Introduction to Hart Crane's *White Buildings*: Why He 'Would Have Done It in a Minute But,'" *Eugene O'Neill Review* 15(1):41–57, Sprg. 1991

Singh, A. K. *The Plays of Eugene O'Neill: A Study in Myths and Symbols*

Smith, M. C., *Eugene O'Neill in Court: Documents in the Case of George Lewys v. Eugene O'Neill, et al*

Smith, M. C., and R. Eaton. "More Roads to Xanadu," *Eugene O'Neill Review* 15(1):27–39, Sprg. 1991

———. "The O'Neill-Komroff Connection: Thirteen Letters from Eugene O'Neill," *Eugene O'Neill Review* 16(2):13, Fall 1992

So, Y. *Eugene O'Neill ui kuk e natanan sooe yangsang kwa chaa tamgu*

Sudo, Y. *Maternal Women in Eugene O'Neill's Later Plays*. M.A. Thesis; Sonoma State U, 1993

Suhajcik, S. S. *Apollo, Dionysus, and Three Sets of Brothers: Nietzsche's The Birth of Tragedy as Applied to O'Neill, Pinter, and Shepard*. M.A. Thesis; Florida Atlantic U, 1991

Swortzell, L. " 'Get My Goat': O'Neill's Attitude toward Children and Adolescents in His Life and Art," 145–63 in R. F. Moorton, Jr., ed. *Eugene O'Neill's Century: Centennial Views on America's Foremost Tragic Dramatist*

Terras, R. "A Spokesman for America: O'Neill in Translation," 87–101 in R. F. Moorton, Jr., ed. *Eugene O'Neill's Century: Centennial Views on America's Foremost Tragic Dramatist*

Tornquist, E. "To Speak the Unspoken: Audible Thinking in O'Neill's Plays," *Eugene O'Neill Review* 16(1):55–70, Sprg. 1992

Torrey, J. "O'Neill's Psychology of Oppression in Men and Women," 165–70 in R. F. Moorton, Jr., ed. *Eugene O'Neill's Century: Centennial Views on America's Foremost Tragic Dramatist*

Wang, Q. "Who Troubled the Waters: A Study of the Motif of Intrusion in Five Modern Dramatists: John Milington Synge, Eugene O'Neill, Edward Albee, Tennessee Williams, and Harold Pinter," (#DA9209537; Indiana U, Pennsylvania) *DAI* 52(12):4325A, Jun. 1992

Waters, J. B. *Eugene O'Neill and Family—The Bermuda Interlude*

Wauschkuhn, D. *Literarischer Dialekt und seine Funktion zur Begrundung einer dramatischen Tradition im Werk von John Millington Synge und Eugene ONeill*

Ah, Wilderness!, 1933

Connolly, T. F. "*Ah, Wilderness!* in Stratford, Ont.," *Eugene O'Neill Review* 15(2):114, Fall 1991

Sidnell, M. J. *Journal of Canadian Studies* 25:137–8, Wntr. 1990/91

Wheeler, B. W. *Harmonious Madness: The Apollonian and Dionysian Tension in Long Day's Journey into Night and Ah, Wilderness*. M.A. Thesis; Sonoma State U, 1991

All God's Chillun Got Wings, 1924

Basile, M. "Semiotic Transformability in *All God's Chillun*," *Eugene O'Neill Review* 16(1):25–37, Sprg. 1992

Cooperman, R. "Unacknowledged Familiarity: Jean Toomer and Eugene O'Neill," *Eugene O'Neill Review* 16(1):39–48, Sprg. 1992

Anna Christie, 1921
Corliss, R. *Time* 141(4):66, 25 Jan. 1993
Gerard, J. *Variety* 349(12):83, 18 Jan. 1993
Griffiths, P. *New Yorker* 68(50):99–102, 1 Feb. 1993
Hornby, R. *Hudson Review* 46:365–7, Summ. 1993
Kanfer, S. *New Leader* 76(3):22–23, 8 Feb. 1993
Kroll, J. *Newsweek* 121(4):59, 25 Jan. 1993
Rich, F. *New York Times* 142:B1(N), 15 Jan. 1993
Richards, D. *New York Times* 142:H5(B), 24 Jan. 1993
Rosen, C. *TheaterWeek* 6(27):26–27, 8 Feb. 1993
Simon, J. *New York* 26(4):69, 25 Jan. 1993
Smith, S. *TheaterWeek* 6(28):17, 15 Feb. 1993
Wilson, E. *Wall Street Journal* A13(W), 3 Feb. 1993

Days Without End, 1933
Shaughnessy, E. L. "O'Neill's Catholic Dilemma in *Days Without End*," *Eugene O'Neill Review* 15(1):5–26, Sprg. 1991

Desire Under the Elms, 1924
Ben Youssef, L. *Violence in Three Plays by Eugene O'Neill: The Emperor Jones, Desire Under the Elms and Long Day's Journey into Night.* M.A. Thesis; Michigan State U, 1992
Desire Under the Elms, Videocassette. Release of 1958 Motion Picture. Paramount, 1991
Narey, W. "Eugene O'Neill's Attic Spirit: *Desire Under the Elms*," *Eugene O'Neill Review* 16(1):49–54, Sprg. 1992
Saur, P. S. "Classifying Rural Dramas: O'Neill's *Desire Under the Elms* and Schonherr's *Erde*," *Modern Austrian Literature* 26(3/4):101, 1993
Weiss, S. A. "O'Neill, Nietzsche, and Cows," *Modern Drama* 34(4):494–98, Dec. 1991

The Emperor Jones, 1920
Ben Youssef, L. *Violence in Three Plays by Eugene O'Neill: The Emperor Jones, Desire Under the Elms, and Long Day's Journey into Night.* M.A. Thesis; Michigan State U, 1992
Conklin, R. "The Expression of Character in O'Neill's *The Emperor Jones* and *The Hairy Ape*," *Philological Papers* 39:101, 1993
The Emperor Jones. Videodisc.
Rogalus, P. W. "Shepard's *Tooth of Crime*, O'Neill's *Emperor Jones*, and the Contemporary American Tragic Hero," *Notes on Contemporary Literature* 22(2):2–3, Mar. 1992
Willis, J. E. *German Expressionism and Its Presence in Eugene O'Neill's The Emperor Jones and Elmer Rice's The Adding Machine.* M. A. Thesis; Central Missouri State U, 1992

The Great God Brown, 1926
"*The Great God Brown*. Gwyn Morgan at the Steiner Theatre," *Plays and Players* (463):26, 1 Oct. 1992

Katsu, K. "*The Great God Brown*: A False Mask," *Chu-Shikoku Studies in American Literature* 27:37–48, Jun. 1991

Sundstrand, J. K. "*The Great God Brown*: Gilmor Brown, The Pasadena Playhouse and the Depression," *Southern California Quarterly* 75(2):143, Summ. 1993

The Hairy Ape, 1922

Andersen-Wyman, D. V. *Art in Tension with Technology: Exploring the Human Dilemmas*. M.A. Thesis; San Jose State U, 1991

Quintero, J., T. Bogard, and E. Bauersfeld. "Directing a Radio Production of Eugene O'Neill's *The Hairy Ape*," *Theatre Journal* 43(3):337–59, Oct. 1991

The Iceman Cometh, 1946

Clarity, J. F. "An O'Neill Classic Enchants Dublin," *New York Times* 142:13(N), 7 Nov. 1992

Eisen, K. " 'The Writing on the Wall': Novelization and the Critique of History in *The Iceman Cometh*," *Modern Drama* 34(1):59–73, Mar. 1991

Gram, J. M. " 'Tomorrow': From Whence *The Iceman Cometh*," *Eugene O'Neill Review* 15(1):79–92, Sprg. 1991

Leadbeater, L. W. "Aristophanes and O'Neill: Hickey as Comic Hero," *Classical and Modern Literature: A Quarterly* 12(4):361–74, Summ. 1992

Maufort, M. "Mirrors of Consciousness: Narrative Patterns in O'Neill's *The Iceman Cometh*," 165–73 in H. Liu and L. Swortzell, eds. *Eugene O'Neill in China: An International Centenary Celebration*

Murray, D. A.. "O'Neill's Transvaluation of Pessimism in *The Iceman Cometh*," *Eugene O'Neill Review* 16(2):73, Fall 1992

Shafer, Y. "A Berlin Diary: *The Iceman Cometh*," *Eugene O'Neill Review* 16(2):81, Fall 1992

————. "*The Iceman Cometh* at the Deutsches Theater," *Western European Stages* 5(2):41, Fall 1993

Lazarus Laughed, 1928

Han, K. "*Lazarus Laughed*: Dionysus and the Birth of Tragedy," *Journal of English Language and Literature* 37(4):993–1005, Wntr. 1991

Long Day's Journey into Night, 1956

Ben Youssef, L. *Violence in Three Plays by Eugene O'Neill: the Emperor Jones, Desire Under the Elms, and Long Day's Journey into Night*. M.A. Thesis; Michigan State U, 1992

Black, S. A. "Reality and Its Vicissitudes: The Problem of Understanding in *Long Day's Journey into Night*," *Eugene O'Neill Review* 16(2):57, Fall 1992

Brown, R. "Causality in O'Neill's Late Masterpieces," 41–54 in R. F. Moorton, Jr., ed. *Eugene O'Neill's Century: Centennial Views on America's Foremost Tragic Dramatist*

Brustein, R. *New Republic* 205(5):30–31, 29 Jul. 1991

Cline, G. S. "The Psychodrama of the 'Dysfunctional Family': Desire, Subjectivity, and Regression in Twentieth-Century American Drama," (#DA9130458; Ohio State U) *DAI* 52(5):1742A, Nov. 1991

Golub, S. "O'Neill and the Poetics of Modernist Strangeness," 17–39 in R. F. Moorton, Jr., ed. *Eugene O'Neill's Century: Centennial Views on America's Foremost Tragic Dramatist*

Gonzalez, J. B. "Homecoming: O'Neill's New London in *Long Day's Journey into Night*," *New England Quarterly* 66(3):450–57, Sep. 1993

Hassell, G. "Return Journey," *Plays and Players* (446):7, 1 Feb. 1991

Meaney, G. "*Long Day's Journey into Night*: Modernism, Post-Modernism and Maternal Loss," *Irish University Review: A Journal of Irish Studies* 21(2):204–18, Fall/Winter 1991

Sewall, R. B. "Eugene O'Neill and the Sense of the Tragic," 3–16 in R. F. Moorton, Jr., ed. *Eugene O'Neill's Century: Centennial Views on America's Foremost Tragic Dramatist*

Simon, J. *New York* 24(27):55–56, 15 Jul. 1991

Smith, M. C., and R. Eaton. "Land and Sea: O'Neill's *Long Day's Journey into Night* and the Humorous Tyrones," *West Virginia University Philological Papers* 37:123–30, 1991

Törnqvist, E. "Strindberg, O'Neill, Noren: A Swedish-American Triangle," *Eugene O'Neill Review* 15(1):64–78, Sprg. 1991

Voglino, B. " 'Games' the Tyrones Play," *Eugene O'Neill Review* 16(1):91–103, Sprg. 1992

Wheeler, B. W. *Harmonious Madness: The Apollonian and Dionysian Tension in Long Day's Journey into Night and Ah, Wilderness.* M.A. Thesis; Sonoma State U, 1991

Windisch, E. *Mary's Pernicious Influence in Long Day's Journey into Night.* M.A. Thesis; Texas A&I U, 1991

Marco Millions, 1928

Smith, M. C., and R. Eaton. "More Roads to Xanadu," *Eugene O'Neill Review* 15(1):27–39, Sprg. 1991

A Moon for the Misbegotten, 1947

Evans, G. *Variety* 348(10):88, 28 Sep. 1992

Frank, G. *TheaterWeek* 4(45):40–41, 10 Jun. 1991

Hampton, W. *New York Times* 142:C16(L), 23 Sep. 1992

Osborn, M. E. *TheaterWeek* 6(39):29–30, 3 May 1993

Simonson, R. *TheaterWeek* 6(13):35, 2 Nov. 1992

Spillane, M. *Nation* 253(1):30–31, 1 Jul. 1991

More Stately Mansions, 1962

Porter, L. "Bakhtin's Chronotope: Time and Space in *A Touch of the Poet* and *More Stately Mansions*," *Modern Drama* 34:369–82, Sep. 1991

Mourning Becomes Electra, 1939

Benchley, R. "Critics' Round Table," *New Yorker* 69(15):66–67, 31 May 1993

Burian, J. M. "*Mourning Becomes Electra* in Prague," *Eugene O'Neill Review* 15(2):110, Fall 1991

Moorton, R. F., Jr. "The Author as Oedipus in *Mourning Becomes Electra* and *Long Day's Journey into Night*," 171–88 in R. F. Moorton, Jr., ed.

Eugene O'Neill's Century: Centennial Views on America's Foremost Tragic Dramatist

Nugel, B. "Von Elektra zu Lavinia: Eugene O'Neills Konzeption der Titelfigur in *Mourning Becomes Electra*," 295–318 in T. Fischer-Seidel, ed. *Frauen und Frauendarstellung in der englischen und amerikanischen Literatur*

Nugent, S. G. "Masking Becomes Electra: O'Neill, Freud, and the Feminine," 55–71 in R. F. Moorton, Jr., ed. *Eugene O'Neill's Century: Centennial Views on America's Foremost Tragic Dramatist*

Peters, J. G. "Ghosts and Guilt: *Mourning Becomes Electra* and Its Mythic Tradition," *Midwest Quarterly* 32(4):474–83, Summ. 1991

Stevenson, R. *TLS* (4593):16, 12 Apr. 1991

S. S. Glencairn (four plays: *The Moon of the Caribbees*; *In the Zone*; *Bound East for Cardiff*, and *The Long Voyage Home*), 1924

Hampton, W. "*S. S. Glencarin* in Four Plays of the Seas," *New York Times* 143:C19(L), 20 Oct. 1993

Strange Interlude, 1928

Smith, M. C., and R. Eaton. "Everything's Up to Date in Kansas City," *Eugene O'Neill Review* 16(1):71–84, Sprg. 1992

A Touch of the Poet, 1957

Bloom, S. F. "Alcoholism and Intoxication in *A Touch of the Poet*," *Dionysus: The Literature and Intoxication TriQuarterly* 2(3):31–39, Wntr. 1991

Gallup, D. "O'Neill's Original 'Epilogue' for *A Touch of the Poet*,' " *Eugene O'Neill Review* 15(2):93–107, Fall 1991

"Theater: *A Touch of the Poet*," *Newsweek* 121(6):62, 8 Feb. 1993

OPPERMAN, DEON

Women in the Wings, 1993

Arthur, T. H. *Theatre Journal* 45:249–50, May 1993

OSBORN, PAUL

On Borrowed Time (based on the novel by L. E. Watkin), 1938

Disch, T. M. *Nation* 253(18):681, 25 Nov. 1991

Filichia, P. "Let's Get Away from It All," *TheaterWeek* 5(13):13, 4 Nov. 1991

Henry, W. A., III. *Time* 138(17):100, 28 Oct. 1991

James, P. *TheaterWeek* 5(14):31, 11 Nov. 1991

Kanfer, S. *New Leader* 74(12):27, 4 Nov. 1991

Oliver, E. *New Yorker* 67(35):108, 21 Oct. 1991

Simon, J. *New York* 24(41):120, 21 Oct. 1991

Weales, G. *Commonweal* 118(21):718–19, 6 Dec. 1991

OSTERMAN, GEORG

Brother Truckers, 1992

Evans, G. *Variety* 348(11):7–71, 5 Oct. 1992

Horwitz, S. "Naughty and Nice," *TheaterWeek* 6(20):22–24, 21 Dec. 1992
Osterman, G. *Brother Truckers*
Rich, F. *New York Times* 142:B1(N), 22 Sep. 1992

OSTROW, STUART

Stages (consists of five "stages" or segments: *Denial, Anger, Bargaining, Depression,* and *Acceptance*), 1978
Rich, F. *New York Times* 142:B3(N), 23 Dec. 1992
Wolf, M. *Variety* 349(7):77, 7 Dec. 1992

OVERMYER, ERIC

Castagno, P. C. "Desultory Structures: Language as Presence in the Works of Overmyer, Wellman, and Jenkin," *Text & Presentation* 11:1–7, 1991

Dark Rapture
Downey, R. "Hot Noir," *American Theatre* 9(4):10 + , Jul/Aug. 1992
Overmyer, E. *Dark Rapture*

The Heliotrope Bouquet, 1993
Greene, A. *TheaterWeek* 6(32):41, 15 Mar. 1993
Overmyer, E. *The Heliotrope Bouquet by Scott Joplin & Louis Chauvin*
Raymond, G. "Making Words Music: Q-and-A with Eric Overmyer," *TheaterWeek* 6(33):24–27, 22 Mar. 1993

Mi vida loca
Overmyer, E. *Mi vida loca*

Native Speech, 1991
Bell, J. *TheaterWeek* 4(41):37, 20 May 1991
Overmyer, E. *Eric Overmyer: Collected Works*

On the Verge, or The Geography of Yearning, 1985
Gaary, D. E. *Windows of Vulnerability: Exploring the Role of Fanny in On the Verge.* M.F.A. Thesis: U of Virginia, 1992
Lilly, M. J. *On the Verge: Embracing the Future Through Eric Overmyer's Drama.* M.F.A. Thesis; DePaul U, 1992
Stadem-Carlson, B. *Eric Overmyer's On the Verge: A Production Focusing on Feminine Values.* M.A. Thesis; U of North Dakota, 1992

OWENS, ROCHELLE

Futz!, 1991
New Yorker 67(37):4, 4 Nov. 1991
Rosen, C. "The Futz Reunion, Minus the Exclamation Point," *TheaterWeek* 5(15):37–39, 18 Nov. 1991

OYAMO (Charles Gordon)

I Am a Man, 1993
> Brustein, R. *New Republic* 209(3/4):29–30, 19 Jul. 1993
> Hampton, W. *New York Times* 142:B3(N), 20 May 1993
> Oyamo. "*I Am a Man*," *American Theatre* 10(11):25–48, 1 Nov. 1993
> Ungaro, J. *TheaterWeek* 6(45):40, 14 Jun. 1993

Let Me Live, 1991
> Ungaro, J. *TheaterWeek* 4(26):36, 4 Feb. 1991

PALMINTERI, CHAZZ

Spano, V. "Vincent Spano and Chazz Palminteri," *American Film* 16(6):46–47, Jun. 1991

A Bronx Tale, 1989
> Reed, J. "DeNiro Direct," *Vogue* 183(9):502–05, Sep. 1993
> Van Gelder, L. "Swamped with Offers," *New York Times* 141:C8(L), 24 Apr. 1992
> Weinraub, B. "2 Tales of Youth and Wilderness, Urban and Rural," *New York Times* 142:B1(N), 13 Sep. 1993

PAPP, JOSEPH

Harris, J. "Joseph Papp: Theater Revolutionary, 1921–1991," 5(15):18+, *TheaterWeek* 18 Nov. 1991
Horn, B. L. *Joseph Papp: A Bio-Bibliography*

PARKER, DOROTHY

Calhoun, R. *Dorothy Parker: A Bio-Bibliography*
De Beaumont, G. *Scusate le ceneri*
Horder, M. "Dorothy Parker: An American Centenary," *Contemporary Review* 263(1535):320–21, Dec. 1993
McCarrell, S. *New York: Visions, Struggles, Voices*
Meade, M. *Dorothy Parker: What Fresh Hell Is This?*
Parker, D. *The Sayings of Dorothy Parker*
Watters, E. *From Major to Minor Paradigms of Literary Value and the Case of Dorothy Parker*. Theses Canadiennes. Ottawa: Bibliotheque nationale du Canada, 1992

PARKER, DOROTHY (with ROSS EVANS)

The Coast of Illyria (based on the life of Charles Lamb), 1949
> Israel, L. "The Theater of Dorothy Parker," *TheaterWeek* 5(42):24–26, 25 May 1992

PARKS, SUZAN-LORI

Robinson, M. "Four Writers," *Theater* 24(1):31–42, Wntr. 1993
Solomon, A. "Signifying on the Signifyin': The Plays of Suzan-Lori Parks,"
Theater 21(3):73, Summ. 1990

The Death of the Last Black Man in the Whole Entire World, 1990
    Brustein, R. *New Republic* 206(15):29, 13 Apr. 1992
    Diamond, L. "Perceptible Mutability in the Word Kingdom," *Theater*
       24(3):86–87, Summ/Fall 1993
    Lamont, R. C., ed. *Women on the Verge: 7 Avant-Garde American Plays*
    Osborn, M. E. "Letter from New Haven: Winterfest Features Experimental
       Plays by Women," *TheaterWeek* 5(32):21–23, 16 Mar. 1992
    Parks, S. "Imperceptible Mutabilities: *The Last Black Man*," Recording.
    ———. "*The Death of the Last Black Man in the Whole Entire World*," in
    Women on the Verge

Devotees in the Garden of Love, 1992
    Osborn, M. E. "Letter from Louisville," *TheaterWeek* 5(38):29, 27 Apr.
    1992

PARNELL, PETER

Flaubert's Latest, 1992
    Gerard, J. *Variety* 347(10):50, 22 Jun. 1992
    Gussow, M. *New York Times* 141:B3(N), 22 Jun. 1992
    Harris, W. "The Evening That Flaubert Came to Stay," *New York Times*
       141:H8(N), 14 Jun. 1992
    Oliver, E. *New Yorker* 68(20):57, 6 Jul. 1992
    Parnell, P. *Flaubert's Latest*.
    Richards, D. *New York Times* 141:H14(N), 28 Jun. 1992
    Simon, J. *New York* 25(27):66, 13 Jul. 1992

PATRICK, ROBERT

The Haunted Host, 1964
    Horwitz, S. "The Substance of Fierstein," *TheaterWeek* 4(42):17–23, 27
    May 1991

PEARSON, SYBILLE

Unfinished Stories, 1992
    Everett, T. *Variety* 348(3):62, 10 Aug. 1992
    Pearson, S. "*Unfinished Stories*," *American Theatre* 9(9):51–69, Jan. 1993
    ———. *Unfinished Stories*

————. "Unfinished Stories," in Goodman, R., and M. Smith, eds. *Women Playwrights: The Best Plays of 1992*
"*Unfinished Stories,*" *Time* 140(4):73, 27 Jul. 1992

PEASLEE, RICHARD. *SEE* CLARKE, MARTHA, RICHARD COE, RICHARD PEASLEE, and STANLEY WALDEN

PERELMAN, SIDNEY JOSEPH

Blair, W., and H. Hill. "Benchley and Perelman," 227–32 in S. Gale, ed. *S. J. Perelman: Critical Essays*
Cole, W., and G. Plimpton. "The Art of Fiction: S. J. Perelman," 3–16 in S. Gale, ed. *S. J. Perelman: Critical Essays*
De Vries, P. "Perelmania," 105–14 in S. Gale, ed. *S. J. Perelman: Critical Essays*
Fowler, D. "Perelman and the Tradition on Falling Out of Fashion," 233–62 in S. Gale, ed. *S. J. Perelman: Critical Essays*
French, P. "Perelman's Revenge or the Gift of Providence, Rhode Island," 95–104 in S. Gale, ed. *S. J. Perelman: Critical Essays*
Gale, S. H. "Around the World in Eighty Ways: S. J. Perelman as Screenwriter," 173–204 in S. Gale, ed. *S. J. Perelman: Critical Essays*
Hasley, L. "The Kangaroo Mind of S. J. Perelman," 87–94 in S. Gale, ed. *S. J. Perelman: Critical Essays*
Kleinzahler, A. "Elevated Shtick: S. J. Perelman," in *Hiding in Plain Sight: Essays in Criticism and Autobiography*
Lahr, J. "Satire as Subversion," 115–16 in S. Gale, ed. *S. J. Perelman: Critical Essays*
MacPherson, M. "Perelman's Rasping Wit Becomes an Anglo-File," 29–36 in S. Gale, ed. *S. J. Perelman: Critical Essays*
Pinsker, S. "Jumping on Hollywood's Bones, or How S. J. Perelman and Woody Allen Found It at the Movies," 159–72 in S. Gale, ed. *S. J. Perelman: Critical Essays*
Stasio, M. "On the Beauty Part," 117–40 in S. Gale, ed. *S. J. Perelman: Critical Essays*
Wain, J. "A Jest in Season: Notes on S. J. Perelman, with a Digression on W. W. Jacobs," 69–86 in S. Gale, ed. *S. J. Perelman: Critical Essays*
Ward, J. A. "The Hollywood Metaphor: The Marx Brothers, S. J. Perelman, and Nathanael West," 141–58 in S. Gale, ed. *S. J. Perelman: Critical Essays*
Yates, N. W. "The Sane Psychoses of S. J. Perelman," 205–26 in S. Gale, ed. *S. J. Perelman: Critical Essays*
Zinsser, W. "That Perelman of Great Price Is Sixty-Five," 17–28 in S. Gale, ed. *S. J. Perelman: Critical Essays*

PERLMAN, ARTHUR. *SEE* LUNDEN, JEFFREY, and ARTHUR PERLMAN

PETERS, CLARKE, and LOUIS JORDAN

Five Guys Named Moe, 1990
"Five Guys Named Moe: Original London Cast Recording," Recording. Gerard, J. *Variety* 346(13):70, 13 Apr. 1992

Harris, J. "An Interview with Cameron Mackintosh," *TheaterWeek* 5(35):16–23, 6 Apr. 1992
Henry, W. A., III. *Time* 139(16):92, 20 Apr. 1992
Kanfer, S. *New Leader* 75(5):23, 6 Apr. 1992
Kroll, J. "Mack Attack: Here Comes Mr. Jordan," *Newsweek* 119(16):79, 20 Apr. 1992
Lazare, L. "Despite Raves, Chi *Moe* Slow Going," *Variety* 350(11):79, 12 Apr. 1993
Lydon, M. *New York Times* 141:H5(N), 5 Apr. 1992
Mandelbaum, K. "Season Preview: The Musicals," *TheaterWeek* 5(1):18 + , 12 Aug. 1991
————. *TheaterWeek* 5(38):33–34, 27 Apr. 1992
McCourtie, C. *Crisis* 99(5):10, Jun/Jul. 1992
Oliver, E. *New Yorker* 68(9):78, 20 Apr. 1992
Rich, F. *New York Times* 141:B3(N), 9 Apr. 1992
————. *New York Times* 142:H5(N), 27 Dec. 1992
Richards, D. *New York Times* 141:H5(N), 19 Apr. 1992
Sandla, R. *Dance Magazine* 66(8):52–53, Aug. 1992
Simon, J. *New York* 25(16):102, 20 Apr. 1992
Stephens, L. "The Men Who Made *Moe*," *TheaterWeek* 5(35):24–25, 6 Apr. 1992
Taylor, M. "Mo' News on *Moe* Show," *Variety* 347(1):49, 20 Apr. 1992
Weiser, J. "Jazz Returns to Broadway," *Down Beat* 59(5):12, May 1992
Witchell, A. "A Home for *Moe*," *New York Times* 140:B4(N), 16 Aug. 1991

PICKERING, STEVE, and CHARLEY SHERMAN

In the Flesh (adaptation of a short story by Clive Barker), 1993
Simonson, R. *TheaterWeek* 6(52):36, 2 Aug. 1993

PIÑERO, MIGUEL

Short Eyes, 1974
Platizky, R. S. "Humane Vision in Miguel Piñero's *Short Eyes*," *Americas Review* 19(1):83–91, Sprg. 1991

PINTAURO, JOSEPH

Slaight, C., ed. *New Plays from A.C.T.'s Young Conservatory*

Men's Lives (adaptation of Peter Matthiessen's book), 1992
Simonson, R. "The Sag Harbor Story," *TheaterWeek* 6(6):24–27, 14 Sep. 1992

Raft of the Medusa, 1991
Beard, J., ed. *The Best Women's Stage Monologues of 1993*
Michaud, Christopher. "Staying Afloat in Troubled Waters," *Advocate* (593):70, 31 Dec. 1991
Pintauro, J. *Raft of the Medusa*
Wontorek, P. *TheaterWeek* 5(23):36, 13 Jan. 1992

POLLOCK, SHARON

Pollock, S. "Walsh" in J. Wasserman, ed. *Modern Canadian Plays*

Getting It Straight
    Pollock, S. *Getting It Straight*, in Doolittle, J., ed. *Heroines: Three Plays*

Blood Relations, 1980 (produced in 1979 as *My Name Is Lisbeth*)
    Shaw, M. B. *Cultivating the Seeds of Art: An Examination of One Actor's Process Through the Role of the Actress in Sharon Pollock's Blood Relations*. M.F.A. Thesis; U of Louisville, 1991

One Tiger to a Hill, 1990
    Sidnell, M. J. *Journal of Canadian Studies* 25:136, Wntr. 1990/91

POST, DOUGLAS

Earth and Sky, 1991
    Chansky, D. *TheaterWeek* 4(28):37, 18 Feb. 1991
    Simon, J. *New York* 24(7):64, 18 Feb. 1991
    Torrens, J. S. *America* 164(7):213, 23 Feb. 1991
    Variety 342(5):116, 11 Feb. 1991

POTOK, CHAIM

Potok, C. "The Invisible Map of Meaning: A Writer's Confrontations," *TriQuarterly* (84):17–45, Sprg/Summ. 1992

POUND, EZRA

Elektra (adaptation of Sophocles's play), 1987
    Simon, J. *New York* 24(12):70, 25 Mar. 1991

PRICE, REYNOLDS

Busch, F. "Reynolds Price: The Art of Fiction CXXVII," *Paris Review* 33(121):150–79, Wntr. 1991
Ketchin, S. "Narrative Hunger and Silent Witness: An Interview with Reynolds Price," *Georgia Review* 47(3):522–42, Fall 1993
Price, R. "Reynolds Price: On Writing for Performance," *American Theatre* 10(4):62, Apr. 1993

PRICE, ROBERT EARL

Price, R. E. "Yardbird's Vamp," *African American Review* 27(1):79–91, Sprg. 1993

PRIDA, DOLORES

Watson, M. "The Search for Identity in the Theater of Three Cuban American Female Dramatists," *Bilingual Review* 16(2/3):188–96, May–Dec. 1991

PRIDEAUX, JAMES

Lyndon (adaptation of *Lyndon: An Oral Biography* by Merle Miller), 1984
    TheaterWeek 4(26):37, 4 Feb. 1991
    Variety 342(2):84, 21 Jan. 1991

PRINCE, HAL

Ansen, D. "Prince Hal in Portland," *Newsweek* 117(15):68, 15 Apr. 1991
Chase, T. "An Interview with Hal Prince," *TheaterWeek* 5(22):18–24, 6 Jan. 1992
Cushman, R. "Theatre: *Show Boat*'s Cool Hand," *Saturday Night* 108(7):19, 1 Sep. 1993
Fennell, T. "Navigating Troubled Waters," *Maclean's* 106(44):72, 1 Nov. 1993
Flatow, S. "Working with Hal," *Opera News* 54(12):14, 3 Mar. 1990
Henry, W. A., III. "Along Comes the *Spider*," *Time* 141(18):70+, 3 May 1993
Murray, K. "Protest Pestering Princely *Show Boat*," *Variety* 350(1):73, 26 Apr. 1993

PUGLIESE, FRANK

Aven' U Boys, 1993
    Kroll, J. *Newsweek* 121(14):61, 5 Apr. 1993
    Pugliese, F. *Aven' U Boys*, in J. Beard, ed. *The Best Men's Stage Monologues of 1993*
    Rich, F. *New York Times* 142:B1(N), 9 Mar. 1993
    Richards, D. *New York Times* 142:H5(N), 21 Mar. 1993

PURDY, JAMES

Purdy, J. "Heatstroke," *Antaeus* (66):395–400, Sprg. 1991

QUINTON, EVERETT, and MARK BENNETT

Linda, 1993
    Ungaro, J. *TheaterWeek* 6(45):40, 14 Jun. 1993

RABE, DAVID

Berkowitz, G. M. *American Drama of the Twentieth Century.* 142+
Carroll, D. "Not-Quite Mainstream Male Playwrights: Guare, Durang, and Rabe," 41–61 in B. King, ed. *Contemporary American Theatre*

Chi, W. *The Role of Language in the Plays of Mamet, Wilson, and Rabe.* Diss.; U
    of Iowa, 1991
Christie, N. B. "Still a Vietnam Playwright After All These Years," 97–115 in T.
    S. Zinman, ed. *David Rabe: A Casebook*
Croyden, M. "Tough Guys Drink Perrier," *TheaterWeek* 4(30):25–27, 4 Mar.
    1991
McDonough, C. J. "Staging Masculinity: The Search for Male Identity in Con-
    temporary American Drama," (#DA9306664; U of Tennessee) *DAI*
    53(11):3910A, May 1993
Rabe, D. "Vietnam Shadows," *American Theatre* 10(7/8):88, Jul/Aug. 1993
Schroeder, E. J. *Vietnam, We've All Been There: Interviews with American Writers*
Stein, H. "The Lost People in David Rabe's Plays," 17–30 in T. S. Zinman, ed.
    David Rabe: A Casebook
Zinman, T. S. "Interview," 3–15 in T. S. Zinman, ed. *David Rabe: A Casebook*
———. "What's Wrong with This Picture? David Rabe's Comic-Strip Plays,"
    31–47 in T. S. Zinman, ed. *David Rabe: A Casebook*

The Basic Training of Pavlo Hummel, 1971
    Geis, D. R. " 'Fighting to Get Down, Thinking It Was Up': A Narratological
        Reading of *The Basic Training of Pavlo Hummel*," 71–83 in T. S. Zinman,
        ed. *David Rabe: A Casebook*

Casualties of War
    Novelli, M. "Spiking the Vietnam Film 'Canon': David Rabe & *Casualties
        of War*," 149–71 in T. S. Zinman, ed. *David Rabe: A Casebook*

Goose and Tomtom
    McMillion, J. "The Cult of Male Identity in *Goose and Tomtom*," 175–87
        in T. S. Zinman, ed. *David Rabe: A Casebook*

Hurlyburly, 1984
    Reinelt, J. "Gender and History in *Hurlyburly*: A Feminist Response," 191–
        205 in T. S. Zinman, ed. *David Rabe: A Casebook*
    Scanlan, R. "Fighting Saints: The Idea of *Hurlyburly*," 207–25 in T. S. Zin-
        man, ed. *David Rabe: A Casebook*
    Stafford, T. J. "The Metaphysics of Rabe's *Hurlyburly*: 'Staring into the
        Eyes of Providence' " *American Drama* 1(2):61–76, Sprg. 1992

In the Boom Boom Room (revision of his 1973 play *Boom Boom Room*), 1974
    Wade, L. "David Rabe and the Female Figure: The Body in the *Boom Boom
        Room*," *Text and Performance Quarterly* 12(1):40–53, Jan. 1992
    Watt, S. "In Mass Culture's Image: The Subject of(in) Rabe's Boom Boom
        Rooms," 49–67 in T. S. Zinman, ed. *David Rabe: A Casebook*

The Orphan, 1973
    Christman, J. "Neglected But Still Family: *The Orphan*," 85–93 in T. S.
        Zinman, ed. *David Rabe: A Casebook*

Sticks and Bones, 1969
> Christy, J. J. "Remembering *Bones*," 119–31 in T. S. Zinman, ed. *David Rabe: A Casebook*
> Davies, L. "Watching the Box: TV on Stage in *Sticks and Bones*," 133–48 in T. S. Zinman, ed. *David Rabe: A Casebook*

Those the River Keeps, 1989
> Weber, B. "Casting Crunch for a New Rabe Play," *New York Times* 142:B4(N), 11 Dec. 1992
> ———. "Will It Be Shepard? Rabe? *New York Times* 142:B2(N), 17 Sep. 1993

RACHEFF, JAMES. *SEE* KOCIOLEK, TED, JAMES RACHEFF, and JAMES RADO

RADO, JAMES. *SEE* KOCIOLEK, TED, JAMES RACHEFF, and JAMES RADO

RAGNI, GEROME

Culver, W. M. *Hair: The American Tribal Love-Rock Musical by Gerome Ragni and James Rado; An Annotated Edition with Introduction.* M.S. Thesis; U of North Texas, 1993
Horn, B. L. *The Age of Hair: Evolution and Impact of Broadway's First Rock Musical*
Shepard, R. F. "Gerome Ragni, 48, a Stage Actor: Co-Author of Broadway's *Hair*," *New York Times* 140:11(N), 13 Jul. 1991

RAPOSO, JOE. *SEE* HARNICK, SHELDON, and JOE RAPOSO

RASHID, STEVE. *SEE* HOLLANDER, NICOLE, ARNOLD APRILL, TOM MULA, STEVE RASHID, and CHERI COONS

REANEY, JAMES

Mayo, J. "Expectations and Compacts in the Beckwith-Reaney Operas: A Case Study," *University of Toronto Quarterly* 63:305–18, Wntr. 1990/91
Parker, G. D. *How to Play: The Theatre of James Reaney*
Reaney, J. "Cutting Up Didoes," *University of Toronto Quarterly* 61(3):372–80, Sprg. 1992
Stingle, R. *James Reaney and His Works*

REBECK, THERESA

Loose Knit, 1993
> Gerard, J. *Variety* 351(10):75, 19 Jul. 1993

Holden, S. *New York Times* 142:B7(N), 2 Jul. 1993
Richards, D. *New York Times* 142:H5(N), 18 Jul. 1993
Simon, J. *New York* 26(27):59, 12 Jul. 1993

Spike Heels, 1992
   Disch, T. M. *Nation* 155(5):187, 17 Aug. 1992
   Evans, G. *Variety* 347(8):62, 8 Jun. 1992
   Goodman, R., and M. Smith, eds. *Women Playwrights: The Best Plays of 1992*
   Oliver, E. *New Yorker* 68(18):84, 22 Jun. 1992
   Rich, F. *New York Times* 141:B3(N), 5 Jun. 1992
   "*Spike Heels*," *Time* 139(24):75, 15 Jun. 1992

REDDIN, KEITH

"10 Writers Receive Whiting Awards," *New York Times* 142:B2(N), 27 Oct. 1992

Life During Wartime, 1990
   Holden, S. *New York Times* 141:C11(L), 11 Aug. 1992
   Resnikova, E. *National Review* 43(14):55, 12 Aug. 1991
   Szentgyorgyi, T. "Happy Endings in Hell," *TheaterWeek* 4(32):29–31, 18 Mar. 1991

Nebraska, 1989
   Holden, S. *New York Times* 141:C15(L), 3 Jun. 1992

REYNOLDS, JONATHAN

Reynolds, J. *Lines Composed a Few Miles above Tintern Abbey, Part II, or How We Got America's Most Wanted and the New York Post, Antaeus* (66):401–6, Sprg. 1991

REYNOLDS, RICK

O'Connor, J. J. "Comedy's Smile Has Turned Wolfish," *New York Times* 142:B2(N), 15 Apr. 1993
Reynolds, R. *Only the Truth Is Funny: My Family and How I Survived It*

Only the Truth Is Funny, 1991
   Lochte, D. *Los Angeles Magazine* 36(11):175, Nov. 1991
   Marowitz, C. *TheaterWeek* 5(14):36, 11 Nov. 1991
   Reynolds, R. *Only the Truth is Funny*. Compact Disc

RIBMAN, RONALD

Ribman, R. *The Rug Merchants of Chaos, and Other Plays*

Dream of the Red Spider, 1993
   Marx, B. "Letter from New England," *TheaterWeek* 6(36):30–31, 12 Apr. 1993

Ribman, R. *Dream of the Red Spider*, in J. Beard, ed. *The Best Men's Stage Monologues of 1993*
Taylor, M. *Variety* 350(6):71, 8 Mar. 1993

RICE, ELMER (Elmer Leopold Reizenstein)

The Adding Machine, 1923
Andersen-Wyman, D. V. *Art in Tension with Technology: Exploring the Human Dilemmas*. M.A. Thesis; San Jose State U, 1991
Gussow, M. *New York Times* 141:B8(N), 16 Sep. 1992
Strand, G. "Treadwell's Neologism: Machinal," *Theatre Journal* 44(2):163–75, May 1992
Wilson, C. P. *White Collar Fictions: Class and Social Representation in American Literature, 1885–1925*

We the People, 1933
Bhatia, N. *Elmer Rice Revisited: A Study of Dramatic Technique in "We the People."* M.A. Thesis; U of Texas at Austin, 1993

RICE, TIM. *SEE* NELSON, RICHARD, TIM RICE, BENNY ANDERSSON, and BJÖRN ULVAEUS

RICHARDSON, JACK

Callens, J. "Of Novices and Scapegoats: Jack Richardson's *In the Final Year of Grace*," *Texas Studies in Literature and Language* 34(1): 41–86, Sprg. 1992

Talmus
Callens, J. "From Miracle Body to Christ Figure: A Reading of Jack Richardson's *Talmus* in the Light of Eliade and Girard," 7–26 in P. L. Michel, E. Gibbs, and A. J. Norris, eds. *BELL: Belgian Essays on Language and Literature*

RICHARDSON, WILLIS

The Chip Woman's Fortune, 1923
Anderson, A. A. "The Ethiopian Art Theatre," *Theatre Survey* 33(2):132–43, Nov. 1992
"Willis Richardson," 159–185 in L. Hamalian and J. V. Hatch, eds. *The Roots of African American Drama*

RIVERA, JOSÉ

Jacobson, L. "An Interview with José Rivera," *Studies in American Drama, 1945-Present* 6(1):49–58, 1991
"10 Writers Receive Whiting Awards," *New York Times* 142:B2(N), 27 Oct. 1992

Each Day Dies with Sleep, 1990
> Rivera, J. "Poverty and Magic in *Each Day Dies with Sleep,*" *Studies in American Drama, 1945-Present* 7(1):163–232, 1992

Marisol, 1990
> Brustein, R. *New Republic* 209(3/4):29–30, 19 Jul. 1993
> Fricker, K. "Another Playwright Confronts an Angel and the Apocalypse," *New York Times* 142:H7(N), 16 May 1993
> Gerard, J. *Variety* 351(4):52, 24 May 1993
> Greene, A. *TheaterWeek* 6(45):38–39, 14 Jun. 1993
> King, R. L. *North American Review* 278:44–47, Mar/Apr. 1993
> Marx, B. "Letter from New England," *TheaterWeek* 6(36):30–31, 12 Apr. 1993
> Osborn, M. E. "Letter from Louisville," *TheaterWeek* 5(38):31, 27 Apr. 1992
> Rich, F. *New York Times* 142:B6(N), 21 May 1993
> Richards, D. "Counting Down to the Year 2000," *New York Times* 142:H5(N), 27 Jun. 1993
> ———. "Good Breeding Can Be the Death of You," *New York Times* 142:H5(N), 30 May 1993
> Rivera, J. "*Marisol,*" *American Theatre* 10(7–8):29–45, Jul/Aug. 1993
> Simon, J. *New York* 26922):59, 31 May 1993
> Simons, T. "José Rivera: We All Think Magically in Our Sleep," *American Theatre* 10(7–8):46–47, Jul/Aug. 1993
> Taylor, M. *Variety* 350(9):88–89, 29 Mar. 1993

Tape, 1993
> Rivera, J. *"Tape"* in M. Smith, ed., *Humana Festival '93: The Complete Plays*

ROBSON, JAMES

King Baby, 1992
> Porter, P. *TLS* (4687):19, 29 Jan. 1992

RODGERS, RICHARD. *SEE* HAMMERSTEIN, OSCAR, II, BENJAMIN F. GLAZER, and RICHARD RODGERS

SEE ALSO HAMMERSTEIN, OSCAR, II, JOSHUA LOGAN, and RICHARD RODGERS

SEE ALSO HAMMERSTEIN, OSCAR, II, and RICHARD RODGERS

ROMAN, FREDDY, and LARRY ARRICK

Catskills on Broadway, 1992
> Evans, G. "*Catskills* Caper Charges Dropped," *Variety* 352(9):193–94, 11 Oct. 1993
> ———. "Long Run for Skim Scam," *Variety* 347(6):1–3, 25 May 1992

————. "Nederlanders to Back *Catskills* Gross Singers," *Variety*
  346(11):83–84, 30 Mar. 1992
James, P. *TheaterWeek* 5(20):36, 23 Dec. 1991
Riedel, M. "Borscht-Belter," *TheaterWeek* 5(26):20+, 3 Feb. 1992

ROME, HAROLD

Collins, G. "Harold Rome, Composer of Songs of Social Conscience, Dies at
  85," *New York Times* 143:B12(N), 27 Oct. 1993
Lichtman, I. "Composer/Lyricist Harold Rome Dies at 85," *Billboard*
  105(45):24, 6 Nov. 1993

ROSE, IRIS

Typhoid Mary 911, 1992
  Bell, J. *TheaterWeek* 6(18):21, 7 Dec. 1992

ROSE, LLOYD

"The Institutional Theater," *Nieman Reports* 46(3):14–26, Fall 1992

ROSEN, LOUIS, and THOM BISHOP

Book of the Night, 1991
  Abarbanel, J. *TheaterWeek* 5(13):30, 4 Nov. 1991
  Chase, T. *TheaterWeek* 5(1):39, 12 Aug. 1991

ROSENBLATT, ROGER

Free Speech in America, 1991
  Simonson, R. *TheaterWeek* 5(20):38, 23 Dec. 1991

ROSENTHAL, RACHEL

Barker, J. M. *Rachel Rosenthal*. M.A. Thesis; San Diego State U, 1991
Hamera, J. "Loner on Wheels as Gaia: Identity, Rhetoric, and History in the
  Angry Art of Rachel Rosenthal," *Text and Performance Quarterly* 11(1):35–
  45, Jan. 1991
Kuczynski, P., director. *Rachel Rosenthal: Searching for a Boon*. Videocassette.
Marranca, B. "A Cosmography of Herself: The Autobiography of Rachel Rosen-
  thal," *Kenyon Review* 15(2):59–67, Sprg. 1993
Meola, D. "Rachel Rosenthal," *Omni* 14(11):57–61, Aug. 1992
Perlmutter, D. *Dance Magazine* 65(1):97, Jan. 1991
Peterson, W. D. *A History of the Instant Theater*. Diss.; U of Texas at Austin, 1991

Pangaean Dreams, 1990
  Peterson, W. D. *Theatre Journal* 43:540–2, Dec. 1991
  Rosenthal, R. *Pangaean Dreams: A Shamanic Journey, a Performance by
  Rachel Rosenthal*. Videocassette.

ROSIE, GEORGE

Carlucco and the Queen of Hearts, 1991
 Bailey, P. *TLS* (4623):29, 8 Nov. 1991
 Rosie, G. *Carlucco and the Queen of Hearts*

ROTH, ARI

Born Guilty, 1991
 Evans, G. *Variety* 350(1):105, 1 Feb. 1993
 Hampton, W. *New York Times* 142:C14(L), 28 Jan. 1993
 Roth, A. *Born Guilty*
 ———. *Born Guilty* in J. Beard, ed. *The Best Men's Stage Monologues of
 1993*
 Simon, J. *New York* 26(7):111, 15 Feb. 1993
 Simonson, R, *TheaterWeek* 4(34):40–41, 1 Apr. 1991
 Ungaro, J. *TheaterWeek* 6(27):32, 8 Feb. 1993

RUBY, HARRY. *SEE* KAUFMANN, GEORGE S., MORRIE RYSKIND, BERT
KALMAR, and HARRY RUBY

RUDKIN, DAVID

Wilcher, R. "The Communal Dream of Myth: David Rudkin's *The Triumph of
 Death,*" *Modern Drama* 35(4):571–84, Dec. 1992

RUDNICK, PAUL

I Hate Hamlet, 1991
 Barron, J. "Hate *Hamlet*? Who Are You Kidding?" *New York Times*
 140:H5(N), 12 May 1991
 Borowski, M. *TheaterWeek* 4(46):17, 24, Jun. 1991
 Disch, T. M. *Nation* 252(18):643–44, 13 May. 1991
 Hornby, R. *Hudson Review* 44:456–8, Autm. 1991
 Kanfer, S. *New Leader* 74(5):21, 8 Apr. 1991
 McGuigan, C. "All's Well That Ends Well: An Unscripted Drama Fires Up
 a Broadway Comedy," *Newsweek* 117(20):55, 20 May 1991
 Rich, F. *New York Times* 140:B1(N), 9 Apr. 1991
 Richards, D. *New York Times* 140:H5(N), 28 Apr. 1991
 Rothstein, M. "What Its Star Dislikes about *I Hate Hamlet*," *New York Times*
 140:B1(N), 15 Apr. 1991
 Rudnick, P. *I Hate Hamlet.*
 ———. "A Playwright Summons the Ghost of John Barrymore," *New York
 Times* 140:H5(N), 7 Apr. 1991
 Simon, J. *New York* 24(16):77, 22 Apr. 1991
 Sneerwell, R. *TheaterWeek* 4(38):33, 29 Apr. 1991
 Torrens, J. S. *America* 164(20)::576, 25 May 1991
 Weales, G. *Commonweal* 118(11):374, 1 Jun. 1991

Witchel, A. "*I Hate Hamlet* Co-Star Walks Out," *New York Times* 140:13(N), 4 May 1991

Wolff, C. "Impromptu Curtain Speech by *I Hate Hamlet* Star," *New York Times* 140:16(L), 22 Jun. 1991

Jeffrey, 1992

Corliss, R. "Laughing on the Inside Too," *Time* 141(18):66–68, 3 May 1993
———. *Time* 141(5):68–69, 1 Feb. 1993

Evans, G. "Closings Crowd Off B'Way," *Variety* 353(6):83–84, 13 Dec. 1993

Grenier, R. "The Homosexual Millennium: Is It Here? Is It Approaching?" *National Review* 45(11):52–56, 7 Jun. 1993

Grode, E. "The Seven Faces of Harriet Harris," *TheaterWeek* 7(6):34–35, 13 Sep. 1993

Harris, J. *Christopher Street* (200):2–3, Apr. 1993

Holden, S. *New York Times* 142:B3(N), 21 Jan. 1993

Kroll, J. *Newsweek* 121(6):64, 8 Feb. 1993

Mufson, D. "Quipping Boy," *Theater* 24(2):116–19, Sprg. 1993

Portantiere, M. *TheaterWeek* 6(29):31, 22 Feb. 1993

Rich, F. *New York Times* 142:B1(N), 3 Feb. 1993

Richards, D. *New York Times* 142:H5(N), 31 Jan. 1993

Scanlan, D. "Paul Rudnick's *Jeffrey*," *TheaterWeek* 6(23):28–31, 11 Jan. 1992

Story, R. D. "The Rudnick Chronicles," *New York* 26(8):42–47, 22 Feb. 1993

Weales, G. "American Theater Watch," *Georgia Review* 47(3):563–73, Fall 1993

RUSH, DAVID

Ellen Universe Joins the Band, 1992

Chase, A. "Reflections: A New Play Series at Geva," *TheaterWeek* 5(51):21–23, 27 Jul. 1992

RYGA, GEORGE

Benson, E. "Canada," 67–81 in B. King, ed., *Post-Colonial English Drama: Commonwealth Drama Since 1960*

Saddlemyer, A. "Crime in Literature: Canadian Drama," 214–30 in M. L. Friedland, ed., *Rough Justice: Essays on Crime in Literature*

The Ecstasy of Rita Joe, 1967

Boire, G. "Tribunalations: George Ryga's Postcolonial Trial 'Play,' " *ARIEL* 22(2):5–20, Apr. 1991

RYSKIND, MORRIE. *SEE* KAUFMAN, GEORGE S., MORRIE RYSKIND, GEORGE GERSHWIN, and IRA GERSHWIN

SEE ALSO KAUFMAN, GEORGE S., MORRIE RYSKIND, BERT KALMAR, and HARRY RUBY

ST. GEORGE, ADRIENNE

Alva!, 1992
  Filichia, P. "Stagestruck: Star!" TheaterWeek 6(26):8–9, 1 Feb. 1993

ST. JOHN, MARY

American Plan, 1933
  Disch, T. M. Nation 252(5):175, 11 Feb. 1991
  Simon, J. New York 24(1):67, 7 Jan. 1991
  Weales, G. Commonweal 118(2):56, 25 Jan. 1991

SALAAM, KALAMU YA

Salaam, K. "Malcolm, My Son," African American Review 27(1):93–115, Sprg.
  1993

SANCHEZ-SCOTT, MILCHA

McFerran, V. D. "Chicana Voices in American Drama: Silviana Wood, Estela
  Portillo Trambley, Cherríe Moraga, Milcha Sanchez-Scott, Josefina Lopez,"
  (#DA9119397; U of Minnesota) DAI 52(6):1946A, Dec. 1991
Sanchez-Scott, M. "The Cuban Swimmer," Antaeus (66):407–20, Sprg. 1991

SAROYAN, WILLIAM

Nuer, H. "Postmarks of Distinction," Writer's Digest 73(2):6, Feb. 1993
Saroyan, W. Warsaw Visitor; Tales from the Vienna Streets: The Last Two Plays
  of William Saroyan

The Hungerers
  Allen, D. "Hungerers on Stage: Hunger Behind the Scenes?" Moscow News
    31(3538):15, 2 Aug. 1992

The Time of Your Life, 1939
  Rich, F. New York Times 141:B3(N), 2 Oct. 1991

SCHECHNER, RICHARD

Langworthy, D. "Devil's Food," American Theatre 10(7/8):12, Jul/Aug. 1993
Schechner, R. "A New Paradigm for Theatre in the Academy," TDR 36(4):7–10,
  Wntr. 1992
———. "A Tale of a Few Cities: Interculturalism on the Road," New Theatre
  Quarterly 7:315–23, Nov. 1991

Dionysus in '69, 1968
  Clemons, L. A. "The Power of Performance: Environmental Theatre and Heterotopia in *Dionysus in '69*," *Theatre Studies* 37:66–73, 1992
  Shephard, W. H. *The Dionysus Group*

SCHENKAR, JOAN

Diamond, E. "Crossing the Corpus Callosum: An Interview with Joan Schenkar," *Drama Review* 35:99–101, Summ. 1991
Schenkar, J. "A New Way to Pay Old Debts: The Playwright Directs Her Own," 253–62 in E. Donkin and S. Clements, eds. *Upstaging Big Daddy: Directing Theater as if Gender and Race Matter*

The Universal Wolf, 1991
  Lamont, R. C., ed. *Women on the Verge: 7 Avant-Garde American Plays*
  Schenkar, J. "*The Universal Wolf*: A Vicious New Version of Little Red Riding Hood," *Kenyon Review* 13(2):76–93, Sprg. 1991

SCHENKKAN, ROBERT

Schenkkan, R. "Family Pride in the 50s: A Comedy of Menace," *Kenyon Review* 15:156–76, Sprg. 1993

The Kentucky Cycle, 1992
  Alleman, R. *Vogue* 183(10):230, Oct. 1993
  Brustein, R. *New Republic* 209(18):28–30, 1 Nov. 1993
  Collins, G. "*Kentucky* Adventure," *New York Times* 142:B2(N), 30 Jul. 1993
  Evans, G. "N.Y. Doesn't Want to Bring *Kentucky* Home," *Variety* 346(13):69 13 Apr. 1992
  ———. "*Cycle* Rolls into Broadway's Red Sea," *Variety* 353(7):55–56, 20 Dec. 1993
  Gerard, J. *Variety* 353(3):32–33, 22 Nov. 1993
  Harris, P. "Post-time Stakes Grow in D.C. *Kentucky* Derby," *Variety* 352(8):71–72, 4 Oct. 1993
  Harris, W. "How a Lone Producer Gambled on an Epic," *New York Times* 143:H5(N), 7 Nov. 1993
  Henry, W. A., III. *Time* 139(6):76, 10 Feb. 1992
  ———. *Time* 142(10):66, 6 Sep. 1993
  ———. *Time* 142(22):72, 22 Nov. 1993
  Horn, M. *U.S. News & World Report* 115(11):72–73, 20 Sep. 1993
  Hornby, R. *Hudson Review* 45(2):293–94, Summ. 1992
  ———. "Regional Theatre Comes of Age," *Hudson Review* 46(3):529–36, Autm. 1993
  Ickes, B. *New York* 26(36):44–45, 13 Sep. 1993
  Kaufman, D. *Nation* 257(20):740–42, 13 Dec. 1993
  Kroll, J. *Newsweek* 122(22):77, 29 Nov. 1993
  Lahr, J. *New Yorker* 69(41):138–40, 6 Dec. 1993
  Marowitz, C. *TheaterWeek* 5(32):29 +, 16 Mar. 1992

Mason, B. A. "Recycling *Kentucky*," *New Yorker* 69(36):50–59, 1 Nov. 1993

Mintz, S. L. "Less Isn't More," *American Theatre* 10(4):20–24, Apr. 1993

O'Steen, K. "Dark Horse Wins Pulitzer," *Variety* 346(13):69, 13 Apr. 1992

Raymond, G. "Season Preview: The Plays," *TheaterWeek* 7(5):14, 6 Sep. 1993

Rich, F. *New York Times* 143:B1(N), 15 Nov. 1993

Richards, D. *New York Times* 143:H5(N), 21 Nov. 1993

Rudd, M. *TheaterWeek* 4(47):32–34, 1 Jul. 1991

Simon, J. *New York* 26(47):79–80, 29 Nov. 1993

Weber, B. "Get Ready for Six Hours of History," *New York Times* 142:B6(N), 5 Mar. 1993

———. "Playing for the *Cycle*," *New York Times* 143:B2(N), 19 Nov. 1993

SCHISGAL, MURRAY

Blatt, K. S. *Murray Schisgal, Playwright.* Diss.; Michigan State U, 1991

Schisgal, M. "Out of the Blue, They Committed," *New York Times* 143:H7(N), 19 Sep. 1993

Simon, N. *One Man Alone.* Videocassete

SCHMIDT, HARVEY. *SEE* JONES, TOM, and HARVEY SCHMIDT

SEE ALSO NASH, RICHARD N., TOM JONES, and HARVEY SCHMIDT

SCHNEEMANN, CAROLEE

Birringer, J. "Imprints and Revisions: Carolee Schneemann's Visual Archeology," *Performing Arts Journal* 45:31–46, May 1993

Constantinides, K. "Carolee Schneemann: Invoking Body Politics," *Michigan Quarterly Review* 30(1):127–45, Wntr. 1991

SCHNEIDER, JOHN

"Winning Writers," *American Theatre* 8(10):62–63, Jan. 1992

SCHUYLER, JAMES

Pace, E. "James Schuyler Dies at 67," *New York Times* 140:9(N), 13 Apr. 1991

Wasserburg, C. "Household Tasks and Daily Work," *Michigan Quarterly Review* 30:747–55, Fall 1991

SCHWARTZ, STEPHEN. *SEE* STEIN, JOSEPH, CHARLES STROUSE, and STEPHEN SCHWARTZ

SEE ALSO TEBELAK, JOHN-MICHAEL, and STEPHEN SCHWARTZ

SCOTT, DOUGLAS

Mountain (about William O. Douglas), 1990
  Filichia, P. *TheaterWeek* 6(27):13, 8 Feb. 1993

SERGEL, CHRISTOPHER, GAYLE SERGEL, and DONOVAN MARLEY

"Christopher Sergel," (Obituary) *Variety* 351(3):115, 17 May 1993

Black Elk Speaks (based on John G. Neihardt's novel of the same name), 1984
  Black Elk Speaks. Videocassette
  Mason, M. S. "The Gospel According to Black Elk," *American Theatre*
    10(12):21–24, Dec. 1993
  Young, A. *Variety* 353(2):42, 15 Nov. 1993

SERGEL, GAYLE. *SEE* SERGEL, CHRISTOPHER, GAYLE SERGEL, and
DONOVAN MARLEY

SERLING, ROD

Brodkin, S. Z. *Seven Plays of Mystery & Suspense*
Sander, G. F. *Serling: The Rise and Twilight of Television's Last Angry Man*

Requiem for a Heavyweight (stage version of his 1956 television play), 1985
  Winchell, M. R. "Rod Serling's *Requiem for a Heavyweight*: A Drama for
    Its Time," *Studies in American Drama, 1945-Present* 8(1):13–20, 1993

SERRAND, DOMINIQUE. *SEE* EPP, STEVEN, FELICITY JONES, and
DOMINIQUE SERRAND

SHANGE, NTOZAKE

Anderlini, S. "Drama or Performance Art? An Interview with Ntozake Shange,"
  Journal of Dramatic Theory and Criticism 6(1):85–87, Fall 1991
Baccolini, R. "Sherazade; L'identita femminile nel teatro contemporaneo in lin-
  gua inglese," 183–96 in R. Baccolini, V. Fortunati, and R. Zacchi, eds. *Il teatro
  e le donne: Forme drammatiche e tradizione al femminile nel teatro inglese*
Charlotte, S. *Creativity: Conversations with 28 Who Excel*
Elder, A. " 'Sassafrass, Cypress & Indigo': Ntozake Shange's Neo-Slave/Blues
  Narrative," *African American Review* 26(1):99–107, Sprg. 1992
Gray, N. *Language Unbound: On Experimental Writing by Women*
Horwitz, S. "The Playwright as Woman," *TheaterWeek* 5(3):22 +, 26 Aug. 1991
Lester, N. A. "At the Heart of Shange's Feminism: An Interview," *Black Ameri-
  can Literature Forum* 24:717–30, Wntr. 1990
McDowell, L., and R. Pringle. *Defining Women: Social Institutions and Gender
  Divisions*
Olaniyan, T. "The Poetics and Politics of 'Othering': Contemporary African, Af-

rican-American, and Caribbean Drama and the Invention of Cultural Identities,'' (#DA9203968; Cornell U) *DAI* 52(8):2922A, Feb. 1992
Shange, N. "However You Come to Me,'' in M. Golden, ed. *Wild Women Don't Wear No Blues: Black Women Writers on Love, Men, and Sex*
————. "Murdering the King's English,'' in M. E. Biggs, ed. *In the Vernacular: Interviews at Yale with Sculptors of Culture*
————. *Three Pieces*
Shinn, T. J. "Living the Answer: The Emergence of African American Feminist Drama,'' *Studies in Humanities* 1792):149–59, Dec. 1990

For Colored Girls Who Have Considered Suicide/When the Rainbow Is Enuf, 1976 (revised 1977)
 Lester, N. A. "Shange's Men: *For Colored Girls* Revisited, and Movement Beyond,'' *African American Review* 26(2):319–28, Summ. 1992
 Shange, N. *For Colored Girls Who Have Considered Suicide*. Videocassette
 ————. *Plays, One*
 Wiley, C. *Theatre Journal* 43:381–3, Oct. 1991

The Love Space Demands, 1992
 Bell, J. *TheaterWeek* 5(37):8, 20 Apr. 1992
 Shange, N. *The Love Space Demands*
 ————. *Plays, One*

Spell #7, 1979
 Cronacher, K. "Unmasking the Minstrel Mask's Black Magic in Ntozake Shange's *Spell #7*,'' *Theatre Journal* 44(2):177–93, May 1992
 Pinkney, M. "Theatrical Expressionism in the Structure and Language of Ntozake Shange's *Spell #7*,'' *Theatre Studies* 37:5–15, 1992
 Shange, N. *Plays, One*
 Wiley, C. *Theatre Journal* 43:381–3, Oct. 1991

SHANGE, NTOZAKE, EMILY MANN, and BAIKIDA CARROLL

Betsey Brown (adaptation of Shange's novel), 1989
 Gussow, M. *New York Times* 140:14(L), 13 Apr. 1991

SHANLEY, JOHN PATRICK

Shanley, J. P. *Thirteen by Shanley*

Beggars in the House of Plenty, 1991
 Gerard, J. *Variety* 345(3):52, 28 Oct. 1991
 Holbrook, C. *TheaterWeek* 5(17):39, 2 Dec. 1991
 Horwitz, S. "J. P. Shanley's Odyssey,'' *TheaterWeek* 5(16):27, 25 Nov. 1991
 Oliver, E. *New Yorker* 67(37):95, 4 Nov. 1991
 Simon, J. *New York* 24(44):119, 11 Nov. 1991

The Big Funk, 1990
Simon J. *New York* 24(1):66, 7 Jan. 1991

SHAPIRO, LEONARD

Collateral Damage: The Private Life of the New World Order, 1991
Raymond, G. "War Dead or *Collateral Damage?*" *TheaterWeek* 4(44):35,
10 Jun. 1991

SHARIF, BINA

One Thousand Hours of Love, 1993
Easton, W. *TheaterWeek* 6(31):38, 8 Mar. 1993

SHAW, PAUL. *SEE* BOURNE, BETTE, PEGGY SHAW, PAUL SHAW, and LOIS
WEAVER

SHAW, PEGGY, and LOIS WEAVER

Anniversary Waltz, 1990
Harris, H. *Theatre Journal* 42:484–88, Dec. 1990

SEE ALSO BOURNE, BETTE, PEGGY SHAW, PAUL SHAW, and LOIS
WEAVER

SEE ALSO MARGOLIN, DEBORAH, and PEGGY SHAW

SHAWN, WALLACE

Brewer, G. "He's Still Falling: Wallace Shawn's Problem of Morality," *American
Drama* 2(1):26–58, Fall 1992
Robinson, M. "Four Writers," *Theater* 24(1):31–42, Wntr. 1993
"Wallace Shawn: Playwright, Author, Actor," *Nation* 253(3):120, 15 Jul. 1991

Fever, 1990
Disch, T. M. *Nation* 252(1):24–25, 7 Jan. 1991
King, W. D. "Dionysus in Santa Barbara: Wallace Shawn's Euripidean
Fever," *Theater Magazine* 23(1):83–87, Wntr. 1992
Posnock, R. "New York Phantasmagoria," *Raritan: A Quarterly Review*
11(2):142–59, Fall 1991
Shawn, W. *The Fever*
————. *Harper's Magazine* 282(1691):42–43, Apr. 1991
Weales, G. *Commonweal* 118(1):18, 11 Jan. 1991

SHEFFER, ISAIAH

The Sheik of Avenue B, 1992
Backalenick, I. "*Avenue B* to Broadway," *TheaterWeek* 6(19):26–27, 14
Dec. 1992

Shepard, R. F. "When Uptown Looks Down," *New York Times* 142:H5(N), 22 Nov. 1992

SHEPARD, SAM

Bednar, R. M. *Sam Shepard: Enacting the Mythic Frontier in Contemporary America.* M.A. Thesis; U of Texas, Austin, 1991

Benet, C. *Sam Shepard on the German Stage: Critics, Politics, Myths*

Bennett, S. "When a Woman Looks: The 'Other' Audience of Shepard's Plays," 168–79 in L. Wilcox, ed. *Rereading Shepard*

Berkowitz, G. M. *American Drama of the Twentieth Century.* 130, 185

Bigelow, E. A. *A Symposium of Voices: Sam Shepard's Theater.* Diss.; State U of New York, Buffalo, 1992

Brienza, S. "Sam Shepard, Anti-Illusion, and Metadrama: Plays on Writing, Acting, and Character," 376–91 in F. Burwick and W. Pape, eds. *Aesthetic Illusion: Theoretical and Historical Approaches*

Busby, M. "Sam Shepard and Frontier Gothic," 84–93 in D. Mogen, S. P. Sanders, and J. B. Karpinski, eds. *Frontier Gothic: Terror and Wonder at the Frontier in American Literature*

Callens, J. "Liege Language and Literature; 'When I Read the Book': Sam Shepard's Action," 33–49 in P. Michel, *BELL: Belgian Essays on Language and Literature*

———. "Sam Shepard: portret van de kunstenaar als ontdekkingsreizinger," *De Vlaamse Gids* 76(3):23–32, May/Jun. 1992

Carroll, D. "Potential Performance Texts for *The Rock Garden* and *4-H Club*," 22–41 in L. Wilcox, ed. *Rereading Shepard*

Carveth, D. L. "The Borderline Dilemma in *Paris, Texas*: Psychoanalytic Approaches to Sam Shepard," *Mosaic* 25(4):99–119, Fall 1992

Cho, E. Y. *Cultural Authorities in Transition and Sam Shepard's Search for Identity.* Diss.; U of Hawaii, 1991

Chocron, I. E. *El Teatro de Sam Shepard: de imagenes a personajes*

Czerepinski, J. N. *Under the Influence: Alcoholic Families in the Plays of Sam Shepard.* Diss.; U of Colorado, 1991

DeRose, D. J. *Sam Shepard*

Dikhit, R. "Opening Closure: The Plays of Sam Shepard," (#DA9112994; New York U) *DAI* 51(12):4120–21A, Jun. 1991

Gordon, R. "Dramatic Deconstruction: The Plays of Sam Shepard," (#DA9110878; U of Kansas) *DAI* 51(11):3743A, May 1991

Grace, S. "Lighting Out for the Territory Within: Field Notes on Shepard's Expressionist Vision," 180–195 in L. Wilcox, ed. *Rereading Shepard*

Graham, L. J. *Sam Shepard, Theme, Image and the Director*

Grant, G. "Shifting the Paradigm: Shepard, Myth, and the Transformation of Consciousness," *Modern Drama* 36(1):120–30, Mar. 1993

———. "Writing as a Process of Performing the Self: Sam Shepard's Notebooks," *Modern Drama* 34(4):549–65, Dec. 1991

Hall, A. C. *A Kind of Alaska: Women in the Plays of O'Neill, Pinter, and Shepard*

Heilman, R. B. "Shepard's Plays: Stylistic and Thematic Ties," *Sewanee Review* 100(4):630–44, Fall 1992

Kovacs, E. E. *From Script to Performance: Directing Sam Shepard's Buried Child.* M.A. Thesis; Arizona State U, 1991

Lincke, N. *"Voice" and Storytelling in Sam Shepard's Family Romances.* M.A. Thesis; U of West Florida, 1993

McDonough, C. J. "Staging Masculinity: The Search for Male Identity in Contemporary American Drama," (#DA9306664; U of Tennessee) *DAI* 53(11):3910A, May 1993

McGhee, J. *True Lies: The Architecture of the Fantastic in the Plays of Sam Shepard*

McKelly, J. C. "The Artist and the West: Two Portraits by Jack Kerouac and Sam Shepard," *Western American Literature* 26(4):293–301, Wntr. 1992

Orr, J. *Tragicomedy and Contemporary Culture: Play and Performance from Beckett to Shepard*

Pugliese, J. "The State of the 'Real': The Screen, the Network, and the Subject," *English Language Notes* 29:75–80, Sep. 1991

Putzel, S. "An American Cowboy on the English Fringe: Sam Shepard's London Audience," *Modern Drama* 36(1):131–46, Mar. 1993

Reaves, G. "Defining the Self in Twentieth Century American Autobiographical Writings: America as Paradigm," (#DA9214834; U of Miami) *DAI* 52(12):4332A, Jun. 1992

Roof, J. "Testicles, Toasters and the 'Real Thing,' " *Studies in the Humanities* 17(2):106–19, Dec. 1990

Rosen, C. "Emotional Territory: An Interview with Sam Shepard," *Modern Drama* 36(1):1–11, Mar. 1993

————. "Marooned But Invincible," *TheaterWeek* 4(44):23–27, 10 Jun. 1991

Sarlin, E. L. *"I Believe in My Mask—The Man I Made Up Is Me": Character and Identity in the Plays of Sam Shepard.* M.A. Thesis; U of Maryland, College Park, 1992

Schvey, H. I. "The Master and His Double: Eugene O'Neill and Sam Shepard," *Journal of Dramatic Theory and Criticism* 5(2):49–60, Sprg. 1991

————. "A Worm in the Wood: The Father-Son Relationship in the Plays of Sam Shepard," *Modern Drama* 36(1):12–26, Mar. 1993

Shepard, A. "The Ominous 'Bulgarian Threat' in Sam Shepard's Plays," *Theatre Journal* 44(1):59–66, Mar. 1992

Shepard, S. "Excerpts from *Slave of the Camera*," *Antaeus* 66:421–9, Sprg. 1991

Suhajcik, S. S. *Apollo, Dionysus, and Three Sets of Brothers: Nietzsche's The Birth of Tragedy as Applied to O'Neill, Pinter, and Shepard.* M.A. Thesis; Florida Atlantic U, 1991

Tucker, M. *Sam Shepard*

Vanden Heuvel, M. "Complementary Spaces: Realism, Performance and a New Dialogics of Theatre," *Theatre Journal* 44(1):47–58, Mar. 1992

————. "The Landlocked Geography of a Horse Dreamer: Performance and Consciousness in the Plays of Sam Shepard" in *Performing Drama/Dramatizing Performance: Alternative Theater and the Dramatic Text*

Weales, G. "Artifacts: The Early Plays Reconsidered," 8–21 in L. Wilcox, ed. *Rereading Shepard*

Wilcox, L. "The Desert and the City: Operation Sidewinder and Shepard's Postmodern Allegory," 42–57 in L. Wilcox, ed. *Rereading Shepard*

Wolter, J. C. "Sam Shepard in German-Speaking Countries: A Classified Bibliography," *Studies in American Drama, 1945-Present* 6(2):195–225, 1991

Wyatt, D. "Shepard's Split," *South Atlantic Quarterly* 91(2):333–60, Sprg. 1992
Young, S. B. *Sam Shepard's Use of Irony in Selected Plays.* Diss.; U of Tennessee, Knoxville, 1992

Angel City, 1976
    Rabillard, S. "Shepard's Challenge to the Modernist Myths of Origin and Originality: *Angel City* and *True West*," 77–96 in L. Wilcox, ed. *Rereading Shepard*
    Wilcox, L. "West's *The Day of the Locust* and Shepard's *Angel City*: Refiguring L.A. Noir," *Modern Drama* 36(1):61–75, Mar. 1993

Buried Child, 1978
    Arnold, L. *The Drama of Alienation: An Interpersonal Examination of Edward Albee's The Zoo Story and Sam Shepard's Buried Child.* M.A. Thesis; U of North Dakota, 1991
    Cho, E. Y. "Cultural Authorities in Transition and Sam Shepard's Search for Identity," (#DA9215010; U of Hawaii) *DAI* 52(12):4327A, Jun. 1992
    DeRose, D. J. "A Kind of Cavorting: Superpresence and Shepard's Family Dramas," 131–149 in L. Wilcox, ed. *Rereading Shepard*
    Francioni, M. " 'London, Texas': Gli elementi pinteriani nel teatro di Sam Shepard," *Confronto Letterario* 8(15):211–25, May 1991
    Hunter, J. W. *Set Design for Buried Child.* M.F.A. Thesis; U of Virginia, 1991
    Lyons, C. R. "Shepard's Family Trilogy and the Conventions of Modern Realism," 115–130 in L. Wilcox, ed. *Rereading Shepard*
    Perry, F. J. *A Reconstruction-Analysis of Buried Child by Playwright Sam Shepard*
    Rivera-Vega, C. H. *Pasts and Presents in Sam Shepard's Family Plays: Buried Child, True West, and Fool for Love.* M.A. Thesis; U of Puerto Rico, 1991
    Shea, L. "The Sacrificial Crisis in Sam Shepard's *Buried Child*," *Theatre Annual* 44:1–9, 1990
    Shields, L. W. *The Fall of the Great Modern American Family Myth in Sam Shepard's Buried Child, A Lie of the Mind, Fool for Love and True West.* M.A. Thesis; Texas Woman's U, 1993
    Urice, A. L. *Directing Sam Shepard's Buried Child.* M.F.A. Thesis; U of Virginia, 1991
    Wilson, A. "True Stories: Reading the Autobiographic in *Cowboy Mouth*, *True Dylan* and *Buried Child*," 97–114 in L. Wilcox, ed. *Rereading Shepard*

Curse of the Starving Class, 1977
    Schlatter, J. F. "Some Kind of a Future: The War for Inheritance in the Work of Three American Playwrights of the 1970s," *South Central Review* 7(1):59–75, Sprg. 1990
    Williams, H. *TLS* (4616):18, 20 Sep. 1991

Fool for Love, 1983
    Callens, J. "Through the Windows of Perception: Shepard's *Fool for Love* on the Screen," 83–112 in J. Callens, ed. *American Literature and the Arts*

Hall, A. C. "Speaking without Words: The Myth of Masculine Autonomy in Sam Shepard's *Fool for Love*," 150–167 in L. Wilcox, ed. *Rereading Shepard*

Londre, F. H. "A Motel of the Mind: *Fool for Love* and *A Lie of the Mind*," 215–224 in L. Wilcox, ed. *Rereading Shepard*

Rivera-Vega, C. H. *Pasts and Presents in Sam Shepard's Family Plays: Buried Child, True West, and Fool for Love.* M.A. Thesis; U of Puerto Rico, 1991

Shields, L. W. *The Fall of the Great Modern American Family Myth in Sam Shepard's Buried Child, A Lie of the Mind, Fool for Love, and True West.* M.A. Thesis; Texas Woman's U, 1993

Geography of a Horse Dreamer
McCarthy, G. "Memory and Mind: Sam Shepard's *Geography of a Horse Dreamer*," 58–76 in L. Wilcox, ed. *Rereading Shepard*

A Lie of the Mind, 1985
Crum, J. A. " 'I Smash the Tools of My Captivity': The Feminine in Sam Shepard's *A Lie of the Mind*," 196–214 in L. Wilcox, ed. *Rereading Shepard*

Haedicke, J. V. " 'A Population (and Theater) at Risk': Battered Women in Henley's *Crimes of the Heart* and Shepard's *A Lie of the Mind*," *Modern Drama* 36(1):83–95, Mar. 1993

Kane, L. "Dreamers and Drunks: Moral and Social Consciousness in Arthur Miller and Sam Shepard," *American Drama* 1(1):27–45, Fall 1991

Lanier, G. W. "Two Opposite Animals: Structural Pairing in Sam Shepard's *A Lie of the Mind*," *Modern Drama* 34(3):410–21, Sep. 1991

Londre, F. H. "A Motel of the Mind: *Fool for Love* and *A Lie of the Mind*," 215–224 in L. Wilcox, ed. *Rereading Shepard*

Rabillard, S. "Destabilizing Plot, Displacing the Status of Narrative: Local Order in the Plays of Pinter and Shepard," *Theatre Journal* 43(1):41–58, Mar. 1991

Shields, L. W. *The Fall of the Great Modern American Family Myth in Sam Shepard's Buried Child, A Lie of the Mind, Fool for Love, and True West.* M.A. Thesis; Texas Woman's U, 1993

Simpatico, 1993
Gussow, M. "As a Play Lies Fallow a Writer Moonlights," *New York Times* 143:B1(N), 27 Dec. 1993

States of Shock, 1991
Hornby, R. *Hudson Review* 44:458–9, Autm. 1991

Kramer, M. *New Yorker* 67(15):78–80, 3 Jun. 1991

Kroll, J. *Newsweek* 117(21):57, 27 May 1991

Rich, F. *New York Times* 140:B1(N), 17 May 1991

Richards, D. *New York Times* 140:H5(N), 26 May 1991

Weales, G. *Commonweal* 118(13):438–39, 12 Jul. 1991

Willadt, S. "States of War in Sam Shepard's *States of Shock*," *Modern Drama* 36(1):147–66, Mar. 1993

The Tooth of Crime, 1972

    Baker-White, R. E. *Popular Theatre and Literary Text in Contemporary Drama: The Dialectic of Appropriation.* (#DA9102223; Stanford U) *DAI* 51(8):2566A, Feb. 1991

    Lanier, G. W. "The Killer's Ancient Mask: Unity and Dualism in Shepard's *The Tooth of Crime*," *Modern Drama* 36(1):48–60, Mar. 1993

    Rogalus, P. W. "Shepard's *Tooth of Crime,* O'Neill's *Emperor Jones,* and the Contemporary American Tragic Hero," *Notes on Contemporary Literature* 22(2):2–3, Mar. 1992

True West, 1980 (revised 1982)

    Hoeper, J. D. "Cain, Canaanites, and Philistines in Sam Shepard's *True West,*" *Modern Drama* 36(1):76–82, Mar. 1993

    Rabillard, S. "Shepard's Challenge to the Modernist Myths of Origin and Originality: *Angel City* and *True West,*" 77–96 in L. Wilcox, ed. *Rereading Shepard*

    Rivera-Vega, C. H. *Pasts and Presents in Sam Shepard's Family Plays: Buried Child, True West, and Fool for Love.* M.A. Thesis; U of Puerto Rico, 1991

    Shields, L. W. *The Fall of the Great Modern American Family Myth in Sam Shepard's Buried Child, A Lie of the Mind, Fool for Love, and True West.* M.A. Thesis; Texas Woman's U, 1993

    Smith, R. H. " *'night Mother* and *True West*: Mirror Images of Violence and Gender," 277–90 in J. Redmond, ed. *Violence in Drama*

SHERMAN, CHARLEY. *SEE* PICKERING, STEVE, and CHARLEY SHERMAN

SHERMAN, JAMES

Beau Jest, 1991

    Sherman, J. *Beau Jest: A Comedy*

    Simon, J. *New York* 24(42):84, 28 Oct. 1991

    Simonson, R. *TheaterWeek* 5(16):41, 25 Nov. 1991

SHERMAN, JONATHAN MARC

Sherman, J. M. *Veins and Thumbtacks*

Women and Wallace, 1988

    Lamb, W., ed. *Ten Out of Ten*

    Moran, T. *TheaterWeek* 6(17):32, 30 Nov. 1992

SHERMAN, MARTIN

Cracks, 1993

    Wolf, M. *Variety* 351(3):106, 17 May 1993

When She Danced, 1991
  O'Connor, P. *TLS* (4612):17, 23 Aug. 1991
  Sherman, M. *When She Danced: A Play*

SHERMAN, RICHARD. *SEE* CAROTHERS, A. J., RICHARD SHERMAN, and
ROBERT SHERMAN

SHERMAN, ROBERT. *SEE* CAROTHERS, A. J., RICHARD SHERMAN, and
ROBERT SHERMAN

SHERWOOD, ROBERT E.

Mishra, K. *American Leftist Playwrights of the 1930's: A Study of Ideology and
  Technique in the Plays of Odets, Lawson, and Sherwood*

Abe Lincoln in Illinois, 1938
  Canby, V. *New York Times* 143:H5(N), 12 Dec. 1993
  Cromwell, J., director. *Abe Lincoln in Illinois*. Videocassette
  Gelderman, C. "Abe's Global Vision," *American Theatre* 10(12):13, Dec.
    1993
  Gerard, J. *Variety* 353(6):43, 13 Dec. 1993
  Henry, W. A., III. *Time* 142(25):81, 13 Dec. 1993
  Mitgang, H. "Why Abraham Lincoln Was an Early New Dealer," *New York
    Times* 143:H6(N), 28 Nov. 1993
  Richards, D. *New York Times* 143:B1(N), 30 Nov. 1993
  Simon, J. *New York* 26(49):108, 13 Dec. 1993
  Waterston, S., ed. *Playbill Lincoln Center Theater at the Vivian Beaumont:
    Abe Lincoln in Illinois*

SHINER, DAVID. *SEE* IRWIN, BILL, and DAVID SHINER

SILLS, PAUL

Adler, T. "The 'How' of Funny," *American Theatre* 10(12):14–18, Dec. 1993

SILVER, JOAN MICKLIN

Hart, C., moderator. *Women in Hollywood*. Videocassette

SILVER, JOAN MICKLIN, and JULIANNE BOYD (and others)

A . . . My Name Is Still Alice, 1992
  Braunagel, D. *Variety* 347(8):67, 8 Jun. 1992
  Chansky, D. *TheaterWeek* 6(27):29, 8 Feb. 1993
  Chase, T. *TheaterWeek* 6(4):24–25, 31 Aug. 1992
  Cook, C. D. *Set and Costume Design for A . . . My Name Is Alice*. M.F.A.
    Thesis; Texas Tech U, 1992

Evans, G. *Variety* 349(5):56, 23 Nov. 1992
Gussow, M. *New York Times/NYTIA* 142:B3(N), 23 Nov. 1992
Mamana, J. "Lashing Back," *TheaterWeek* 6(12):26–27, 26 Oct. 1992
Richards, D. *New York Times* 142:H5(N), 29 Nov. 1992
Silver, J. M. *A . . . My Name Is Still Alice*
Simon, J. *New York* 25(49):106, 14 Dec. 1992
Wasserman, L. "Julianne Boyd & Joan Micklin Silver: A Smooth-as-Silk Partnership," *American Theatre* 9(4):32–33, Jul/Aug. 1992

SILVER, NICKY

Pterodactyls, 1993
Brantley, B. *New York Times* 143:B5(N), 22 Oct. 1993
Evans, G. *Variety* 352(12):35, 1 Nov. 1993
Richards, D. *New York Times* 143:H5(N), 24 Oct. 1993
Simon, J. *New York* 26(44):85, 8 Nov. 1993

SILVER, R. S. (ROBERT SIMPSON)

The Bruce, 1991
Stevenson, R. *TLS* (4614):17, 6 Sep. 1991

SIMO, ANA MARIA

Simo, A. M. *Going to New England*
Watson, M. "The Search for Identity in the Theater of Three Cuban American Female Dramatists," *Bilingual Review* 16(2/3):188–96, May–Dec. 1991

SIMON, BARNEY

Branch, W. B. "Black Dramatists in the Diaspora: The Beginnings," in W. B. Branch, ed. *Crosswinds*

Born in the RSA, 1990
Schlossman, D. *Theatre Journal* 42:501–5, Dec. 1990

SIMON, LUCY. *SEE* NORMAN, MARSHA, and LUCY SIMON

SIMON, MAYO

The Old Lady's Guide to Survival, 1992
Osborn, M. E. "Letter from Louisville," *TheaterWeek* 5(38):29, 27 Apr. 1992
Simons, T. *American Theatre* 9(2):52–53, May 1992

SIMON, NEIL

Berkowitz, G. M. *American Drama of the Twentieth Century*. 153, 173
"The Best Theater of 1992," *Time* 141(1):67, 4 Jan. 1993
Bryer, J. R. "An Interview with Neil Simon," *Studies in American Drama, 1945-Present* 6(2):153–76, 1991
Richards, D. "The Last of the Red Hot Playwrights," *New York Times Magazine* 140:30, 17 Feb. 1991
Snow, L. "Doc's Grand Slam," *TheaterWeek* 4(45):20–21, 10 Jun. 1991
Wilson, E. interviewer. *Neil Simon*. 2 videocassettes

Brighton Beach Memoirs (the first play of his semiautobiographical trilogy), 1983
Lipton, J. "Neil Simon: The Art of Theater X," *Paris Review* 34(125):167–204, Wntr. 1992

Broadway Bound (the third play of his semiautobiographical trilogy), 1983
Terry, P. S. *Shared Comedic Elements of Three Plays in Modern American Theater: Six Degrees of Separation, I'm Not Rappaport, and Broadway Bound*. M.A. Thesis; U of Nevada, Las Vegas, 1992

Jake's Women, 1988
Disch, T. M. *Nation* 254(18):642–43, 11 May 1992
Dwyer, V. *Maclean's* 105(20):56–57, 18 May 1992
Gerard, J. *Variety* 346(11):84–85, 30 Mar. 1992
Kramer, M. *New Yorker* 68(7):79, 6 Apr. 1992
Lochte, D. *Los Angeles Magazine* 38(6):129, Jun. 1993
Marowitz, C. *TheaterWeek* 6(41):29–31, 17 May 1993
Moran, T. "A Family Affair," *TheaterWeek* 6(8):24–25, 28 Sep. 1992
Popkin, H. *TheaterWeek* 5(37):38, 20 Apr. 1992
Richards, D. *New York Times* 141:H5(N), 5 Apr. 1992
Rothstein, M. "Neil Simon Detour," *New York Times* 140:B3(N), 30 Aug. 1991
Simon, J. *New York* 25(14):106–07, 6 Apr. 1992
Weales, G. "American Theater Watch, 1991–1992," *Georgia Review* 46(3):524–37, Fall 1992
———. *Commonweal* 119(17):23, 9 Oct. 1992

Laughter on the 23rd Floor, 1993
Clarke, E. "Theater," *New York* 26(36):46–47, 13 Sep. 1993
Collins, G. "Neil Simon Opens a Door to the Past and Finds a Roomful of Vying Jokesters," *New York Times* 143:H5(N), 21 Nov. 1993
Gerard, J. *Variety* 353(5):33–34, 6 Dec. 1993
Henry, W. A., III. *Time* 142(24):76, 6 Dec. 1993
Kroll, J. "Broadway Unbound," *Newsweek* 119(7):60–61, 17 Feb. 1992
———. *Newsweek* 122(23):81, 6 Dec. 1993
Raymond, G. "Season Preview: The Plays," *TheaterWeek* 7(5):14, 6 Sep. 1993
Rich, F. *New York Times* 143:B1(N), 23 Nov. 1993
Richards, D. *New York Times* 143:H27(N), 28 Nov. 1993

Simon, J. *New York* 26(48):131, 6 Dec. 1993

Weber, B. "Drama on *Laughter*," *New York Times* 143:B9(N), 15 Oct. 1993

Lost in Yonkers, 1991

Dalva, N. *Dance Magazine* 65(8):53, Aug. 1991

Disch, T. M. *Nation* 252(13):460, 8 Apr. 1991

Heilpern, J. "Irene Worth and Mercedes Ruehl—Neil Simon's Two Newest Leading Women," *Vogue* 181(3):280–81, Mar. 1991

Henry, W. A., III. *Time* 137(9):70, 4 Mar. 1991

Hevesi, D. "Pulitzer Prizes in Letters Go to Updike and Simon," *New York Times* 140:A11(N), 10 Apr. 1991

Hornby, R. *Hudson Review* 44(2):289–91, Summ. 1991

Kanfer, S. *New Leader* 74(3):22, 11 Feb. 1991

Kroll, J. *Newsweek* 117(9):60, 4 Mar. 1991

Lazare, L. "*Lost in Yonkers* Finds Home in Chicago," *Variety* 348(5):67, 24 Aug. 1992

Rothstein, M. "A Pair of Winners Say Adieu to *Yonkers*," *New York Times* 140:C3(L), 23 Aug. 1991

———. "*Yonkers* and *Will Rogers* Win the Top Tony Awards," *New York Times* 140:C11(L), 3 Jun. 1991

Simon, N. *Lost in Yonkers: The Illustrated Screenplay of the Film*

Torrens, J. S. *America* 164(17):496–97, 4 May, 1991

Variety 342(2):84, 21 Jan. 1991

Weales, G. *Commonweal* 118(9):293–94, 3 May 1991

Weinraub, B. "Beyond Valley Girls and Sunshine Boys," *New York Times* 142:B3(N), 26 Apr. 1993

Wolf, M. "*Lost in Yonkers* May Be Found in London," *Variety* 349(5):55–56, 23 Nov. 1992

The Odd Couple, 1965 (revised 1985)

Rothstein, M. "*Odd Couple* Returns for a Good Deed," *New York Times* 140:B3(N), 20 Jun. 1991

SIMON, NEIL, MARVIN HAMLISCH, and DAVID ZIPPEL

The Goodbye Girl (adaptation of Simon's screen play)

Boehlert, E. *Billboard* 105(12):49, 20 Mar. 1993

Buckley, M. "The Goodbye Boy: Q-and-A with Martin Short," *Theater-Week* 6(30):15–18, 1 Mar. 1993

Evans, G. "Test of a Salesman for Two Tough Shows," *Variety* 350(7):69–70, 15 Mar. 1993

———. *Variety* 350(6):69, 8 Mar. 1993

Gerard, J. "Brutal B.O. Prompts *Girl* to Bid Goodbye," *Variety* 351(12):39–40, 2 Aug. 1993

Harris, J. E. *Christopher Street* (201):6–7, May 1993

Henry, W. A., III. *Time* 141(11):69, 15 Mar. 1993

Kanfer, S. *New Leader* 76(5):23, 5 Apr. 1993

Lazare, L. *Variety* 349(10):72, 4 Jan. 1993

Mandelbaum, K. *TheaterWeek* 6(33):28–31, 22 Mar. 1993

Oliver, E. *New Yorker* 69(4):122, 15 Mar. 1993

Rich, F. *New York Times* 142:B1(N), 5 Mar. 1993
Richards, D. *New York Times* 142:H1(N), 14 Mar. 1993
Shapiro, L. *Newsweek* 121(11):82, 15 Mar. 1993
Simon, J. *New York* 26(11):73, 15 Mar. 1993
Weber, B. "*Goodbye Girl* in Progress," *New York Times* 142:C2(L), 5 Feb. 1993
————. "A Jaunty Jester Finds a New Voice on Broadway," *New York Times* 142:H5(N), 28 Feb. 1993
————. "Michael Kidd Replaces Gene Saks as Director of *The Goodbye Girl*," *New York Times* 142:B1(N), 8 Jan. 1993
————. "Saks Tells His Story, Angrily," *New York Times* 142:B8(N), 15 Jan. 1993
————. " 'Simon Gets a Scene Right, or Rather Correct," *New York Times* 142:B8(N), 12 Feb. 1993

SLOAN, JUDITH

She's Just a Feminist, 1991
Chansky, D. *TheaterWeek* 4(44):35, 10 Jun. 1991

SMEAL, DENNIS RAYMOND

Change Partners & Dance, 1992
Filichia, P. *TheaterWeek* 6(27):12, 8 Feb. 1993

SMITH, ANNA DEAVERE

"Art," *Time* 141(26):67, 28 Jun. 1993
"Bio," *People Weekly* 40(9):95, 30 Aug. 1993
Blaszczyk, C. Producer. *Anna Deavere Smith: In Her Own Words*. Audiocassette.
Johnson, R. "Jamison Offers a Hymn to Ailey," *Dance Magazine* 67(12):28, Dec. 1993
Lewis, B. "The Circle of Confusion: A Conversation with Anna Deavere Smith," *Kenyon Review* 15(4):54–64, Fall 1993
Neill, H. "Conflicting Answers," *TLS* (4006):44, 9 Apr. 1993
"Prizes for Two Playwrights," *New York Times* 143:B3(N), 20 Oct. 1993
Rayner, R. "Word of Mouth: In Her New One-Woman Show, Anna Deavere Smith Articulates the Language of Urban Unrest," *Harper's Bazaar* 3376:248, 1 Apr. 1993
Richards, S. L. "Caught in the Act of Social Definition: On the Road with Anna Deavere Smith," in *Acting Out: Feminist Performances*
Rothstein, M. "Racial Turmoil in America: Tales from a Woman Who Listened," *New York Times* 141:E7(N), 5 Jul. 1992
Rugoff, R. "One-Woman Chorus," *Vogue* 183(4):224–26, Apr. 1993
Schechner, R. "Anna Deavere Smith: Acting Is Incorporation," *TDR* 37(4):63 +, Wntr. 1993
Simon, D. E. V. "29 Characters in Search of Community," *Ms. Magazine* 3(2):67, Sep/Oct. 1992

Weber, B. "Examining Current Events," *New York Times* 142:B7(N), 23 Apr. 1993

Fires in the Mirror, 1992

Brustein, R. *New Republic* 207(2):29–30, 6 Jul. 1992

Caplan, B. *New Statesman & Society* 6(246):21–22, 2 Apr. 1993

Clines, F. X. "Giving Voice to a Neighborhood's Anguish," *New York Times* 141:B1(N), 10 Jun. 1992

Kroll, J. *Newsweek* 119(22):74, 1 Jun. 1992

Laris, K. *Theatre Journal* 45(1):117–19, Mar. 1993

Martin, C. "Anna Deavere Smith: The Word Becomes You," *TDR* 37(4):45–62, Wntr. 1993

Rich, F. *New York Times* 141:B1(N), 15 May 1992

Richards, D. *New York Times* 141:H5(N), 17 May 1992

Simon, J. *New York* 25(27):66, 13 Jul. 1992

Smith, A. D. *Fires in the Mirror*. Videocassette

Stayton, R. "A Fire in a Crowded Theatre: Anna Deavere Smith Relives the Los Angeles Riots," *American Theatre* 10(7/8):20–26, Jul/Aug. 1993

Witchel, A. "About *Fires* Before It Got Hot," *New York Times* B2(N), 22 May, 1992

Wright, D. "A Seance with History," *New York Times* 141:H14(N), 10 May 1992

Twilight: Los Angeles, 1992

Blanchard, B. *Progressive* 57(12):35–36, Dec. 1993

Henry, W. A., III. *Time* 141(26):73, 28 Jun. 1993

Hornby, R. *Hudson Review* 46:534–5, Autm. 1993

Kroll, J. *Newsweek* 121(26):62–63, 28 Jun. 1993

Lahr. J. *New Yorker* 69(19):90–94, 28 Jun. 1993

Meeks, C. *Variety* 351(8):28–29, 28 Jun. 1993

Smith, A. "On *Twilight*," *American Theatre* 10(7/8):23, Jul/Aug. 1993

Weinraub, B. "Condensing a Riot's Cacophony into the Voice of One Woman," *New York Times* 142:B1(N), 16 Jun. 1993

SOLIS, OCTAVIO

Solis, O. *Man of the Flesh*. 109–167 in *Plays from South Coast Repertory*

Prospect, 1993

Harvey, D. *Variety* 351(2):246, 10 May 1993

Santos & Santos, 1993

Jamison, L. "Welcome to El Paso," *American Theatre* 10(12):8–9, Dec. 1993

SOMSEN, PENNELL

One Tit, A Dyke, & Gin, 1991

Somsen, P. *One Tit, A Dyke, & Gin*, 112–147 in T. Helbing, ed. *Gay and Lesbian Plays Today*

SONDHEIM, STEPHEN

Banfield, S. *Sondheim's Broadway Musicals*
Evans, G. "Top-Line Playwrights Write Off Broadway," *Variety* 348(6):63, 31 Aug. 1992
Gordon, J. L. *Art Isn't Easy: The Theater of Stephen Sondheim*
Gottfried, M. *Sondheim*
Hischak, T. S. *Word Crazy: Broadway Lyricists from Cohan to Sondheim*
Kirsch, C. *Conditions of Harmony in Stephen Sondheim's Sunday in the Park with George*. M.A. Thesis; U of Texas, Dallas, 1993
Loney, G. "Beyond the Broadway Musical: Crossovers, Confusions and Crisis," 151–76 in B. King, ed. *Contemporary American Theatre*
McClatchy, J. D. "Laughter in the Soul," *Antaeus* (71/72):86–91, Autm. 1993
Pasqual, D. "Lorenz Hart: Side by Side by Sondheim," *TheaterWeek* 5(4):33–37, 2 Sep. 1991
Steyn, M. *Stephen Sondheim*

Anyone Can Whistle, 1964
   Filichia, P. "We're Opening Doors," *TheaterWeek* 6(13):14–15, 2 Nov. 1992
   Mandelbaum, K. *TheaterWeek* 6(16):29–32, 23 Nov. 1992

Assassins, 1991
   Henry, W. A., III. *Time* 137(5):62, 4 Feb. 1991
   Kroll, J. *Newsweek* 117(5):72, 4 Feb. 1991
   Mandelbaum, K. *TheaterWeek* 4(27):17–21, 11 Feb. 1991
   Simon, J. *New York* 24(5):38, 4 Feb. 1991
   Weiss, B. "Letter from San Jose," *TheaterWeek* 6(28):24–25, 15 Feb. 1993

Putting It Together, 1993
   Ames, K. *Newsweek* 121(15):61, 12 Apr. 1993
   Gerard, J. *Variety* 350(10):184, 5 Apr. 1993
   Henry, W. A., III. *Time* 141(15):71, 12 Apr. 1993
   Kirkpatrick, M. *Wall Street Journal* A12(W), 7 Apr. 1993
   Mandelbaum, K. *TheaterWeek* 6(37):27–28, 19 Apr. 1993
   Rich, F. *New York Times* 142:B1, 2 Apr. 1993
   Richards, D. *New York Times* 142:H5, 11 Apr. 1993
   Simon, J. *New York* 26(15):66–67, 12 Apr. 1993
   Weber, B. *New York Times* 142:B3, 28 Oct. 1992

SEE ALSO FURTH, GEORGE, and STEVEN SONDHEIM

SEE ALSO LAPINE, JAMES, and STEVEN SONDHEIM

SPENCER, DAVID. *SEE* MENKEN, ALAN, ALAN BENNERT, and DAVID SPENCER

STAVIS, BARRIE

Goldstein, E. "An Interview with Barrie Stavis," *Studies in American Drama, 1945-Present* 6(1):71, 1991

STEEN, DAVID

Avenue A, 1991
   Marowitz, C. *TheaterWeek* 4(52):40–41, 5 Aug. 1991

STEIN, GERTRUDE

Grabes, H. " 'If It Can Be Done Why Do It'—Gertrude Steins unmögliche Dramenasthetik," 161–80 in T. Fischer-Seidel, ed. *Frauen und Frauendarstellung in der englischen und amerikanischen Literatur*
Kostelanetz, R. "Gertrude Stein," 29–39 in R. Kostelznetz, ed., *American Writing Today*
Miller, L. C. "Writing Is Hearing and Saying: Gertrude Stein on Language and in Performance," *Text and Performance Quarterly* 13(2):154, 1 Apr. 1993
Robinson, M. "Gertrude Stein, Forgotten Playwright," *South Atlantic Quarterly* 91(3):620–43, Summ. 1992

Accents in Alsace
   Giesenkirchen, M. "Where English Speaks More than One Language: Accents in Gertrude Stein's *Accents in Alsace*," *Massachusets Review* 34(1):45–62, Sprg. 1993

Dr. Faustus Lights the Lights, 1938
   Brustein, R. "On Theater: Wilson Lights Steins Lights," *New Republic* 107(7):27, 10 Aug. 1992
   Callens, J. "Ter plaatse fietsen: Wilson regisseert Stein," *De Vlaamse Gids* 77(3):13–18, May/Jun. 1993
   Greene, A. "Festival Review," *TheaterWeek* 6(2):32–34, 17 Aug. 1992
   Savran, D. "Whistling in the Dark," *Performing Arts Journal* 45:25–27, Jan. 1993
   Stevenson, R. *TLS* (4719):19, 10 Sep. 1993

STEIN, JOSEPH, and MARK BLITZSTEIN

Juno (based on Sean O'Casey's *Juno and the Paycock*), 1959
   Filichia, P. "*Juno* and the Playwright," *TheaterWeek* 6(16):12–13, 23 Nov. 1992
   Mandelbaum, K. *TheaterWeek* 6(16):29–32, 23 Nov. 1992

STEIN, JOSEPH, CHARLES STROUSE, and STEPHEN SCHWARTZ

Rags, 1991
   Filichia, P. "Brand New World," *TheaterWeek* 5(17):16, 2 Dec. 1991
   Mandelbaum, K. *TheaterWeek* 5(20):32 +, 23 Dec. 1991

STEIN, JOSEPH, JERRY BOCK, and SHELDON HARNICK

Fiddler on the Roof (musical version of stories by S. Aleichem), 1964
   Disch, T. M. *Nation* 252(1):26 +, 7 Jan. 1991

STEPPLING, JOHN

Sea of Cortez, 1992
   Marowitz, C. *TheaterWeek* 5(47):34–36, 29 Jun. 1992

STERNER, JERRY

Schempp, W. D., director. *Judith Ehrlich and Jerry Sterner.* Videocassette

Other People's Money, 1989
   Marowitz, C. *TheaterWeek* 4(51):40, 29 Jul. 1991
   Sterner, J. *Other People's Money: The Ultimate Seduction*

STEVENS, WALLACE

Brint, S. D. "A Necessary Distance; Wallace Stevens: The Epigram and the
   Play," *Durham University Journal* 83(1):85–90,Jan. 1991

STEWART, ELLEN

Chast, S. L. *Ellen Stewart and La Mama: A Study of Theatrical Spaces.* Diss.; U
   of California, Berkeley, 1991
Ostroska, B. *Ellen Stewart's Global "Pushcart": Twenty-six Years of Internation-
   alism at La Mama.* Diss.; U of Colorado, 1991
———. "Interview with Ellen Stewart of La Mama Experimental Theatre Club,"
   Journal of Dramatic Theory and Criticism 6(1):99–105, Fall 1991

Yunus Emre, 1992
   Lamont, R. C. "Multiculturalism at La MaMa E.T.C.," *TheaterWeek*
   6(24):26–28, 18 Jan. 1993

STONE, PETER, and SHERMAN EDWARDS

1776, 1969
   Filichia, P. "Let Freedom Sing," *TheaterWeek* 4(50):11–13, 22 Jul. 1991

STROUSE, CHARLES. *SEE* LAURENTS, ARTHUR, CHARLES STROUSE,
and RICHARD MALTBY, JR.

SEE ALSO MEEHAN, THOMAS, MARTIN CHARNIN, and CHARLES
STROUSE

SEE ALSO STEIN, JOSEPH, CHARLES STROUSE, and STEPHEN
SCHWARTZ

STURGES, PRESTON

Henderson, B. "Cartoon and Narrative in the Films of Frank Tashlin and Preston
    Sturges," in A. Horton, ed. *Comedy/Cinema/Theory*
Jacobs, D. *Christmas in July: The Life and Art of Preston Sturges*
Pinck, D. "Preston Sturges: The Wizard of Hollywood," *American Scholar*
    61(3):402–08, Summ. 1992
Sturges, S., ed. *Preston Sturges on Preston Sturges*

A Cup of Coffee, written 1931, first produced 1988
    Marowitz, C. *TheaterWeek* 6(4):31, 31 Aug. 1992

STYNE, JULE. *SEE* COMDEN, BETTY, ADOLPH GREEN, and JULE STYNE

SEE ALSO COMDEN, BETTY, ADOLPH GREEN, JULE STYNE, MOOSE
CHARLAP, and CAROLYN LEE

SEE ALSO NORMAN, MARSHA, and JULE STYNE

SULLIVAN, DANIEL

Inspecting Carol
    Sullivan, D. *Inspecting Carol*

SWADOS, ROBIN

A Quiet End, 1986
    Swados, R. *A Quiet End*, 151–212 in T. Helbing, ed. *Gay and Lesbian Plays
    Today*

SWEET, JEFFREY

Sweet, J. *American Enterprise: A Play with Music*
———. *The Dramatist's Toolkit: The Craft of the Working Playwright*

The Value of Names (a one-act 1983 play expanded to full-length)
    Filichia, P. *TheaterWeek* 4(51):14, 29 Jul. 1991

SWEET, JEFFREY, SUSAN BIRKENHEAD, and HOWARD MARREN

What About Luv? (musical version of Murray Schisgal's *Luv*), 1991
    Filichia, P. *TheaterWeek* 5(24):11, 20 Jan. 1991

SWERLING, JO. *SEE* BURROWS, ABE, JO SWERLING, and FRANK
LOESSER

TACCONE, TONY

Volpone, 1993
    Schechter, J. "Exposing *Volpone*," *American Theatre* 10(5–6):7, May/Jun. 1993

TALLY, TED

Parnell, S. *Performing the Role of Kathleen Scott in Terra Nova by Ted Tally.* M.F.A. Thesis; U of Florida, 1992
Van Gelder, L. "Recalling Dr. Lecter," *New York Times* 141:13(N), 1 Feb. 1992

TANNER, JUSTIN

Party Mix, 1991
    Marowitz, C. *TheaterWeek* 4(28):39, 18 Feb. 1991

TEBELAK, JOHN-MICHAEL, and STEPHEN SCHWARTZ

Godspell (based on the Gospel of Matthew), 1971
    Murray, K. "*Godspell* Case Resurrected for Radner," *Variety* 348(8):55, 14 Sep. 1992

TELSON, BOB. *SEE* BREUER, LEE, and BOB TELSON

TEMPLE, ROBERT

He Who Saw Everything (a verse translation of *The Epic of Gilgamesh*), 1993
    Ray, J. *TLS* (4704):20, 28 May 1993

TERRY, MEGAN

Headlights, 1988
    Babnich, J. " 'Turn Your Headlights On': An Interview with Megan Terry," *University of Mississippi Studies in English* 10:191–203, 1992

TERRY, MEGAN, JO ANN SCHMIDMAN, and SORA KIMBERLAIN

De La Vars, L. P., ed. *Images of the Self as Female*
Terry, M., J. Schmidman, and S. Kimberlain. "Gender Is Attitude," in L. Senelick, ed. *Gender in Performance: The Presentation of Difference in the Performing Arts*

TESICH, STEVE

Coen, S. "Steve Tesich: The Only Kind of Real Rebel Left, He Figures, Is a Moral Person," *American Theatre* 9(4):30–31, Jul/Aug. 1992
"Tesich, Steve," *Current Biography* 52(8):50–55, Aug. 1991

On the Open Road, 1992
  Gerard, J. *Variety* 350(4):231, 22 Feb. 1993
  Greene, A. *TheaterWeek* 6(30):26, 1 Mar. 1993
  Lazare, L. *Variety* 346(12):172–73, 6 Apr. 1992
  Moran, T. "Beware of Actor," *TheaterWeek* 6(30):22, 1 Mar. 1993
  Rich, F. *New York Times* 142:B3(N), 17 Feb. 1993
  Richards, D. *New York Times* 142:H5(N), 21 Feb. 1993
  Simon, J. *New York* 26(9):115–16, 1 Mar. 1993
  Tesich, S. *On the Open Road*
  Weales, G. *Commonweal* 118(8):261, 19 Apr. 1991

The Speed of Darkness, 1989
  Evans, G. *Variety* 342(8):59, 4 Mar. 1991
  Queenan, J. *American Spectator* 24(5):41–42, May 1991
  Sneerwell, R. *TheaterWeek* 4(31):32, 11 Mar. 1991
  Snow, L. *TheaterWeek* 4(30):15–19, 4 Mar. 1991
  Tesich, S. *The Speed of Darkness*
  Weales, G. *Commonweal* 118(8):261, 19 Apr. 1991

THOMAS, AUDREY CALLAHAN

Cooke, M. N. *The Fictive Confessions of Audrey Thomas and Mary di Michele*,
  (U of Toronto) *DAI* 51(10):3415A, Apr. 1991
Thomas, A. C. *Graven Images*

THOMPSON, JUDITH

Bessai, D. "Sharon Pollock and Judy Thompson," 97–117 in B. King, ed. *Post-
  Colonial English Drama: Commonwealth Drama Since 1960*
Knowles, R. P. "The Dramaturgy of the Perverse," *Theatre Research Interna-
  tional* 17(3):226–35, Autm. 1992

THOMSON, VIRGIL

O'Connor, P. "Virgil Thomson: The Discipline of Spontaneity," *Opera*
  42(2):161, 1 Feb. 1991
Rorem, N. "Virgil (1944)," *Antaeus* (71/72):63–82, Autm. 1993
Yellin, V. F. "Sullivan and Thomson, Gilbert and Stein," *Journal of Musicology*
  11(4):478–98, Fall 1993

TILLMAN, KATHERINE D. CHAPMAN

Aunt Betsey's Thanksgiving, 1914
  "Katherine D. Chapman Tillman," 124–133 in L. Hamalian and J. V. Hatch,
    eds. *The Roots of African American Drama*

TOCE, THOMAS. *SEE* BOLT, JONATHAN, DOUGLAS J. COHEN, and
THOMAS TOCE

TOLAN, KATHLEEN

Approximating Mother, 1991
    Evans, G. *Variety* 345(5):60, 11 Nov. 1991
    Miles, J., ed. *Playwriting Women: 7 Plays from the Women's Project*
    Simonson, R. *TheaterWeek* 5(18):35, 9 Dec. 1991

TOLINS, JONATHAN

Twilight of the Golds, 1993
    Anderson, P. *Advocate* (642):90–91, 16 Nov. 1993
    Brantley, B. *New York Times* 143:B5(N), 22 Oct. 1993
    Gerard, J. *Variety* 352(12):34–35, 1 Nov. 1993
    Harris, J. E. *Christopher Street* (205):4, 1 Sep. 1993
    Kanfer, S. *New Leader* 76(13):22, 15 Nov. 1993
    Marowitz, C. *TheaterWeek* 6(28):29, 15 Feb. 1993
    Neher, E. "Breaking the Code," *TheaterWeek* 6(30):19–21, 1 Mar. 1993
    Oliver, E. *New Yorker* 69(36):126, 1 Nov. 1993
    Raymond, G. "Season Preview: The Plays," *TheaterWeek* 7(5):17, 6 Sep.
        1993
    Richards, D. *New York Times* 143:H5(N), 31 Oct. 1993
    Simon, J. *New York* 26(44):84–85, 8 Nov. 1993
    Talenti, P. C. "The Dawning of a Playwright," *Advocate* (638):54–57, 21
        Sep. 1993
    Tolins, J. "A Playwright's Insight—and Warning," *Time* 142(4):38–39, 26
        Jul. 1993
    Weber, B. *New York Times* 143:B9(N), 29 Oct. 1993

TOOMER, JEAN

Cooperman, R. "Unacknowledged Familiarity: Jean Toomer and Eugene
    O'Neill," *Eugene O'Neill Review* 16(1):39–48, Sprg. 1992
Hutchinson, G. B. "Jean Toomer and the 'New Negroes' of Washington," *Ameri-*
    can Literature 63(4):683–92, Dec. 1991
———. "Jean Toomer and American Racial Discourse," *Texas Studies in Litera-*
    ture and Language 35(2):226–40, Summ. 1993
Miller, R. B. "Black in His Cellar: The Personal Tragedy of Jean Toomer," *Lang-*
    ston Hughes Review 11(1):36, Sprg. 1992

TOWNS, GEORGE A.

The Sharecropper, 1932
    "George A. Towns," 287–306 in L. Hamalian and J. V. Hatch, eds. *The*
    Roots of African American Drama

TRAMBLEY, ESTELA PORTILLO

McFerran, V. D. "Chicana Voices in American Drama: Silviana Wood, Estela
    Portillo Trambley, Cherríe Moraga, Milcha Sanchez-Scott, Josefina Lopez,"
    (#DA9119397; U of Minnesota) *DAI* 52(6):1946A, Dec. 1991

TREADWELL, SOPHIE

Machinal, 1928
   Dolan, J. "Machinal," *Theatre Journal* 44(1):96–97, Mar. 1992
   Lahr, J. *New Yorker* 69(39):112–16, 22 Nov. 1993
   Morley, S. "*Machinal*: Looking Through a Glass Onion: It's a Great Big
       Shame," *Spectator* 271(8624):53, 23 Oct. 1993
   Nordern, B. *TLS* (4725):20, 22 Oct. 1993
   Strand, G. "Treadwell's Neologism: *Machinal*," *Theatre Journal* 44(2):163–
       75, May 1992
   Wolf, M. *Variety* 353(5):34–35, 6 Dec. 1993

TREMBLAY, MICHEL

Findlay, B. "Translating Tremblay into Scots," *Theatre Research International*
   17(2):138–45, Summ. 1992
Godin, J. C. "Le 'tant qu'a ca' d'Albertine," *Quebec Studies* 11:111–16, Fall/
   Wntr. 1990–91
Homel, D. "Sacred Monsters," *Books in Canada* 21(1):16, 1 Jan. 1992
Lavoie, P. "Michel Tremblay, Dramaturge-Demiurge," *Theatre Research Inter-
   national* 17(3):180–89, Autm. 1992
Leblanc, A. "D'Aristophane a Michel Tremblay: Le Trivial dans le theatre que-
   becois," *L'Action Nationale* 81(5):674–86, May 1991

Forever Yours, Marie-Lou
   Sidnell, M. J. *Journal of Canadian Studies* 25:135–6, Wntr. 1991

Les Belles Soeurs, 1970
   Babington, D. "The Shared Voice of Michel Tremblay," *Queen's Quarterly*
       99(4):1074–81, Wntr. 1992
   Lafon, D. "Entre Cassandre et Clytemnestre: le theatre quebecois," *Theater
       Research International* 17(3):236–45, Autm. 1992

TWAIN, MARK

The Gilded Age (his revision of G. Densmore's dramatization of Twain's novel),
   1874
   Wolter, J. C. *The Dawning of American Drama: American Dramatic Criti-
       cism 1746–1915*. 328, 476

UHRY, ALFRED

"Behind the Scenes: Alfred Uhry; Fantastic Fantasticks; Other News," *Dramatists Guild Quarterly* 28(2):56, Summ. 1991

Driving Miss Daisy, 1987
   "Judge Dismisses *Miss Daisy* Suit," *New York Times* 142:B7(N), 10 Dec.
       1992

ULVAEUS, BJÖRN. *SEE* NELSON, RICHARD, TIM RICE, BENNY ANDERSSON, and BJÖRN ULVAEUS

VALDEZ, LUIS

Gross, T. "Interviews with Daniel Valdez and Luis Valdez," *San Jose Studies* 19(1):53, Wntr. 1993
Morales, E. "Shadowing Valdez," *American Theatre* 9(7):14–19, Nov. 1992

Zoot Suit, 1978
    Fregoso, R. "The Representation of Cultural Identity in *Zoot Suit*," *Theory and Society* 22(5):659, 1 Oct. 1993

VALENTI, MICHAEL. *SEE* ALLEN, RALPH, JIMMY McHUGH, and MICHAEL VALENTI

van ITALLIE, JEAN-CLAUDE

Chakravartee, M. "Open Theatre and 'Closed Society': Jean-Claude van Itallie and Mamet Reconsidered," *Literary Criterion* 26(3):48, 1991
Harris, W. "Plays Are for Questions, Not Answers," *New York Times* 142:H5(N), 23 May 1993

Ancient Boys: A Requiem, 1989 (later revised)
    Ungaro, J. *TheaterWeek* 4(30):36, 4 Mar. 1993

Master and Margarita (adaptation of Mikhail Bulgakov's novel), 1993
    Lamont, R. C. *TheaterWeek* 6(46):34, 21 Jun. 1993

VAN PEEBLES, MELVIN

"The Hollywood Shuffle," *Economist* 318(7700):87, 30 Mar. 1991

VAWTER, RON

Goldberg, R. *Artforum* 31(1):101, Sep. 1992
Harris, J. "Strange Fruit," *Christopher Street* (181):6–7, 22 Jun. 1992
Holden, S. "Two Strangers Meet Through an Actor," *New York Times* 141:H5(N), 3 May 1992
Schechner, R. "Ron Vawter: For the Record," *TDR* 37(3):17–41, Fall 1993
Stevens, A. "Finding a Devil Within to Portray Roy Cohn," *New York Times* 142:H1(N), 18 Apr. 1993
Yablonsky, L. "Two Sides of a Queer Coin," *Advocate* (604):83, 2 Jun. 1992

VIDAL, GORE

Parini, J. "An Interview with Gore Vidal," *New England Review* 14(1):93–101, Fall 1991

VINAVER, MICHAEL

Bradby, D. "A Theatre of Everyday: The Plays of Michael Vinaver," *New Theatre Quarterly* 7:261–83, Aug. 1991

Vinaver, M. "Decentralization as Chiaroscuro," *New Theatre Quarterly* 7:64–76, Feb. 1991

VOGEL, PAULA

Coen, S. "Paula Vogel: No Need for Gravity," *American Theatre* 10(4):26–27, Apr. 1993

"Paula Vogel: In Her Dark, Audacious Comedies," *Mirabella* 5(1):48, 1 Jun. 1993

The Baltimore Waltz, 1992
> Brustein, R. *New Republic* 206(15):28, 13 Apr. 1992
> Disch, T. M. *Nation* 254(11):389–90, 23 Mar. 1992
> Goodman, R. and M. Smith, eds. *Women Playwrights: The Best Plays of 1992*
> Harris, J. *Christopher Street* 14(18):9–10, 16 Mar. 1992
> King, R. L. *North American Review* 278:44–48, Mar/Apr. 1993
> Raymond, G. "Magical Mystery Tour," *TheaterWeek* 5(30):28–30, 2 Mar. 1992
> Rich, F. *New York Times* 141:B1(N), 12 Feb. 1992
> Richards, D. *New York Times* 141:H17(N), 16 Feb. 1992
> Roman, D. *Theatre Journal* 44(4):520–2, Dec. 1992
> Smith, R. "*Waltz* in Three Dimensions," *American Theatre* 9(3):54–56, Jun. 1992
> Ungaro, J. *TheaterWeek* 5(34):31, 30 Mar. 1992
> Vogel, P. "*The Baltimore Waltz*," *American Theatre* 8(6):36, 1 Sep. 1991
> Weales, G. *Commonweal* 119(8):18–19, 24 Apr. 1992

WADE, KEVIN

Key Exchange, 1981
> Boston Conservatory Recording. *Senior Directing Scene Workshops*. Videocassette.

WAGNER, JANE

The Search for Signs of Intelligent Life in the Universe, 1985
> Brown, J. *Taking Center Stage: Feminism in Contemporary U.S. Drama*

WAGNER, SHEL

Tattle Tales, 1993
> Peimer, J. *Theatre Journal* 45:386–7, Oct. 1993

WAITS, TOM. *SEE* WILSON, ROBERT, TOM WAITS, and WILLIAM S. BURROUGHS

WALCOTT, DEREK

Hamner, R. *Derek Walcott*
————. "Dramatizing the New World's African King: O'Neill, Walcott and Cesaire on Christophe," *Journal of West Indian Literature* 5(1–2):30–47, Aug. 1992
Jonsson, S. "La literatura es mestiza: Entrevista a Derek Walcott," *Quimera: Revista de Literatura* 115:29–31, 1992
Olaniyan, T. "Dramatizing Postcoloniality: Wole Soyinka and Derek Walcott," *Theatre Journal* 44(4):485, Dec. 1992
————. "The Poetics and Politics of 'Othering': African, African-American, and Caribbean Drama and the Invention of Cultural Identities," (#DA9203968; Cornell U) *DAI* 52(8):2922A, Feb. 1992
Valdes, A. "Un Nobel difenente," *Quimera: Revista de Literatura* 115:26–27, 1992

Dream on Monkey Mountain, 1967
Olaniyan, T. "Corporal/Discursive Bodies and the Subject: *Dream on Monkey Mountain* and the Poetics of Identity," 155–71 in H. Ryan-Ransom, ed. *Imagination, Emblems and Expressions: Essays on Latin American, Caribbean, and Continental Culture and Identity*

The Odyssey (a dramatization of Homer's *Odyssey*), 1993
Hamner, R. "*The Odyssey*: Derek Walcott's Dramatization of Homer's *Odyssey*," 24(4):101–08, Oct. 1993
King, R. L. *North American Review* 278:43, Mar/Apr. 1993

WALDEN, STANLEY. *SEE* CLARKE, MARTHA, RICHARD COE, RICHARD PEASLEE, and STANLEY WALDEN

WALKER, GEORGE F.

Borkowski, A. "Theatre of the Improbable: George F. Walker," *Canadian Forum* 70(802):16–19, Sep. 1991
Haff, S. "Slashing the Pleasantly Vague: George F. Walker and the Word," *Essays in Theatre* 10(1):59–69, Nov. 1991
Johnson, C. "George F. Walker," 82–96 in B. King, ed. *Post-Colonial English Drama: Commonwealth Drama Since 1960*
Smith, C. M. "Parody in the Plays and Productions of George F. Walker," (U of Toronto) *DAI* 51(10):3272A, Apr. 1991

Escape from Happiness
King, R. L. *North American Review* 278:44–48, Mar/Apr. 1993

Nothing Sacred, 1991
Easton, T. *Analog Science Fiction-Science Fact* 111(13):162–64, Nov. 1991
Evans, G. *Variety* 349(1):76, 26 Oct. 1992

Raymond, G. "Growing Up Onstage," *TheaterWeek* 6(17):23–24, 30 Nov. 1992
Van Gelder, L. *New York Times* 142:B3(N), 27 Oct. 1992

WALKER, PAUL

Under Control, 1992
Bruckner, D. J. R. *New York Times* 142:C25(L), 22 Oct. 1992

WARREN, MERCY OTIS

Barker-Benfield, G. J. *Portraits of American Women: From Settlement to the Present*
Baym, N. "Between Enlightenment and Victorian: Toward a Narrative of American Women Writers Writing History," *Critical Inquiry* 18(1):22–41, Autm. 1991
———. "Mercy Otis Warren's Gendered Melodrama of Revolution," *South Atlantic Quarterly* 90(3):531–54, Summ. 1991
Dykeman, T. B., ed. *American Women Philosophers 1650–1930*
Grundy, E. A. *Planted by the Feminine Hand: Mercy Otis Warren and Republican Motherhood*. M.A. Thesis; Sarah Lawrence College, 1991
Kern, J. B. "Mercy Otis Warren: Dramatist of the American Revolution," 247–59 in M. A. Schofield and C. Macheski, eds. *Curtain Calls: British and American Women and the Theater, 1660–1820*
Nicolay, T. F. *Transforming the Traditional: Gender Roles, Literary Authority, and the American Woman Writer*. Diss.; U of Rochester, 1993
Oreovicz, C. Z. "Heroic Drama for an Uncertain Age: The Plays of Mercy Warren," 192–210 in K. Z. Derounian-Stodola, ed. *Early American Literature and Culture: Essays Honoring Harrison T. Meserole*

WASSERSTEIN, WENDY

Berkowitz, G. M. *American Drama of the Twentieth Century*. 198+
Biggs, M. E. *In the Vernacular: Interviews at Yale with Sculptors of Culture*
Kachur, B. "Women Playwrights on Broadway: Henley, Howe, Norman, and Wasserstein," 15–40 in B. King, ed. *Contemporary American Theatre*
Rosen, C. "An Unconventional Life: Q & A with Wendy Wasserstein," *TheaterWeek* 6(13):17–27, 2 Nov. 1992
Wasserstein, W. *Life in the Theatre*. Recording.
———. "Tender Offer," *Antaeus* 66:452–58, Sprg. 1991

The Heidi Chronicles, 1988
Jacobson, L. B., director. *Heidi Chronicles*. Videocassette.
Keyssar, H. "Drama and the Dialogic Imagination: *The Heidi Chronicles* and *Fefu and Her Friends*," *Modern Drama* 34(1):88–106, Mar. 1991
Wasserstein, W. *The Heidi Chronicles and Other Plays*

The Sisters Rosenweig, 1992
Brantly, B. *New York Times* 143:B3(N), 24 Sep. 1993
Brustein, R. *New Republic* 207(24):34, 7 Dec. 1992

Finn, W. "Sister Act," *Vogue* 182(9):360–61, Sep. 1992
Gerard, J. *Variety* 349(1):75, 26 Oct. 1992
——. *Variety* 350(8):56, 22 Mar. 1993
Greene, A. *TheaterWeek* 6(35):32, 5 Apr. 1993
Henry, W. A., III. *Time* 140(18):69, 2 Nov. 1992
Hornby, R. *Hudson Review* 46:367–9, Summ. 1993
Kanfer, S. *New Leader* 76(5):22–23, 5 Apr. 1993
Kroll, J. *Newsweek* 120(18):104, 2 Nov. 1992
Kron, J. *New York Times* 142:B1(N), 8 Dec. 1992
Miller, J. "The Secret Wendy Wasserstein," *New York Times* 142:H1(N), 18 Oct. 1992
Oliver, E. *New Yorker* 68(37):105, 2 Nov. 1992
Richards, D. *New York Times* 142:H5(N), 1 Nov. 1992
Rothstein, M. "Kahn's Way," *TheaterWeek* 6(31):20–24, 8 Mar. 1993
Simon, J. *New York* 26(14):85, 5 Apr. 1993
Wasserstein, W. *The Sisters Rosenweig*

WEAVER, LOIS. *SEE* BOURNE, BETTE, PAUL SHAW, PEGGY SHAW, and LOIS WEAVER

SEE ALSO SHAW, PEGGY, and LOIS WEAVER

WEILL, KURT

Lucchesi, J. "Neues zu Kurt Weill—in Wort, Bild und Ton: Eine Sammelbesprechung," *The Brecht Yearbook* 18:201–15, 1993

WEINSTOCK, JACK. *SEE* BURROWS, ABE, JACK WEINSTOCK, WILLIE GILBERT, and FRANK LOESSER

WEISS, ADRIENNE

Celestial Alphabet Event, 1991
    Bell, J. *TheaterWeek* 5(12):38, 28 Oct. 1991

WEISS, JEFF

Hot Keys, 1992
    Bell, J. *TheaterWeek* 5(33):16, 23 Mar. 1992
    Solomon, A. "A New York (Theater) Diary, 1992," *Theater* 24(1):7–18, Wntr. 1993
    Wright, D. "How Jeff Weiss Found His Pulpit on the Stage," *New York Times* 142:H5(N), 30 May 1993

WELLMAN, MAC

Castagno, P. C. "Desultory Structures: Language as Presence in the Works of Overmyer, Wellman, and Jenkin," *Text & Presentation* 11:1–7, 1991

————. "Varieties of Monologic Strategy: The Dramaturgy of Len Jenkin and Mac Wellman," *New Theatre Quarterly* 9(34):134–46, May 1993
Overmyer, E. "Mac Wellman's Horizontal Avalanches," *Theater* 21(3):54–56, Summ/Fall 1990
Robinson, M. "Four Writers," *Theater*, 24(1):31–42, Wntr. 1993
Wellman, M. "From *A Murder of Crows*," *Kenyon Review* (15):65–68, Sprg. 1993

7 Blowjobs, 1991
    Phillips, M. *TheaterWeek* 5(22):35, 6 Jan. 1992

Terminal Hip, 1992
    Robinson, M. "Figure of Speech: An Interview with Mac Wellman," *Performing Arts Journal* (40):43–51, Jan. 1991
    Wellman, M. *"Terminal Hip," Performing Arts Journal* (40):52–73, Jan. 1992

WERTENBAKER, TIMBERLAKE

Carlson, S. "Issues of Identity, Nationality, and Performance: The Reception of Two Plays by Timberlake Wertenbaker," *New Theatre Quarterly* 9(35):267–89, Aug. 1993
Dahl, M. K. "Constructing the Subject: Timberlake Wertenbaker's *The Grace of Mary Traverse*," *Journal of Dramatic Theory and Criticism* 7(2):149–59, Sprg. 1993
DiGaetani, J. L. "Timberlake Wertenbaker," 265–73 in J. L. DiGaetani, ed. *A Search for a Postmodern Theater: Interviews with Contemporary Playwrights*
Gussow, M. "A Woman of the World," *New York Times* 141:B2(N), 28 Feb. 1992
Inverso, M. "Der Straf-block: Performance and Execution in Barnes, Griffiths, and Wertenbaker," *Modern Drama* 36(3):420–30, 1 Sep. 1993
Sachelaridou, E. "E Problematike tes Istorias kai tes Mythologias sto Gynaikeio Theatriko Logo: E Periptose tes Timberlake Winter," *Gramma: Journal of Theory and Criticism* 8:155–75, 1993
Sullivan, E. B. "Hailing Ideology, Acting in the Horizon, and Reading between Plays by Timberlake Wertenbaker," *Theatre Journal* 45(2):139–54, 1 May 1993
Wilson, A. "Forgiving History and Making New Worlds: Timberlake Wertenbaker's Recent Drama," 146–61 in J. Acheson, ed. *British and Irish Drama Since 1960*

The Love of the Nightingale, 1992
    Chansky, D. *TheaterWeek* 6(27):29, 8 Feb. 1993
    Cook, R. *Theatre Journal* 45:381–2, Oct. 1993
    Ungaro, J. *TheaterWeek* 7(4):37, 30 Aug. 1993

Our Country's Good (adaptation of Keneally's *The Playmaker*)
    Bell, M. "Novel and Theatre in Thomas Keneally's *The Playmaker*: Historical and Generic Models of the Self," 228–36 in W. G. Busse, ed., *Anglistentag 1991, Dusseldorf: Proceedings*

Davis, J. "Festive Irony: Aspects of British Theatre in the 1980s," *Critical Survey* 3(3):339–50, 1991
————. "A Play for England: The Royal Court Adapts *The Playmaker*," 175–90 in P. Reynolds, ed., *Novel Images: Literature in Performance*
Hornby, R. *Hudson Review* 44(3):455–56, Autm. 1991
King, R. L. *Massachusetts Review* 32(1):153–55, Sprg. 1991
Rich, F. *New York Times* 140:B1(N), 30 Apr. 1991
Richards, D. "*Our Country's Good*," *New York Times* 140:H28(N), 19 May 1991
Rothstein, M. "It's 2nd Play May be Fateful for Broadway Cost Plan," *New York Times* 140:B1(N), 23 Apr. 1991
Taylor, V. "Mothers of Invention: Female Characters in *Our Country's Good* and *The Playmaker*," *Critical Survey* 3(3):331–38, 1991
Wilson, A. "*Our Country's Good*: Theatre, Colony and Nation in Wertenbaker's Adaptation of *The Playmaker*," *Modern Drama* 34(1):23–34, Mar. 1991

Three Birds Alighting on a Field, 1991
MacCarthy, F. *TLS* (4616):18, 10 Sep. 1991

WEST, CHERYL

Madison, C. "West Probes Traumas—with No Flinching," *American Theatre* 8(12):46–47, Mar. 1992

Before It Hits Home, 1989
Simon, J. *New York* 25(12):70–71, 23 Mar. 1992
Simonson, R. *TheaterWeek* 4(34):40–41, 1 Apr. 1991
Springer, P. Gregory. *Advocate* (570):66+, 12 Feb. 1991
Ungaro, J. *TheaterWeek* 5(36):36, 13 Apr. 1992
Weales, G. *Commonweal* 119(8):19, 24 Apr. 1992

Jar the Floor
Goodman, R., and M. Smith, eds. *Women Playwrights: The Best Plays of 1992*

WEST, MAE

Allen, R. C. *Horrible Prettiness: Burlesque and American Culture*. 27, 274–83
Fields, A., and L. M. Fields. *From the Bowery to Broadway: Lew Fields and the Roots of American Popular Theater*. 484, 489
Pela, R. L. "Way Out West," *Advocate* (612):56–57, 22 Sep. 1992
Robertson, P. " 'The Kinda Comedy That Imitates Me': Mae West's Identification with the Feminist Camp," 156–72 in D. Bergman, ed. *Camp Grounds: Style and Homosexuality*

The Drag, 1926
>   Hamilton, M. "Mae West Live: *SEX*, *The Drag*, and 1920s Broadway," *TDR* 36(4):82–100, Wntr. 1992

Pleasure Man, 1928
>   Hamilton, M. " 'I'm the Queen of the Bitches': Female Impersonation and Mae West's *Pleasure Man*," 107–10 in L. Ferris, ed., *Crossing the Stage: Controversies on Cross-Dressing*

SEX, 1926
>   Hamilton, M. "Mae West Live: *SEX*, *The Drag*, and 1920s Broadway," *TDR* 36(4):82–100, Wntr. 1992

WHITE, EDMUND

Trios, 1993
>   Dyson, J. *TLS* (4713):19, 30 Jul. 1993

WIDDEMER, MARGARET

The Rose-Garden Husband
>   Mann, B. J. "Tennessee Williams and *The Rose-Garden Husband*," *American Drama* 1(1):16–26, Fall 1991

WILDER, THORNTON

Berkowitz, G. M. *American Drama of the Twentieth Century*. 60
Bryer, J. *Conversations with Thornton Wilder*
Konkle, L. E. "Errand into the Theatrical Wilderness: The Puritan Narrative Tradition in the Plays of Wilder, Williams, and Albee," (#DA9134329; U of Wisconsin, Madison) *DAI* 52(10):3611A, Apr. 1992

The Matchmaker (revision of his play *The Merchant of Yonkers*, an adaptation of J. N. Nestroy's play *Einen Jux will er sich machen*), 1954
>   Simonson, R. *TheaterWeek* 5(8):36, 30 Sep. 1991

Our Town, 1939
>   Clines, F. X. "Through the Looking Glass and into *Our Town*," *New York Times* 142:H5(N), 1 Aug. 1993
>   Torrens, J. S. *America* 165(9):224, 5 Oct. 1991

Wilder, Wilder, Wilder
>   Bell, J. "*Wilder, Wilder, Wilder*," *TheaterWeek* 6(33):14, 22 Mar. 1993
>   Disch, T. M. *New York Times* 142:H6(N), 28 Feb. 1993
>   Hampton, W. *New York Times* 142:C13(L), 21 Dec. 1992
>   Oliver, E. *New Yorker* 68(44):127, 21 Dec. 1992
>   Richards, D. *New York Times* 142:H20(N), 7 Mar. 1993
>   Ungaro, J. "*Wilder, Wilder, Wilder*: Three by Thornton," *TheaterWeek* 6(21):32, 28 Dec. 1992

WILLIAMS, TENNESSEE

Adam, J. *Versions of Heroism in Modern American Drama: Redefinitions by Miller, Williams, O'Neill and Anderson*

Babcock, G. *Rewriting the Masculine: The National Subject in Modern American Drama*. Diss.; Louisiana State U, 1993

Bak, J. S. *Tennessee Williams and the Southern Dialectic: In Search of Androgyny*. Diss.; Ball State U, 1993

Berkowitz, G. M. *American Drama of the Twentieth Century*. 75, 86, 161

Blanchard, L. "The Fox and the Phoenix: Tennessee Williams's Strong Misreading of D. H. Lawrence," 15–30 in K. Cushman and D. Jackson, eds. *D. H. Lawrence's Literary Inheritors*

Brayton, J. A. "The Ancestry of Thomas Lanier 'Tennessee' Williams," *NEHGS NEXUS* 8(3/4):108–13, Jun/Aug. 1991

———. "Corrections to 'The Ancestry of Thomas Lanier 'Tennessee' Williams,'" *NEXUS* 8(6):180, Dec. 1991

Bruhm, S. "Blackmailed by Sex: Tennessee Williams and the Economics of Desire," *Modern Drama* 34(4):528–37, Dec. 1991

Budd, D. R. "Tennessee Williams: Dreadfulness and the Ethics of Human Choice," in M. G. Newton, ed. *Ethics in Modern American Literature: Rivers to Skyscrapers*

Choukri, M. *Jean Genet et Tennessee Williams à Tanger*

Clum, J. M. " 'Something Cloudy, Something Clear': Homophobic Discourse in Tennessee Williams," 43–61 in W. R. Dynes and S. Donaldson, eds. *Homosexual Themes in Literary Studies*

Colanzi, R. M. "Caged Birds: Bad Faith in Tennessee Williams's Drama," *Modern Drama* 35(3):451–65, Sep. 1992

———. " 'A Flame Burning Nothing': Tennessee Williams' Existential Drama," (#DA9107889; Temple U) *DAI* 51(11):3741A, May 1991

Coleman, T. S. *Tennessee Williams in Tinseltown*. M.A. Thesis; California State U, Chico, 1993

Crandell, G. W. *Tennessee Williams: A Descriptive Bibliography*

Cunningham, J. C. *Memory and Fantasy in Three Works by Tennessee Williams*. M.A. Thesis; San Francisco State U, 1992

Dubois, F. *Tennessee Williams: l'oiseau sans pattés*

Egri, P. "Dramatic Exposition and Resolution in O'Neill, Williams, Miller, and Albee," *Neohelicon: Acta Comparationis Litterarum Universarum* 19(1):175–84, 1992

Gunn, D. W. *Tennessee Williams, a Bibliography*

Hale, A. "The Secret Script of Tennessee Williams," *Southern Review* 27(2):363–75, Sprg. 1991

Hayman, R. *Tennessee Williams: Everyone Else Is an Audience*

Holditch, W. K. "South Toward Freedom: Tennessee Williams," 61–75 in R. S. Kennedy, ed. *Literary New Orleans: Essays and Meditations*

Hood, S. "Tennessee in Texas," *Tennessee Williams Literary Journal* 2(2):51,

Kataria, G. R. *The Faces of Eve: A Study of Tennessee Williams's Heroines*

Kolin, P. C. "Tennessee Williams Sends His Autobiography to Mexico," *Mississippi Quarterly* 46(2):255–56, Sprg. 1993

Konkle, L. E. "Errand into the Theatrical Wilderness: The Puritan Narrative Tradition in the Plays of Wilder, Williams, and Albee,'' (#DA9134329; U of Wisconsin, Madison) *DAI* 52(10):3611A, Apr. 1992

Leahy, S. L. *Tennessee Williams' Two River County: From the Kingdom of Earth to the Kingdom of Heaven.* Diss.; U of Notre Dame, 1993

Long, J. M. *Tennessee Williams' Women.* M.A. Thesis; California State U, Dominguez Hills, 1992

Murphy, B. *Tennessee Williams and Elia Kazan: A Collaboration in the Theatre*

Pagan, N. O. *Rethinking Literary Biography: A Postmodern Approach to Tennessee Williams*

———. ''Tennessee Williams's Theater as Body,'' *Philological Quarterly* 72(1):97–115, Wint. 1993

Qun, Z. L., and S. Shao. ''A Bibliography of Tennessee Williams in China,'' *Studies in American Drama, 1945-Present* 8(2):214–16, 1993

Rhodes, K. *Tennessee Williams: A Repressed, Divided Understanding.* Diss.; U of Essex, 1993

Russo, V. ''A Brief Encounter with Tennessee Williams,'' *Advocate* (613):108–11, 6 Oct. 1992

Savran, D. ''By Coming Suddenly into a Room That I Thought Was Empty': Mapping the Closet with Tennessee Williams,'' *Studies in the Literary Imagination* 24(2):57–74, Fall 1991

———. *Communists, Cowboys, and Queers: The Politics of Masculinity in the Work of Arthur Miller and Tennessee Williams*

Speer, R. *Tennessee Williams, Sentenced to Solitary Confinement.* M.A. Thesis; Laredo State U, 1992

Spurk, T. L. *The Colors of Butterfly Wings: A Study of the Significance of Color Symbolism in Selected Works of Tennessee Williams.* M.A. Thesis; Mississippi College, 1992

Taylor, J. B. ''Fragile and Flawed Female Characters in the Drama of Tennessee Williams,'' *Mount Olive Review* 6:110–14, Sprg. 1992

Thomas, S. *The Spectators and the Performers: Reflection Versus Action in the Plays of Tennessee Williams.* M.A. Thesis; Bibliotheque Nationale du Canada, 1991

Unger, E. K. *Against the Tragic Myth: The Surprisingly Successful Heroines of Tennessee Williams.* Diss.; Lehigh U, 1993

Wang, Q. ''Who Troubled the Waters: A Study of the Motif of Intrusion in Five Modern Dramatists: John Millington Synge, Eugene O'Neill, Edward Albee, Tennessee Williams, and Harold Pinter,'' (#DA9209537; Indiana U, Pennsylvania) *DAI* 52(12):4325A, Jun. 1992

Wang, Qun. ''On the Dramatization of the Illusory World in Tennessee Williams, Arthur Miller and Edward Albee's Major Plays,'' (#DA9101987; U of Oregon) *DAI* 51(8):2569A, Feb. 1991

Williams, T. *''The Chalky White Substance,''* *Antaeus* 66:467–73, Sprg. 1991

Zeineddine, N. *Because It Is My Name: Problems of Identity Experienced by Women, Artists, and Breadwinners in the Plays of Henrik Ibsen, Tennessee Williams, and Arthur Miller*

Camino Real, 1953

Hammons, S. E. *Interpreting the Role of Marguerite Gautier in Camino Real.* M.F.A. Thesis; San Diego State U, 1993

Cat on a Hot Tin Roof, 1955

Hurd, M. R. "Cats and Catamites: Achilles, Patroclus, and Williams' *Cat on a Hot Tin Roof*," *Notes on Mississippi Writers* 23(2):63–66, Jun. 1991

Inge, M. T. "The South, Tragedy, and Comedy in Tennessee Williams's *Cat on a Hot Tin Roof*," 157–65 in V. Lerda, et al, eds. *The United States South: Regionalism and Identity*

Weimer, C. B. "Journeys from Frustration to Empowerment: *Cat on a Hot Tin Roof* and Its Debt to Garcia Lorca's *Yerma*," *Modern Drama* 35(4):520–29, Dec. 1992

The Glass Menagerie, 1944

Bak, J. S. " 'Celebrate Her with Strings': Leitmotifs and the Multifaceted 'Strings' in Williams's *The Glass Menagerie*," *Notes on Mississippi Writers* 24(2):81–87, Jul. 1992

Diemert, B. "Tennessee Williams's *The Glass Menagerie*: A Possible Source in Virginia Woolf's *The Years*," *English Language Notes* 29(4):79–81, Jun. 1992

Harris, L. "*Menagerie* in Manila and Other Cross-Cultural Affinities: The Relevance of the Plays of Tennessee Williams on the Filipino Stage," *Studies in American Drama, 1945-Present* 8(2):163–74, 1993

Koel, L. H. *The Contents of an Actor's Performance Journal.* M.F.A. Thesis; DePaul U, 1992

Lewis, K. *The Search for Personal Dignity in Three Modern American Dramas.* M.A. Thesis; Florida State U, 1991

Mann, B. J. "Tennessee Williams and *The Rose-Garden Husband*," *American Drama* 1(1):16–26, Fall 1991

Morrow, L. and E. Morrow. "Humpty-Dumpty Lives! Complexity Theory as an Alternative to the Omelet Scenario in *The Glass Menagerie*," *Studies in American Drama, 1945-Present* 8(2):127–39, 1993

Reynolds, J. "The Failure of Technology in *The Glass Menagerie*," *Modern Drama* 34(4):522–27, Dec. 1991

Simonson, R. *TheaterWeek* 4(26):40–41, 4 Feb. 1991

Usui, M. " 'A World of Her Own' in Tennessee Williams's *The Glass Menagerie*," *Studies in Culture and the Humanities* 1:21–37, 1992

Warshauer, S. C. *The Making of a Victim: The Transformation in the Character of Laura in Revisions of Tennessee Williams' The Glass Menagerie.* M.A. Thesis; U of Texas, Austin, 1991

Kingdom of Earth (*The Seven Descents of Myrtle*), 1968

Kolin, P. C. "Sleeping with Caliban: The Politics of Race in Tennessee Williams's *Kingdom of Earth*," *Studies in American Drama, 1945-Present* 8(2):140–62, 1993

The Night of the Iguana, 1959

Lochte, D. *Los Angeles Magazine* 36(11):174+, Nov. 1991

Orpheus Descending (revision of his *Battle of Angels*), 1957

Egan, R. B. "Orpheus Christus Mississippiensis: Tennessee Williams's Xavier in Hell," *Classical and Modern Literature* 14(1):61–98, Fall 1993

Hall, P., director. *Orpheus Descending.* Videodisc.

Keller, J. R. "Tennessee Williams' *Orpheus Descending* and Joe Orton's *Entertaining Mr. Sloane,*" *Notes on Contemporary Literature* 22(2):8–10, Mar. 1992

Out Cry (revision of his two-character play), 1971
Wickstrom. G. M. *Theatre Journal* 43:534–5, Dec. 1991

A Streetcar Named Desire, 1947
   Bedient, C. "There Are Lives That Desire Does Not Sustain: *A Streetcar Named Desire,*" 45–58 in P. C. Kolin, ed. *Confronting Tennessee Williams's A Streetcar Named Desire: Essays in Cultural Pluralism*
   Blau, H. "Readymade Desire," 19–25 in P. C. Kolin, ed. *Confronting Tennessee Williams's A Streetcar Named Desire: Essays in Cultural Pluralism*
   Bray, R. "A Streetcar Named Desire: The Political and Historical Subtext," 183–97 in P. C. Kolin, ed. *Confronting Tennessee Williams's A Streetcar Named Desire: Essays in Cultural Pluralism*
   Cardullo, B. "Birth and Death in *A Streetcar Named Desire,*" 167–80 in P. C. Kolin, ed. *Confronting Tennessee Williams's A Streetcar Named Desire: Essays in Cultural Pluralism*
   Cline, G. S. "The Psychodrama of the 'Dysfunctional' Family: Desire, Subjectivity, and Regression in Twentieth Century American Drama," (#DA9130458; Ohio State U) *DAI* 52(5):1742–43A, Nov. 1991
   Conroy, M. "Acting Out: Method Acting, the National Culture, and the Middlebrow Disposition in Cold War America," *Criticism* 35:239–63, Sprg. 1993
   Dwyer, V. *Maclean's* 105(20):56–57, 18 May 1992
   Elacqua, V. and J. Shatzky. "Looking Back at *Streetcar*: The Influence of Tennessee Williams on John Osborne," *Tennessee Williams Literary Journal* 2(2):41, Wntr. 1991
   Gronbeck-Tedesco, J. L. "Absence and the Actor's Body: Marlon Brando's Performance in *A Streetcar Named Desire* on Stage and in Film," *Studies in American Drama, 1945-Present* 8(2):115–26, 1993
   Harris, L. J. "Perceptual Conflict and the Perversion of Creativity in *A Streetcar Named Desire,*" 83–103 in P. C. Kolin, ed. *Confronting Tennessee Williams's A Streetcar Named Desire: Essays in Cultural Pluralism*
   Henry, W. A., III. *Time* 139(16):93, 20 Apr. 1992
   Holditch, W. K. "The Broken World: Romanticism, Realism, Naturalism in *A Streetcar Named Desire,*" in P. C. Kolin, ed., *Confronting Tennessee Williams's A Streetcar Named Desire: Essays in Cultural Pluralism*
   Kailo, K. "Blanche Dubois and Salome as New Women: Old Lunatics in Modern Drama," 119–36 in J. Redmond, ed. *Madness in Drama*
   Kelly, L. "The White Goddess, Ethnicity, and the Politics of Desire," 121–32 in P. C. Kolin, ed. *Confronting Tennessee Williams's A Streetcar Named Desire: Essays in Cultural Pluralism*
   Kleb, W. "Marginalia: *Streetcar*, Williams, and Foucault," 27–43 in P. C. Kolin, ed. *Confronting Tennessee Williams's A Streetcar Named Desire: Essays in Cultural Pluralism*
   Kolin, P. C. "Eunice Hubbell and the Feminist Thematics of *A Streetcar Named Desire,*" 105–20 in P. C. Kolin, ed. *Confronting Tennessee Williams's A Streetcar Named Desire: Essays in Cultural Pluralism*

————. "The First Critical Assessments of *A Streetcar Named Desire*: The *Streetcar* Tryouts and the Reviewers," *Journal of Dramatic Theory and Criticism* 6(1):45–67, Fall 1991

————. "Olivier to Williams: An Introduction," *Missouri Review* 13(3):143–57, 1991

————. "Our Lady of the Quarter: Blanche DuBois and the Feast of the Mater Dolorosa," *ANQ* (4):81–7, Apr. 1991

————. "Rutting in *A Streetcar Named Desire*," *Notes on Contemporary Literature* 22(1):2–3, Jan. 1992

————. "Williams in Ebony: A Black and Multi-Racial Production of *A Streetcar Named Desire*," *Black American Literature Forum* 25:147–81, Sprg. 1991

Kolin, P. C., and J. Wolter. "Williams's *A Streetcar Named Desire*," *Explicator* 49:241–4, Summ. 1991

Kramer, M. *New Yorker* 68(10):84–85, 27 Apr. 1992

Kroll, J. *Newsweek* 119(17):67, 27 Apr. 1992

Lant, K. M. "A Streetcar Named Misogyny," 225–38 in J. Redmond, ed. *Violence in Drama*

Morrow, L., and E. Morrow. "The Ontological Potentialities of Antichaos and Adaptation in *A Streetcar Named Desire*," 59–70 in P. C. Kolin, ed. *Confronting Tennessee Williams's A Streetcar Named Desire: Essays in Cultural Pluralism*

Phillips, G. D. "*A Streetcar Named Desire*: Play and Film," 223–35 in P. C. Kolin, ed. *Confronting Tennessee Williams's A Streetcar Named Desire: Essays in Cultural Pluralism*

Rich, F. *New York Times* 141:B1(N), 13 Apr. 1992

Richards, D. *New York Times* 141:H5(N), 19 Apr. 1992

Rosen, C. "A Private Art," *TheaterWeek* 5(42):16–23, 25 May 1992

Schleuter, J. " 'We've Had This Date with Each Other from the Beginning': Reading Toward Closure in *A Streetcar Named Desire*," 71–81 in P. C. Kolin, ed. *Confronting Tennessee Williams's A Streetcar Named Desire: Essays in Cultural Pluralism*

Simon, J. *New York* 25(17):83, 27 Apr. 1992

Winchell, M. R. "The Myth Is the Message: Or, Why *Streetcar* Keeps Running," 133–45 in P. C. Kolin, ed. *Confronting Tennessee Williams's A Streetcar Named Desire: Essays in Cultural Pluralism*

Wolter, J. C. "The Cultural Context of *A Streetcar Named Desire* in Germany," 199–221 in P. C. Kolin, ed. *Confronting Tennessee Williams's A Streetcar Named Desire: Essays in Cultural Pluralism*

Suddenly Last Summer

Colanzi, R. M. "Tennessee Williams's Revision of *Suddenly Last Summer*," *Journal of Modern Literature* 16:651–52, Sprg. 1990

Evans, R. " 'Or Else This Were a Savage Spectacle': Eating and Troping Southern Culture," *Southern Quarterly* 30(2/3):141–49, Wint/Sprg. 1992

Hoffman, J. "Taking on His Own Reflection—and Tennessee Williams," *New York Times* 142:H28(N), 3 Jan. 1993

Raymond, G. "*Suddenly Last Summer*: Director Richard Eyre on the TV Version of Williams's Play," *TheaterWeek* 6(22):24–25, 4 Jan. 1993

Summer and Smoke, 1948
Portes, L. *Summer and Smoke, by Tennessee Williams.* M.F.A. Thesis; U of California, San Diego, 1992

Sweet Bird of Youth, 1956
Smith, C. W. *Patterns of Progression: Tennessee Williams's Sweet Bird of Youth, from Manuscripts Through Published Text.* Diss.; Lehigh U, 1993

The Two-Character Play, 1967 (revised 1969)
LaBelle, T. K. *Reality and Representation: A Postmodern Reading of Tennessee Williams's The Two-Character Play.* M.A. Thesis; Auburn U, 1993

Vieux Carré, 1977
Clinton, C. "The Reprise of Tennessee Williams' *Vieux Carré*: An Interview with Director Keith Hack," *Studies in American Drama, 1945-Present* 7(2):265–75, 1992

WILLIAMSON, GLEN

The Boy Who Saw True, 1992
Portantiere, M. *TheaterWeek* 6(17):33, 30 Nov. 1992

WILSON, AUGUST

Arthur, T. H. "Looking for My Relatives: The Political Implications of 'Family' in Selected Work of Athol Fugard and August Wilson," *South African Theatre Journal* 6(2):5–16, Sep. 1992
Berkowitz, G. M. *American Drama of the Twentieth Century.* 144, 194
DiGaetani, J. L. "August Wilson," 275–84 in J. L. DiGaetani, ed. *A Search for a Postmodern Theater: Interviews with Contemporary Playwrights*
Huang, N. S. "August Wilson Wants His Ham," *M* 9(7):72, Apr. 1992
McDonough, C. J. "Staging Masculinity: The Search for Male Identity in Contemporary American Drama," (#DA9306664; U of Tennessee) *DAI* 53(11):3910A, May 1993
Pereira, K. "The Search for Identity in the Plays of August Wilson: An Exploration of the Themes of Separation, Migration, and Reunion," (#DA9132980; Florida State U) *DAI* 52(6):1946A, Dec. 1991
Plum, J. "Blues, History, and the Dramaturgy of August Wilson," *African American Review* 27(4):561–67, Wntr. 1993
Rocha, M. W. "Black Madness in August Wilson's *Down the Line* Cycle," 191–201 in J. Redmond, ed. *Madness in Drama*
Shafer, Y. "August Wilson: A New Approach to Black Drama," *Zeitschrift fur Anglistik und Amerikanistik* 39(1):17–27, 1991
Shannon, S. G. "Blues, History, and Dramaturgy: An Interview with August Wilson," *African American Review* 27(4):539–59, Wntr. 1993
———. "From Lorraine Hansberry to August Wilson: An Interview with Lloyd Richards," *Callaloo* 14(1):124–35, Wntr. 1991

————. "The Good Christian's Come and Gone: The Shifting Role of Christianity in August Wilson Plays," *MELUS* 16(3):127–42, Fall 1989/1990
Wilson, A. "Testimonies," *Antaeus* 66:474–79, Sprg. 1991

Joe Turner's Come and Gone, 1987
  Abarbanel, J. *TheaterWeek* 4(30):35, 4 Mar. 1991

Ma Rainey's Black Bottom, 1984
  McKelly, J. C. "Hymns of Sedition: Portraits of the Artist in Contemporary African-American Drama," *Arizona Quarterly* 48(1):87–107, Sprg. 1992
  Shannon, S. G. "The Long Wait: August Wilson's *Ma Rainey's Black Bottom*," *Black American Literature Forum* 25(1):135–46, Sprg. 1991

Two Trains Running, 1990
  Ansen, D. *Newsweek* 119(17):70, 27 Apr. 1992
  Disch, T. M. *Nation* 254(22):799–800, 8 Jun. 1992
  Dwyer, V. *Maclean's* 105(20):56–57, 18 May 1992
  Gerard, J. *Variety* 345(7):46, 25 Nov. 1991
  ————. *Variety* 347(1):50, 20 Apr. 1992
  Henry, W. A., III. *Time* 139(17):65, 27 Apr. 1992
  Kanfer, S. *New Leader* 75(6):21, 4 May 1992
  Kramer, M. *New Yorker* 68(10):85, 27 Apr. 1992
  Lochte, D. *Los Angeles Magazine* 37(3):123, Mar. 1992
  Marowitz, C. *TheaterWeek* 5(38):35–36, 27 Apr. 1992
  Rich, F. *New York Times* 141:B1(N), 14 Apr. 1992
  Simon, J. *New York* 25(17):82, 27 Apr. 1992
  Weales, G. *Commonweal* 119(11):18, 5 Jun. 1992
  Wilde, L. "Reclaiming the Past: Narrative and Memory in August Wilson's *Two Trains Running*," *Theater* 22(1):73–74, Wntr. 1990/1991
  Williams, L. *Time* 138(21):20, 25 Nov. 1991

WILSON, LANFORD

Berkowitz, G. M. *American Drama of the Twentieth Century.* 135, 181
Chi, W. *The Role of Language in the Plays of Mamet, Wilson, and Rabe.* Diss.; U of Iowa, 1991
Copperman, R. "Lanford Wilson: A Bibliography," *Bulletin of Bibliography* 48(3):125–35, Sep. 1991
DiGaetani, J. L. "Lanford Wilson," 285–93 in J. L. DiGaetani, ed. *A Search for a Postmodern Theater: Interviews with Contemporary Playwrights*
Konas, G. "Tennessee Williams and Lanford Wilson at the Missouri Crossroads," *Studies in American Drama, 1945-Present* 5:23–41, 1990
Tibbetts, J. C. "An Interview with Lanford Wilson," *Journal of Dramatic Theory and Criticism* 5(2):175–80, Sprg. 1991
Wilson, L. "The Moonshot Tape," *Antaeus* 66:480–92, Sprg. 1991

Eukiah, 1992
  Osborn, M. E. "Letter from Louisville," *TheaterWeek* 5(38):32, 27 Apr. 1992

5th of July, 1978 (revised *Fifth of July*, 1980)
> Schlatter, J. F. "Some Kind of a Future: The War for Inheritance in the Work of Three American Playwrights of the 1970s," *South Central Review* 7(1):59–75, Sprg. 1990

Redwood Curtain, 1992
> Brown, M. *Variety* 345(13):75, 13 Jan. 1992
> Gallo, C. "Arbor Days," *TCI* 27(4):8, Apr. 1993
> Gelb, H. *Nation* 254(13):462–464, 6 Apr. 1992
> Gerard, J. *Variety* 350(10):184, 5 Apr. 1993
> Greene, A. *TheaterWeek* 6(36):26–27, 12 Apr. 1993
> Hornby, R. *Hudson Review* 46:370–1, Summ. 1993
> Kanfer, S. *New Leader* 76(6):22, 3 May 1993
> Kroll, J. *Newsweek* 121(15):61, 12 Apr. 1993
> Lahr, J. *New Yorker* 69(8):107, 12 Apr. 1993
> Rich, F. *New York Times* 142:B1, 31 Mar. 1993
> Richards, D. *New York Times* 142:H5, 11 Apr. 1993
> Riedel, M. "The Man from Missouri," *TheaterWeek* 6(39):21–26, 3 May 1993
> Simon, J. *New York* 26(15):66, 12 Apr. 1993
> Weber, B. "Raising the *Redwood Curtain*," *New York Times* 142:B2, 4 Dec. 1992
> Wilson, E. *Wall Street Journal* A14, 5 Apr. 1993

WILSON, ROBERT M.

Arens, K. "Robert Wilson: Is Postmodern Performance Possible?" *Theatre Journal* 43(1):14–40, Mar. 1991

Armstrong, G. S. "Political and Practical Ideologies," *Performing Arts Journal* 43(15):38–41, Jan. 1993

Birringer, J. "Wilson/Wagner," *Performing Arts Journal* 43(15):62–65, Jan. 1993

Callens, J. "Ter plaatsefietsen: Wilson regisseert Stein," *De Vlaamse Gids* 77(3):13–18, May/Jun. 1993

Dasgupta, G. "Personalizing History," *Performing Arts Journal* 43(15):31–37, Jan. 1993

Dietrich, D. Y. "Archetypal Dreams: The Quantum Theater of Robert Wilson," (#DA9303728; U of Michigan) *DAI* 53(10):3411A, Apr. 1993

Fairbrother, T. "Two Chairs and a Bed," *Artforum* 29:79–81, Jan. 1991

"Fechas, imagenes y palabras," *Primer acto* 246:56–63, Nov/Dec. 1992

Kostelanetz, R. "Writing and Performance: A Conversation among Linda Mussman, Richard Foreman, Robert Wilson, and Richard Kostelanetz," 489–509 in R. Kostelanetz, ed. *American Writing Today*

Langworthy, D. " 'Listen to the Pictures'—Robert Wilson & German Theater Criticism," *Theater* 23(1):35–40, Wntr. 1992

Loney, G. "Beyond the Broadway Musical: Crossovers, Confusions and Crisis," 151–76 in B. King, ed. *Contemporary American Theatre*

Marranca, B. "Robert Wilson and the Idea of the Archive: Dramaturgy as an Ecology," *Performing Arts Journal* 43(15):66–79, Jan. 1993

McCombie, M. "Robert Wilson," *Arts Magazine* 66:71, Sep. 91

Rogoff, G. "Time, Wilson, and What a Play Should Do," *Theater* 22(3):52–53, Summ/Fall 1991

Savran, D. "Whistling in the Dark," *Performing Arts Journal* 43:25–27, Jan. 1993

Vanden Heuvel, M. " 'Of Our Origins: In Ghostlier Demarcations, Keener Sounds': Robert Wilson's Search for a New Order of Vision," in M. Vanden Heuvel, ed. *Performing Drama/Dramatizing Performance: Alternative Theater and the Dramatic Text*

Wirth, A. "The Don Juan Myth Radiantly Transformed," *Performing Arts Journal* 43(15):42–45, Jan. 1993

———. "The Thrust Stage as Guillotine," *Performing Arts Journal* 43(15):59–61, Jan. 1993

WILSON, ROBERT, and PHILIP GLASS

the CIVIL warS: a tree is best measured when it is down, 1982–1984 (others also collaborated on this project)

    Dietrich, D. Y. "Space/Time and the Tapestry of Silence: The Quantum Theater of Robert Wilson," *Word & Image: A Journal of Verbal/Visual Enquiry* 8(3):173–82, Jul/Sep. 1992

    Kubiak, A. "Reforming Content: Meaning in Postmodern Performance," *Studies in the Literary Imagination* 24(2):29–36, Fall 1991

Einstein on the Beach, 1976

    Bell, J. *TheaterWeek* 6(20):12–14, 21 Dec. 1992

    Ladra, D. "*Einstein on the Beach* y Don Juan ultimo," *Primer acto* 246:48–55, Nov/Dec. 1992

WILSON, ROBERT, TOM WAITS, and WILLIAM S. BURROUGHS

The Black Rider, 1993

    Roberts, M. "Take a Ride with Robert Wilson's *The Black Rider*," *Interview* 23(11):72, Nov. 1993

    Rockwell, J. "*The Black Rider* Rides Again," *Opera News* 58(5):28–29, Nov. 1993

WOLFE, GEORGE C.

Keene, J. "George C. Wolfe: A Brief Biography," *Callaloo* 16(3):593–94, Summ. 1993

Rowell, C. H. " 'I Just Want to Keep Telling Stories': An Interview with George C. Wolfe," *Callaloo* 16(3):602–23, Summ. 1993

Simpson, J. C. "A Jam Session with George C. Wolfe," *TheaterWeek* 6(12):18–21, 26 Oct. 1992

The Colored Museum, 1986

    Elam, H. J., Jr. "Signifyin(g) on African-American Theatre: *The Colored Museum* by George Wolfe," *Theatre Journal* 44(3):291–303, 1 Oct. 1992

Jelly's Last Jam, 1992
>Heilpern, J. "With *Jelly's Last Jam*, Renegade Writer/Director George C.
>Wolfe Redefines the Black American Musical," *Vogue* 182(5):144+, May
>1992
>Henry, W. A., III. *Time* 139(18):78, 4 May 1992
>Kroll, J. *Newsweek* 119(18):66, 4 May 1992
>Mandelbaum, K. "Season Preview: The Musicals," *TheaterWeek* 5(1):18+,
>12 Aug. 1991
>———. *TheaterWeek* 5(41):35–37, 18 May 1992
>Oliver, E. *New Yorker* 68(12):78, 11 May 1992
>Rich, F. *New York Times* 141:B1(N), 27 Apr. 1992
>Sandla, R. "Meet the Hunnies and a Honey," *Dance Magazine* 66(11):76,
>Nov. 1992
>Simon, J. *New York* 25(20):61, 18 May 1992

Spunk: Three Tales by Zora Neale Hurston (dramatization of stories by Hurston:
"Sweat," "Story in Harlem Slang," and "The Gilded Six-Bits"), 1989
>Lochte, D. *Los Angeles Magazine* 36(11):175, Nov. 1991
>Over, W. *Theatre Journal* 43:119–21, Mar. 1991

WOLFF, RUTH

The Abdication, 1969
>Perkins, S. J. "The Performance of Gender: A Rhetorical Analysis of Con-
>temporary Feminist Theater," (#DA9238691; U of Kansas) *DAI*
>53(8):2603A, Feb. 1993

WONG, ELIZABETH

Letters to a Student Revolutionary, 1991
>Chansky, D. *TheaterWeek* 4(43):41, 3 Jun. 1991
>Gussow, M. *New York Times* 140:C18, 16 May 1991
>Lamont, R. C., ed. *Women on the Verge: 7 Avant-Garde American Plays*

WOOD, SILVIANA

McFerran, V. D. "Chicana Voices in American Drama: Silviana Wood, Estela
Portillo Trambley, Cherríe Moraga, Milcha Sanchez-Scott, Josefina Lopez,"
(#DA9119397; U of Minnesota) *DAI* 52(6):1946A, Dec. 1991

WRANGLER, JACK, HAL HACKADY, and ROBERT HABER

The Valentine Touch (based on O. Henry's short story "A Retrieved Reforma-
tion"), 1992
>Weiss, B. "From Porn Star to Playwright," *TheaterWeek* 6(24):23–25, 18
>Jan. 1993

WRIGHT, RAE C. *SEE* MARGOLIN, DEBORAH, and RAE C. WRIGHT

WRIGHT, ROBERT. *SEE* DAVIS, LUTHER, ROBERT WRIGHT, GEORGE
FOREST, and MAURY YESTON

YAMAUCHI, WAKAKO

Yogi, S. ''Subversive Narratives in the Stories of Wakako Yamauchi and Hisaye
Yamamoto,'' 131–50 in S. G. Lim and A. Ling, eds. *Reading the Literatures of
Asian America*

The Chairman's Wife (about Madame Mao Tse-Tung), 1990
    Houston, V. H. *The Politics of Life: Four Plays by Asian American Women*

YANKOWITZ, SUSAN

Night Sky
    Miles, J., ed. *Playwriting Women: 7 Plays from the Women's Project*

YELLOW ROBE, WILLIAM S.

Rosenberg, S. ''When Earth Becomes a Character,'' *American Theatre* 9(4):38–
39, Jul/Aug. 1992

YEP, LAWRENCE

Yep, L. ''Dragonwings,'' *American Theatre* 9(5):P1–13, Sep. 1992

YESTON, MAURY

History Loves Company, 1991
    Abarbanel, J. *TheaterWeek* 5(13):30, 4 Nov. 1991

SEE ALSO KOPIT, ARTHUR, and MAURY YESTON

SEE ALSO DAVIS, LUTHER, ROBERT WRIGHT, GEORGE FOREST, and
MAURY YESTON

YORINKS, ARTHUR

Milvy, E. ''From Sendak's Kitchen,'' *American Theatre* 10(4):33–34, Apr. 1993

YOUNG, ANDREW

Thanksgiving Day, 1993
    Filichia, P. ''Thanksgiving in May,'' *TheaterWeek* 6(40):15, 10 May 1993

YOUNGBLOOD, SHAY

Allen, D. "Shay Youngblood Urges Teachers to Nurture Students," *Language Arts* 68(2):166, Feb. 1991

ZEAL, ELEANOR

Breaking the Bank, 1992
    Horspool, D. *TLS* (4721):19, 24 Sep. 1992

ZIGUN, DICK

Martin, D. "The Rebirth of a Sideshow at Coney Island," *New York Times* 141:C1(L), 4 Sep. 1992
Paran, J. "Dick Zigun," *American Theatre* 9(6):34–36, Oct. 1992

ZIMET, PAUL

Baron Bones (first of a trilogy, *The Blue Sky Is a Curse*; the second is *Brown Dog Is Dead* by Ellen Maddow, and the third is *The Plumber's Helper* by Zimet and Maddow), 1993
    Bell, J. *TheaterWeek* 6(28):15, 15 Feb. 1993

Fata Morgana, 1991
    Bell, J. "Words Become Music," *TheaterWeek* 4(27):22–27, 11 Feb. 1991
    ———. *TheaterWeek* 4(41):35–6, 20 May 1991

ZIMET, PAUL, and ELLEN MADDOW

The Plumber's Helper, 1993
    Bell, J. *TheaterWeek* 6(28):16, 15 Feb. 1993

ZIMMERMAN, MARY

The Notebooks of Leonardo da Vinci (based on the notebooks of Leonardo da Vinci; an earlier version of this play was staged in 1989 at the Lookingglass Theatre), 1993
    Griffin, G. "Exposing da Vinci," *American Theatre* 10(11):10, Nov. 1993

ZINDEL, PAUL

DiGaetani, J. L. "Paul Zindel," 295–303 in J. L. DiGaetani, ed. *A Search for a Postmodern Theater: Interviews with Contemporary Playwrights*

And Miss Reardon Drinks a Little, 1967
    Keller, J. R. "A Fellowship of Madness: Williams' Blanche Dubois and Zindel's Anna Reardon," *Notes on Contemporary Literature* 23(5):2–3, Nov. 1993

The Effect of Gamma Rays on Man-in-the-Moon Marigolds, 1965 (later revised)
  Loomis, J. B. ''Female Freedoms, Dantesque Dreams, and Paul Zindel's
  Anti-Sexist *The Effect of Gamma Rays on Man-in-the-Moon Marigolds*,''
  Studies in American Drama, 1945-Present 6(2):123–33, 1991

ZIPPEL, DAVID. *SEE* GELBART, LARRY, CY COLEMAN, and DAVID ZIPPEL

SEE ALSO SIMON, NEIL, MARVIN HAMLISCH, and DAVID ZIPPEL

LIST OF BOOKS INDEXED

Acheson, James, ed. *British and Irish Drama Since 1960*. Houndmills, England: Macmillan, 1993.

Adam, Julie. *Versions of Heroism in Modern American Drama: Redefinitions by Miller, O'Neill, and Anderson*. New York: St. Martin's P, 1991.

Alexander, Doris. *Eugene O'Neill's Creative Struggle: The Decisive Decade, 1924–1933*. University Park: Pennsylvania State U P, 1992.

Allen, Robert C. *Horrible Prettiness: Burlesque and American Culture*. Chapel Hill: U. of North Carolina P, 1991.

Anderson, Jane. *The Baby Dance: A Drama in Two Acts*. New York: S. French, 1992.

———. *Food and Shelter: A Drama in Two Acts*. New York: S. French, 1992.

Anderson, Laurie. *Empty Places: A Performance*. New York: Harper Perennial, 1991.

Baccolini, Raffaella, Vita Fortunati, and Romana Zacchi, eds. *Il teatro e le donne: Forme drammatiche e tradizione al femminile nel teatro inglese*. Urbino: Quattroventi, 1991.

Baker, Isadore Lewis. *Brodie's Notes on Arthur Miller's The Crucible*. London: Pan, 1991.

Banfield, Stephen. *Sondheim's Broadway Musicals*. Ann Arbor: U. of Michigan P, 1993.

Barbour, Douglas. *Michael Ondaatje*. New York: Twayne, 1993.

Barker-Benfield, G. J. *Portraits of American Women: From Settlement to the Present*. New York: St. Martin's P, 1991.

Beard, Jocelyn, ed. *The Best Men's Stage Monologues of 1993*. Newbury, VT: Smith and Kraus, 1993.

———. *The Best Women's Stage Monologues of 1993*. Newbury, VT: Smith and Kraus, 1993.

Benet, Carol. *Sam Shepard on the German Stage: Critics, Politics, Myths*. New York: P. Lang, 1993.

Bergman, David, ed. *Camp Grounds: Style and Homosexuality*. Amherst: U. of Massachusetts P, 1993.

Berkowitz, Gerald M. *American Drama of the Twentieth Century*. New York: Longman, 1992.

Charlotte, Susan. *Creativity: Conversations with 28 Who Excel.* Troy, MI: Momentum Books, 1993.

———. *Creativity in Film: Conversations with 14 Who Excel.* Troy, MI: Momentum Books, 1993.

Chocron, Isaac E. *El teatro de Sam Shepard: de imagenes a personajes.* Caracas, Venezuela: Monte Avila Editores, 1991.

Choukri, Mohamed. *Jean Genet et Tennessee Williams a Tanger.* Paris: Quai Voltaire, 1992.

Cohn, Ruby. *New American Dramatists, 1960–1990.* New York: St. Martin's, 1991.

Cole, Susan Letzler. *Directors in Rehearsal: A Hidden World.* New York: Routledge, 1992.

Crandell, George W. *Tennessee Williams: A Descriptive Bibliography.* Pittsburgh: U of Pittsburgh P, 1993.

Cushman, Keith, and Dennis Jackson, eds. *D. H. Lawrence's Literary Inheritors.* New York: St. Martin's, 1991.

Deats, Sara Munson, and Lagretta Tallent Lenken, eds. *The Aching Hearth: Family Violence in Life and Literature.* New York: Plenum, 1991.

De Beaumont, Gaia. *Scusate le ceneri.* Venezia: Marsilio, 1993.

Demastes, William W. *Clifford Odets: A Research and Production Sourcebook.* New York: Greenwood, 1991.

De La Vars, Lauren Pringle, ed. *Images of the Self as Female: The Achievement of Women Artists in Re-Envisioning Feminine Identity.* Lewiston: Edwin Mellen P, 1992.

DeRose, David J. *Sam Shepard.* New York: Twayne, 1992.

Derounian-Stodola, Kathryn Zabelle, ed. *Early American Literature and Culture: Essays Honoring Harrison T. Meserole.* Newark: U of Delaware P, 1992.

DiGaetani, John L., ed. *A Search for a Postmodern Theater: Interviews with Contemporary Playwrights.* New York: Greenwood P, 1991.

Donkin, Ellen, and Susan Clements, eds. *Upstaging Big Daddy: Directing Theater as if Gender and Race Matter.* Ann Arbor: U of Michigan P, 1993.

Doolittle, Joyce, ed. *Heroines: Three Plays.* Red Deer: Red Deer College P, 1992.

Dubois, Felicie. *Tennessee Williams: l'oiseau sans pattes.* Paris: Editions Balland, 1992.

Dykeman, Therese Boos, ed. *American Women Philosophers 1650-1930.* Lewiston: Edwin Mellen P, 1993.

Dynes, Wayne R., and Stephen Donaldson. *Homosexual Themes in Literary Studies.* New York: Garland, 1992.

Farber, Donald C., and Robert Viagas. *The Amazing Story of The Fantasticks: America's Longest Running Play.* New York: Citadel P, 1991.

Ferguson, Mary Anne, ed. *Images of Women in Literature.* 5th ed. Boston: Houghton Mifflin, 1991.

Ferris, Lesley, ed. *Crossing the Stage: Controversies on Cross-Dressing.* London: Routledge, 1993.

Fields, Armond, and L. Marc Fields. *From the Bowery to Broadway: Lew Fields and the Roots of American Popular Theater.* Oxford: Oxford U P, 1993.

Fischer-Seidel, Therese. *Frauen und Frauendarstellung in der englischen und amerikanischen Literatur.* Turbinger: Narr, 1991.

Friedland, M. L., ed. *Rough Justice: Essays on Crime in Literature.* Toronto: U of Toronto P, 1991.

Friesen, Lauren, ed. *Theatre and Religion*. Goshen, IN: Theatre and Religion Forum Group, 1992.

Gale, Steven H., ed. *S. J. Perelman: Critical Essays*. New York: Garland, 1992.

Garebian, Keith. *The Making of My Fair Lady*. Toronto: ECW P, 1993.

Garrett-Groag, Lillian. *The White Rose*. New York: Dramatist's Play Service, 1993.

Gintsburg, Adi, ed. *Naftule zeman: otobiyografyah*. Tel Aviv: Devir, 1991.

Glassman, Steve, and Kathryn Lee Seidel, eds. *Zora in Florida*. Orlando: U of Central Florida, 1991.

Golden, Marita, ed. *Wild Women Don't Wear No Blues: Black Women Writers on Love, Men, and Sex*. New York: Doubleday, 1993.

Goodman, Robyn, and Marisa Smith, eds. *Women Playwrights: The Best Plays of 1992*. Newbury, VT: Smith and Kraus, 1993.

Gordon, Joanne Lesley. *Art Isn't Easy: The Theater of Stephen Sondheim*. New York: Da Capo P, 1992.

Gottfried, Martin. *Sondheim*. New York: H. N. Abrams, 1993.

Graham, Laura J. *Sam Shepard: Theme, Image, and the Director*. New York: P. Lang, 1993.

Gray, Nancy. *Language Unbound: On Experimental Writing by Women*. Urbana: U of Illinois P, 1992.

Gross, Robert F. *S. N. Behrman: A Research and Production Sourcebook*. Westport, CT: Greenwood P, 1992.

Gspann, Veronika. *Edward Albee Dramai*. Budapest: Akademiai Kiado, 1992.

Gunn, Drewey Wayne. *Tennessee Williams, a Bibliography*. Metuchen, NJ: Scarecrow P, 1991.

Hall, Ann C. *A Kind of Alaska: Women in the Plays of O'Neill, Pinter, and Shepard*. Carbondale: Southern Illinois U P, 1993.

Hamalian, Leo, and James V. Hatch, eds. *The Roots of African American Drama: An Anthology of Early Plays, 1858–1938*. Detroit: Wayne State U P, 1991.

Hamner, Robert. *Derek Walcott*. New York: Twayne, 1993.

Hart, Lynda, and Peggy Phelan, eds. *Acting Out: Feminist Performances*. Ann Arbor: U of Michigan P, 1993.

Hatch, James V. *Sorrow Is the Only Faithful One: The Life of Owen Dodson*. Chicago: U of Illinois P, 1993.

Hayman, Ronald. *Tennessee Williams: Everyone Else Is an Audience*. New Haven: Yale U P, 1993.

Hazelton, Nancy J. Doran, and Kenneth Krauss, eds. *Maxwell Anderson and the New York Stage*. Monroe, NY: Library Research, 1991.

Helbing, Terry. *Gay and Lesbian Plays Today*. Portsmouth, NH: Heinemann, 1992.

Heller, Adele, and Lois Rudnick, eds. *1915, The Cultural Moment: The New Politics, the New Woman, the New Psychology, the New Art & the New Theatre in America*. New Brunswick: Rutgers U P, 1991.

Hemphill, Essex, ed. *Brother to Brother: New Writings by Black Gay Men*. Boston: Alyson, 1991.

Hillwood Art Museum Collection. *Edward Albee's Other Eye: Sculptural Objects from the Edward Albee and Edward F. Albee Foundation Collections* (includes essay by Albee). Brookville, NY: Hillwood Art Museum, 1993.

Hischak, Thomas S. *Word Crazy: Broadway Lyricists from Cohan to Sondheim*. New York: Praeger, 1991.

Horn, Barbara Lee. *The Age of Hair: Evolution and Impact of Broadway's First Rock Musical.* New York: Greenwood P, 1991.

————. *Joseph Papp: A Bio-Bibliography.* New York: Greenwood P, 1992.

Horton, Andrew, ed. *Comedy/Cinema/Theory.* Berkeley: U of California P, 1991.

Houchin, John H. *The Critical Response to Eugene O'Neill.* Westport, CT: Greenwood P, 1993.

Houston, Velina Hasu. *The Politics of Life: Four Plays by Asian American Women.* Philadelphia: Temple U P, 1993.

Howell, John. *Laurie Anderson.* Emeryville, CA: Thunder's Mouth P, 1992.

Inge, Luther C. *Travels in Search of the Past: The Ancestry of William Motter Inge, Playwright.* Oklahoma City: L. C. Inge, 1991.

Jacobs, Diane. *Christmas in July: The Life and Art of Preston Sturges.* Berkeley: U of California P, 1992.

Jansen, Wolfgang. *My Fair Lady: die deutsche Erstauffuhrung 1961 im Berliner Theater des Westens.* Berlin: Weidler, 1992.

Joki, Ilkka. *Mamet, Baktin, and the Dramatic: The Demotic as a Variable of Addressivity.* Abo: Abo Akademis Forslag, 1993.

Jones, Nesta Wyn, and Steven Dykes, eds. *File on Mamet.* London: Methuen Drama, 1991.

Kallenberg-Schroder, Andrea. *Autobiographisches in Arthur Millers familienzentrierten Dramen.* Frankfurt am Main: Lang, 1993.

Kane, Leslie, ed. *David Mamet: A Casebook.* New York: Garland, 1991.

Kataria, Gulshan Rai. *The Faces of Eve: A Study of Tennessee Williams's Heroines.* New Delhi: Sterling, 1992.

Kennedy, Richard S. *Literary New Orleans: Essays and Meditations.* Baton Rouge: Louisiana State U P, 1992.

Khare, R. R. *Eugene O'Neill & His Visionary Quest.* New Delhi: Mittal Publications, 1992.

King, Bruce, ed. *Contemporary American Theatre.* New York: St. Martin's P, 1991.

————. *Post-Colonial English Drama: Commonwealth Drama Since 1960.* New York: St. Martin's P, 1992.

King, Larry L., and Ben Z. Grant. *The Kingfish: A One-Man Play Loosely Depicting the Life and Times of the Late Huey P. Long of Louisiana.* Dallas: Southern Methodist U P, 1992.

Kintz, Linda. *The Subject's Tragedy: Political Poetics, Feminist Theory, and Drama.* Ann Arbor: U of Michigan P, 1992.

Kolin, Philip C., ed. *Confronting Tennessee Williams's A Streetcar Named Desire: Essays in Cultural Pluralism.* Westport, CT: Greenwood, 1993.

Kostelanetz, Richard, ed. *American Writing Today.* Troy, NY: Whitston Publishing Co., 1991.

Krutch, Joseph Wood, ed. *Nine Plays by Eugene O'Neill.* New York: Modern Library, 1993.

Lamb, Wendy., ed. *Ten Out of Ten: Ten Winning Plays Selected from the Young Playwrights Festival, 1982–1991, Produced by the Foundation of the Dramatists Guild.* New York: Delacorte P, 1992.

Lal, D. K. *Myth and Mythical Concept in O'Neill's Plays.* New Delhi, Atlantic Publishers & Distributors, 1992.

Lamont, Rosette C., ed. *Women on the Verge.* New York: Applause Theatre Books, 1993.

Leiter, Samuel L. *From Belasco to Brook: Representative Directors of the English-Speaking Stage.* New York, Greenwood P, 1991.

Lerda, Valeria, et. al., eds. *The United States South: Regionalism and Identity.* Rome: Bulzoni, 1991.

Leshem-Ezra, Danah. *Artur Miler, Moto shel sokhen.* Tel Aviv: Or-am, 1993.

Lesser, Wendy, ed. *Hiding in Plain Sight: Essays in Criticism and Autobiography.* San Francisco: Mercury House, 1993.

Lim, Shirley Geok-lin, and Amy Ling, eds. *Reading the Literatures of Asian America.* Philadelphia: Temple U P, 1992.

Liu, Hai-ping, and Lowell Swortzell, eds. *Eugene O'Neill in China: An International Centenary Celebration.* Westport, CT: Greenwood, 1992.

Loesser, Susan. *A Most Remarkable Fella: Frank Loesser and the Guys and Dolls in His Life; A Portrait by His Daughter.* New York: D. K. Fine, 1993.

Makowsky, Veronica. *Susan Glaspell's Century of American Women: A Critical Interpretation of Her Work.* New York: Oxford U P, 1993.

Mamet, David. *The Cabin: Reminiscence and Diversions.* New York: Vintage Books, 1993.

Mancini, Anne. *Focus on The Crucible by Arthur Miller.* Melbourne: Longman Cheshire, 1992.

Martine, James J. *The Crucible: Politics, Property, and Pretense.* New York: Twayne, 1993.

McCarrell, Stuart. *New York: Visions, Struggles, Voices.* Chicago: Xenia, 1991.

McClure, Arthur F. *A Bibliographical Guide to the Works of William Inge (1913–1973).* Lewiston, NY: Mellen P, 1991.

McConachie, Bruce A. *Melodramatic Formations: American Theatre and Society, 1820–1870.* Iowa City: U of Iowa P, 1992.

McDonough, Edwin J. *Quintero Directs O'Neill.* Chicago: A Cappella Books, 1991.

McDowell, Linda, and Rosemary Pringle. *Defining Women: Social Institutions and Gender Divisions.* New York: Polity P, 1992.

McGhee, Jim. *True Lies: The Architecture of the Fantastic in the Plays of Sam Shepard.* New York: P. Lang, 1993.

McKnight, Russell, and Robert Tauber, eds. *An Inaugural Commemorative Keepsake: The Thurber Center Opening, December 1992.* Columbus, OH: Logan Elm P, 1992.

Meade, Marion. *Dorothy Parker: What Fresh Hell Is This?* New York: Minerva, 1991.

Michel, Pierre, ed. *BELL: Belgian Essays on Language and Literature.* Brussels: U de Liege, 1991.

Miles, Julia, ed. *Playwriting Women: 7 Plays from the Women's Project.* Portsmouth, NH: Heinemann, 1993.

Miller, Gabriel, ed. *Critical Essays on Clifford Odets.* Boston: G. K. Hall, 1991.

Mishra, Kshamanidhi. *American Leftist Playwrights of the 1930's: A Study of Ideology and Technique in the Plays of Odets, Lawson, and Sherwood.* New Delhi: Classical Publishing Co., 1991.

Mogen, David, Scott P. Sanders, and Joanne B. Karpinski, eds. *Frontier Gothic: Terror and Wonder at the Frontier in American Literature.* Rutherford, NJ: Fairleigh Dickinson U P, 1993.

Moore, Barbara, and David G. Yellin. *Horton Foote's Three Trips to Bountiful.* Dallas: Southern Methodist U P, 1993.

Moorton, Richard F., Jr., ed. *Eugene O'Neill's Century: Centennial Views on America's Foremost Tragic Dramatist* (Contributions in Drama and Theatre Studies 36). Westport, CT: Greenwood P, 1991.

Muller, Kurt. *Inszenierte Wirklichkeiten: die Erfahrung der Moderne im Leben und Werk Eugene O'Neills*. Darmstadt: Wissenschaftliche Buchgesellschaft, 1993.

Murphy, Brenda. *Tennessee Williams and Elia Kazan: A Collaboration in the Theatre*. Cambridge, England: Cambridge U P, 1992.

Murphy, Patrick D., ed. *Staging the Impossible: The Fantastic Mode in Modern Drama*. Westport, CT: Greenwood P, 1992

Nelson, Emmanuel S., ed. *AIDS: The Literary Response*. New York: Twayne, 1992.

Newton, Mark G., ed. *Ethics in Modern American Literature: Rivers to Skyscrapers*. Saint Leo, FL: Saint Leo College P, 1991.

Noren, Lars. *Och ge oss skuggorna*. Stockholm: Bonnier, 1991.

Nourse, Joan Thellusson. *Artur Miler Tsayad ha-mekhashefot: Zikhronot mi-shene yeme Sheni: Mareh me-al ha-gesher: Le-ahar ha-nefilah: Takrit be-Vishi*. Tel Aviv: Or-am, 1991.

Oates, Joyce Carol. *I Stand Before You Naked*. New York: S. French, 1991.

Olive, John. *Evelyn and the Polka King*. New York: Theatre Communications Group, 1992.

Orr, John. *Tragicomedy and Contemporary Culture: Play and Performance from Beckett to Shepard*. Houndmills: Macmillan, 1991.

Osterman, Georg. *Brother Truckers*. New York: French, 1993.

Overmyer, Eric. *Don Quixote de la Jolla*. New York: Broadway Play Publishing, 1993.

————. *Dark Rapture*. New York: Broadway Play Publishing, 1993.

————. *Eric Overmyer: Collected Plays*. Newbury, VT: Smith and Kraus, 1993.

————. *The Heliotrope Bouquet by Scott Joplin & Louis Chauvin*. New York: Broadway Play Publishing, 1993.

————. *Mi vida loca*. New York: Broadway Play Publishing, 1991.

Pagan, Nicholas. *Rethinking Literary Biography: A Postmodern Approach to Tennessee Williams*. London: Fairleigh Dickinson U P, 1993.

Papke, Mary E. *Susan Glaspell: A Research and Production Sourcebook*. Westport, CT: Greenwood P, 1993.

Parker, Dorothy. *The Sayings of Dorothy Parker*. London: Duckworth, 1992.

Parker, Gerald D. *How to Play the Theatre of James Reaney*. Toronto: ECW P, 1991.

Payne, James Robert, ed. *Multicultural Autobiography: American Lives*. Knoxville: U of Tennessee P, 1992.

Pearson, Sybille. *Unfinished Stories*. New York: Dramatists Play Service, 1993.

Perry, Frederick J. *A Reconstruction-Analysis of Buried Child by Playwright Sam Shepard*. Lewiston, NY: Mellen Research U P, 1992.

Pinder, Brenda. *Arthur Miller, Death of a Salesman, The Crucible, A Workshop Approach: A Photocopiable Resource*. Rozelle, NSW: St. Clair P, 1991.

Pintauro, Joseph. *Raft of the Medusa*. New York: Dramatists Play Service, 1992.

Plays from South Coast Repertory. New York: Broadway Play Publishing, 1993.

Prasad, Sheela. *Tradition and Experiment in the Plays of Eugene O'Neill*. Delhi: Capital Publishing House, 1991.

Rabkin, Eric S. *Lifted Masks and Other Works*. Ann Arbor: U of Michigan P, 1992.

Redmond, James, ed. *Madness in Drama*. Cambridge: Cambridge U P, 1993.
————. *Melodrama*. Cambridge: Cambridge U P, 1992.
————. *Violence in Drama*. Cambridge: Cambridge U P, 1991.
Reynolds, Peter, ed. *Novel Images: Literature in Performance*. London: Routledge, 1993.
Reynolds, Rick. *Only the Truth Is Funny: My Family and How I Survived It*. New York: Hyperion, 1992.
Ribman, Ronald. *The Rug Merchants of Chaos, and Other Plays*. New York: Theatre Communications Group, 1992.
Rosie, George. *Carlucco and the Queen of Hearts; The Blasphemer*. Edinburgh: Chapman, 1992.
Roth, Ari. *Born Guilty*. New York: Theatre Communications Group, 1991.
Roy, Irene. *Le Theatre Repere: du ludique au poetique dans le theatre de recherche*. Quebec: Nuit Blanche, 1993.
Ryan-Ransom, Helen, ed. *Imagination, Emblems and ExPions: Essays on Latin American, Caribbean, and Continental Culture and Identity*. Bowling Green, OH: Popular, 1993.
Rudnick, Paul. *I Hate Hamlet*. Garden City, NY: Fireside Theatre, 1991.
Sander, Gordon F. *Serling: The Rise and Twilight of Television's Last Angry Man*. New York: Dutton, 1992.
Saroyan, William. *Warsaw Visitor; Tales from the Vienna Streets: The Last Two Plays of William Saroyan*. Fresno: California State U P, 1991.
Savran, David. *Communists, Cowboys, and Queers: The Politics of Masculinity in the Work of Arthur Miller and Tennessee Williams*. Minneapolis: U of Minnesota P, 1992.
Scharine, Richard G. *From Class to Caste in American Drama: Political and Social Themes Since the 1930s*. New York: Greenwood P, 1991.
Schneemann, Carolee. *Carolee Schneemann Video Burn*. San Francisco: San Francisco Art Institute, 1992.
Schofield, Mary Anne, and Cecilia Macheski, eds. *Curtain Calls: British and American Women and the Theater, 1660–1820*. Athens: Ohio U P, 1991.
Schroeder, Erik James, ed. *Vietnam, We've All Been There: Interviews with American Writers*. Westport, CT: Praeger, 1992.
Senelick, Laurence, ed. *Gender in Performance: The Presentation of Difference in the Performing Arts*. Hanover, NH: U P of New England, 1992.
Shange, Ntozake. *The Love Space Demands: A Continuing Saga*. New York: St. Martin's, 1991.
————. *Plays, One*. London: Methuen Drama, 1992.
————. *Three Pieces*. New York: St. Martin's, 1992.
Shanley, John Patrick. *13 by Shanley*. New York: Applause Books, 1992.
Shawn, Wallace. *The Fever*. New York: Dramatists Play Service, 1992.
Shephard, William Hunter. *The Dionysus Group*. New York: P. Lang, 1991.
Sherman, James. *Beau Jest: A Comedy*. New York: S. French, 1992.
Sherman, Jonathan Marc. *Veins and Thumbtacks*. New York: Dramatists Play Service, 1992.
Sherman, Martin. *When She Danced: A Play*. London: S. French, 1992.
Silver, Joan Micklin. *A . . . My Name Is Still Alice*. London: French, 1993.
Simo, Ana Maria. *Going to New England*. New York: Theatre Communications Group, 1991.

Simon, Neil. *Neil Simon's Lost in Yonkers: The Illustrated Screenplay of the Film.* New York: Newmarket P, 1993.

Singh, Avadhesh K. *The Plays of Eugene O'Neill: A Study in Myths and Symbols.* New Delhi: Creative Publishers, 1991.

Slaight, Craig, ed. *New Plays from A.C.T.'s Young Conservatory.* Newbury, VT: Smith and Kraus, 1993.

Smith, Jessie Carney. *Epic Lives: One Hundred Black Women Who Made a Difference.* Detroit: Visible Ink P, 1993.

Smith, Madeline. *Eugene O'Neill in Court: Documents in the Case of George Lewys v. Eugene O'Neill, et al.* New York: P. Lang, 1993.

Smith, Marisa, ed. *Humana Festival '93: The Complete Plays.* Newbury, VT: Smith and Kraus, 1993.

So, Yong-duk. *Eugene O'Neill ui kuk e natanan sooe yangsang kwa chaa tamgu.* Soul Tukpyolsi: Hansin Munhwasa, 1992.

Sterner, Jerry. *Other People's Money: The Ultimate Seduction.* New York: Penguin, 1991.

Steyn, Mark. *Stephen Sondheim.* London: Josef Weinberger, 1993.

Stingle, Richard. *James Reaney and His Works.* Toronto: ECW P, 1991.

Sturges, Sandy, ed. *Preston Sturges on Preston Sturges.* New York: Faber and Faber, 1991.

Sullivan, Daniel. *Inspecting Carol.* New York: S. French, 1992.

Sweet, Jeffrey. *American Enterprise: A Play with Music.* Chicago: Chicago Plays, 1991.

———. *The Dramatist's Toolkit: The Craft of the Working Playwright.* Portsmouth, NH: Heinemann, 1993.

Tesich, Steve. *On the Open Road: A New Play.* New York: Applause, 1993.

———. *The Speed of Darkness.* New York: S. French, 1991.

Thomas, Audrey Callahan. *Graven Images.* New York: Viking, 1993.

Torres, Tereska. *Les maisons hantees de Meyer Levin.* Paris: Danoel, 1991.

Tucker, Martin. *Sam Shepard.* New York: Continuum, 1992.

Vanden Heuvel, Michael. *Performing Drama/Dramatizing Performance: Alternative Theater and the Dramatic Text.* Ann Arbor: U of Michigan P, 1991.

Wasserman, Jerry, ed. *Modern Canadian Plays.* Vancouver: Talon Books, 1993.

Wasserstein, Wendy. *The Heidi Chronicles and Other Plays.* New York: Penguin Books, 1991.

———. *The Sisters Rosenweig.* New York: Harcourt Brace Jovanovich, 1993.

Waters, J. B. *Eugene O'Neill and Family—The Bermuda Interlude.* Warwick, Bermuda: Waters, 1992.

Waterston, Sam, ed. *Playbill Lincoln Center Theater at the Vivian Beaumont: Abe Lincoln in Illinois.* New York: Playbill, Inc., 1993.

Wauschkuhn, Doris. *Literarischer Dialekt und seine Funktion zur Begrundung einer dramatischen Tradition im Werk von John Millington Synge und Eugene ONeill.* Trier: Wissenschaftlicher Verlag Trier, 1993.

Wilcox, Leonard. *Rereading Shepard: Contemporary Critical Essays on the Plays of Sam Shepard.* New York: St. Martin's P, 1993.

Wilson, Christopher Pierce. *White Collar Fictions: Class and Social Representation in American Literature, 1885–1925.* Athens: U of Georgia P, 1992.

Women on the Verge: 7 Avant-Garde American Plays. New York: Applause, 1993.

Woods, Jeannie Marlin. *Theatre to Change Men's Souls: The Artistry of Adrian Hall.* Newark: U of Delaware P, 1993.

Zaman, Niaz, ed. *Migration, Migrants, and the United States*. Dhaka, Bangladesh: Bangladesh Association for American Studies, 1992.

Zeineddine, Nada. *Because It Is My Name: Problems of Identity Experienced by Women, Artists, and Breadwinners in the Plays of Henrik Ibsen, Tennessee Williams, and Arthur Miller*. Braunton, Devon: Merlin Books, 1991.

Zinman, Toby Silverman. *David Rabe: A Casebook*. New York: Garland, 1991.

LIST OF AUDIOVISUAL MATERIALS INDEXED

Adult Learning Satellite Service, PBS. Videocassette. *Emanuel Azenberg; David Henry Hwang; Larry Gelbert; Robert Whitehead.* Taped from satellite broadcast, 19 Feb. 1991.

Angelou, Maya, and Hendrick Hertzberg, Moderators. *Michael Ondaatje.* Videocassette. WNYE-TV, 1993.

———. *Amiri Baraka.* Videocassette. WNYE-TV, 1993.

Banner, Bob, Executive Producer. *A Tribute to Arthur Miller.* Videocassette recorded on the occasion of Miller receiving the Algur H. Meadows Award for Excellence in the Arts. 9 Mar. 1991.

Black Elk Speaks. Videocassette. A world premiere of Christopher Sergel's revised script of his adaptation of John G. Neihardt's book. Performed at Bristol Community College Arts Center Theatre, Fall River, MA, Nov. 1992.

Blaszczyk, Connie, Producer. *Anna Deavere Smith: In Her Own Words.* 1 Sound Cassette. Boston: WGBH Radio, 1993.

Boston Conservatory Recording. *Senior Directing Scene Workshops.* Videocassette. Special Guest Speaker Michael Allosso. Recorded by the Boston Conservatory. 14 Oct. 1992.

Coon, Becca, Director. *I Stand Before You Naked.* Videocassette. Recorded by Butler University. 18 Apr. 1993.

Cromwell, John, Director. *Abe Lincoln in Illinois.* Videocassette. A Turner Home Entertainment release of the 1940 motion picture, 1991.

Desire Under the Elms, Videocassette. Release of 1958 film. Paramount, 1991.

The Emperor Jones. Videodisc. Release of 1933 motion picture. A joint venture of Janus Films and Voyager P, 1993.

"Five Guys Named Moe: Original London Cast Recording," Recording. US: Relativity/First Night Records, 1991.

Hall, Peter, Director. *Orpheus Descending.* Videodisc. Turner Pictures release of 1990 film, 1992.

Hart, Carol, Moderator. *Women in Hollywood.* Videocassette. New York Network/ SUNYSAT, 1993.

Heller, Adele, and Lois Rudnick, Directors. *Beginnings: The First Season of Plays Staged by the Provincetown Players, 1915.* Videocassete. Rutgers U P, 1991 (accompanies the book, *1915, the Cultural Moment*).

Jacobson, Leslie B., Director. *Heidi Chronicles*. Videocassettes. George Washington Theatre & Dance Department, 1993.

Kentucky Center for the Arts. *Kentucky Voices: A Bicentennial Celebration of Writing: Marsha Norman*. Sound cassette (Vol. 2), 1992.

Kuczynski, Pawel, Director. *Rachel Rosenthal: Searching for a Boon*. Videocassette. Los Angeles Workshop on Performance Art, 1992.

Lapine, James, Director. *Into the Woods*. 3 Videocassettes. American Playhouse: WETA-TV, 1991.

MacAdams, Lewis, Interviewer. *Amiri Baraka*. Videocassette. Los Angeles: Lannan Foundation, 1991.

Parks, Suzan-Lori. *Imperceptible Mutabilities: The Last Black Man*. Recording. (1 Sound Cassette) Seattle: U. of Washington, 1991.

Reynolds, Rick. *Only the Truth Is Funny*. Compact Disc. Larkspur, CA: Gang of Seven, 1992.

Rosenthal, Rachel. *Pangaean Dreams: A Shamanic Journey, a Performance by Rachel Rosenthal*. Videocassette. An adaptation of a live performance commissioned by the L. A. Festival; co- sponsored by the Santa Monica Museum of Art, 1991.

Schempp, William D., Director. *Judith Ehrlich and Jerry Sterner*. Videocassette. Panel discussion of greed. New York: CUNY, 1991.

Shange, Ntozake. *For Colored Girls Who Have Considered Suicide When the Rainbow Is Enuf*. Videocassette. Recorded at Butler University, Indianapolis, IN, Apr. 1993.

Shapiro, Larry. Producer. *Literatti*. (Tape 1) Videocassettes. World Affairs Production in Association with WNYE-TV New York, 1993.

Simon, Noah. *One Man Alone*. Videocassete. Produced by Jordan College of Fine Arts, Butler U., Indianapolis, IN, 1993.

Smith, Anna Deavere. *Fires in the Mirror*. Videocassette. American Playhouse: PBS Video, 1993.

Wasserstein, Wendy. *Life in the Theatre*. Recording (60 minute sound cassette). Lecture sponsored by New York Society Library, 17 Mar. 1992.

Wilson, Edwin, Interviewer. *David Henry Hwang, Playwright*. Videocassette. Audio Visual Services, U. of California, Santa Cruz, 1991.

———. *Eric Bentley*. Videocassette. PBS Adult Learning Satellite Service. Taped 26–27 May, 1993.

———., Producer. *Spotlight IV: 407 & 408*. Videocassette. 1992.

———., Interviewer. *Jerry Zaks; Christopher Durang; Walter Kerr; Tommy Tune*. Videocassette. PBS Adult Learning Satellite Service. Taped Apr. 1991.

———. *Neil Simon*. 2 Videocassettes. PBS Adult Learning Satellite Service. Taped May 1993.

LIST OF JOURNALS INDEXED

(* ceased publication).

ABA Journal: The Lawyer's Magazine. Chicago, IL.
Academic Medicine: Journal of the Association of American Medical Colleges. Washington, DC.
ATQ. Kingston, RI.
Advocate. Los Angeles, CA.
African American Review. Terre Haute, IN.
Amerasia Journal. Los Angeles, CA.
America. New York, NY.
American Drama. New York, NY.
American Film: The Magazine of the Film and Television Arts. New York, NY.
American Forests. Washington, DC.
American Heritage. New York, NY.
American Literature: A Journal of Literary History, Criticism, and Bibliography. Durham, NC.
American Music. Champaign, IL.
American Poetry Review. Philadelphia, PA.
American Record Guide. Cincinnati, OH.
American Scholar. Washington, DC.
American Spectator. Arlington, VA.
American Studies. Warsaw, Poland.
American Theatre: The Monthly Forum for News, Features and Opinions. New York, NY.
American Visions. Washington, DC.
American Writing Today. Washington, DC.
Americas. Washington, DC.
Americas Review: A Review of Hispanic Literature and Art of the USA. Houston, TX.
Analog Science Fiction-Science Fact. New York, NY.
Antaeus. New York, NY.
Antioch Review. Yellow Springs, OH.
Architectural Digest. Los Angeles, CA.
ARIEL: A Review of Arts and Letters in Israel. Jerusalem, Israel.

The Arizona Quarterly: A Journal of American Literature, Culture, and Theory. Tucson, AZ.
Art America. New York, NY.
Art & Auction. New York, NY.
Art in America. New York, NY.
Art Papers. Atlanta, GA.
ArtForum. New York, NY.
ARTnews. New York, NY.
Arts Magazine. New York, NY.
Artspace. Albuquerque, NM.
The Atlantic. Boston, MA.
Bilingual Review/ Revista Bilingue. Tempe, AZ.
Billboard. New York, NY.
Biography. Honolulu, HI.
Black American Literature Forum. Terre Haute, IN.
Black Collegian. New Orleans, LA.
Booklist. Chicago, IL.
Books in Canada. Toronto, Ontario.
*Brecht Yearbook. Detroit, MI.
Bulletin of Bibliography. Westport, CT.
CEA Critic. Youngstown, OH.
Callaloo: An Afro-American and African Journal of Arts and Letters. Baltimore, MD.
Canadian Forum. Vancouver, British Columbia.
Canadian Literature/Litterature Canadienne: A Quarterly of Criticism and Review. Vancouver, British Columbia.
Canadian Review of American Studies. London, Ontario.
Canadian Theatre Review. Toronto, Ontario.
Chicago. Chicago, IL.
Chimaera: Revista de Literatura. Barcelona, Spain
Christopher Street. New York, NY.
Chronicle of Higher Education. Washington, DC.
Chu-Shikoku Studies in American Literature.
Cineaste. New York, NY.
Classical and Modern Literature: A Quarterly. Terre Haute, IN.
Clues. Lincoln, NE.
College English. Urbana, IL.
College Language Association Journal. Atlanta, GA.
Commentary. Singapore, Singapore.
Common Knowledge. New York, NY.
Commonweal. New York, NY.
Communication Education. Annandale, VA.
Confronto Letterario. Pavia, Italy
Connecticut Historical Society Bulletin. Hartford, CT.
Connoisseur. New York, NY.
Conradiana: A Journal of Joseph Conrad Studies. Lubbock, TX.
Contemporary American Theatre. New York, NY.
Contemporary Theatre Review: An International Journal. New York, NY.
Contemporary Review. London, England.
Crisis. New York, NY.
Critical Inquiry. Chicago, IL.

Critical Quarterly. Oxford, England.
Critical Review: An Interdisciplinary Journal. Chicago, IL.
Critical Survey. Oxford, England.
Criticism: A Quarterly for Literature and the Arts. Detroit, MI.
Current Biography. Bronx, NY.
*Dance. New York, NY
Dance Magazine. New York, NY.
Dance Pages Magazine. New York, NY.
Dancing Times. London, England.
De Vlaamse Gids. Antwerp, Belgium.
Die Neueren Sprachen: Zeitschrift fuer Forschung, Unterricht und Kontaktstudium auf dem Fachgebiet der modernen Fremdsprachen. Frankfurt, Germany.
Dionysos: The Literature and Intoxication TriQuarterly. Superior, WI.
Discourse: Journal for Theoretical Studies in Media and Culture. Bloomington, IN.
Dispositio: Revista Hispanica de Semiotica Literaria. Ann Arbor, MI.
Dissent. New York, NY.
Dissertation Abstracts International, Section A: Humanities and Social Sciences. Ann Arbor, MI.
Down Beat: Jazz, Blues, and Beyond. Elmhurst, IL.
Dramatics: Devoted to the Advancement of Theatre Arts in the Secondary Schools. Cincinnati, OH.
Dramatists Guild Quarterly. New York, NY.
Durham University Journal. Durham, England.
Ebony. Chicago, IL.
Economist. New York, NY.
English Journal. Urbana, IL.
English Language Notes. Boulder, CO.
Esquire. New York, NY.
Essays in Theatre. Guelph, Ontario.
Etudes Anglaises. Grande-Bretagne, Etas-Unis. Paris, France.
Eugene O'Neill Review. Boston, MA.
Explicator. Washington, DC.
Facts on File World News Digest with Index. New York, NY.
Feminisms. Columbus, OH.
Feminist Teacher. Bloomington, IN.
Film Comment. New York, NY.
Films in Review. New York, NY.
Flannery O'Connor Bulletin. Milledgeville, GA.
Flash Art Italia. Milan, Italy.
Forbes. New York, NY.
Frontiers: A Journal of Women's Studies. Albuquerque, NM.
Genders. Austin, TX.
Gentlemen's Quarterly. New York, NY.
Georgia Review. Athens, GA.
Gestos: Teoria y Practica del Teatro Hispanico. Irvine, CA.
Gettysburg Review. Gettysburg, PA.
Glamour. New York, NY.
Gramma: Journal of Theory and Criticism. Thessalonike, Greece.
Grand Street. New York, NY.

Guitar Review. New York, NY
Harper's Bazaar. New York, NY.
Harper's Magazine. New York, NY.
High Performance: A Quarterly Magazine for the New Arts Audience.
     Santa Monica, CA.
Hispanic: The Magazine of Contemporary Hispanic. Washington, DC.
Hudson Review: A Magazine of Literature and the Arts. New York, NY.
Humanist. Amherst, NY.
Index on Censorship. London, England.
Insight. New York, NY.
Iris: A Journal About Women. Charlottesville, VA.
Irish University Review: A Journal of Irish Studies. Dublin, Ireland.
Italian Journal. Dobbs Ferry, NY.
James Joyce Quarterly. Tulsa, OK.
Jewish Currents. New York, NY.
Journal of American Culture. Bowling Green, OH.
Journal of American Drama and Theatre. New York, NY.
Journal of American Studies. Cambridge, England.
Journal of Black Studies. Newbury Park, CA.
Journal of Canadian Studies/Revue D'etudes Canadiennes.
     Peterborough, Ontario.
Journal of Dramatic Theory and Criticism. Lawrence, KS.
Journal of English Language and Literature. Seoul, Korea.
Journal of Evolutionary Psychology. Philadelphia, PA.
Journal of Homosexuality. Binghamton, NY.
Journal of Musicology: A Quarterly Review Music History, Criticism, Analysis,
     and Performance Practice. Berkeley, CA.
Journal of Popular Culture. Bowling Green, OH.
Journal of Popular Film and Television. Washington, DC.
Journal of West Indian Literature. Bridgetown, Barbados.
Kenyon Review. Gambier, OH.
L'Action Nationale. Paris, France.
Langston Hughes Review. Providence, RI.
Language Arts. Urbana, IL.
*Lear's: For the Woman Who Wasn't Born Yesterday. New York, NY.
Legacy. Amherst, MA.
Life. New York, NY.
Literary Criterion. Bangalore, India.
Literature and Psychology: A Quarterly Journal of Literary Criticism as Informed
     by Depth Psychology. Providence, RI.
Literature-Film Quarterly. Salisbury, MD.
London Theatre News. New York, NY.
Los Angeles Magazine, Los Angeles, CA.
Maclean's. Toronto, Ontario.
Massachusetts Review: A Quarterly of Literature, Arts and Public Affairs.
     Amherst, MA.
Media Week. New York, NY.
MELUS. Amherst, MA.
Mexican Studies-Estudios Mexicanos. Berkeley, CA.
Michigan Quarterly Review. Ann Arbor, MI.

Midamerica: A Historical Review. Chicago, IL.
Midwest Quarterly: A Journal of Contemporary Thought. Pittsburg, KS.
*Mime Journal. Allendale, MI.
Minnesota Review: A Journal of Committed Writing, Fiction, Poetry, Essays, Reviews. Stony Brook, NY.
Mirabella. New York, NY.
Mississippi Quarterly: The Journal of Southern Culture. Mississippi State, MS.
Missouri Review. Columbia, MO.
Modern Austrian Literature. Riverside, CA.
Modern Drama. Downsview, Ontario.
Modern Fiction Studies: A Critical Quarterly Devoted to Criticism, Scholarship and Bibliography of American, English and European Fiction Since about 1880. West Lafayette, IN.
Modern Language Studies. London, England.
Mosaic: A Review of Jewish Thought and Culture. Cambridge MA.
Moscow News. Moscow, Russia.
Mother Jones. San Francisco, CA.
Mount Olive Review. Mount Olive, NC.
Ms. Magazine. New York, NY.
Musical Quarterly. New York, NY.
Nation. New York, NY.
National Catholic Reporter. Kansas City, MO.
National Review: A Journal of Fact and Opinion. New York, NY.
Nation's Business. Washington, DC.
Neohelicon: Acta Comparationis Litterarum Universarum. Amsterdam, Netherlands.
New England Quarterly: A Historical Review of New England Life and Letters. Boston, MA.
New England Review: Middlebury Series. Hanover, NH.
New Leader: A Bi-Weekly of News and Opinion. New York, NY .
New Mexico Magazine. Santa Fe, NM.
New Orleans Review. New Orleans, LA.
New Republic: A Journal of Opinion. Washington, DC.
New Statesman & Society: An Independent Political and Literary Review. London, England.
New Theatre Quarterly. Cambridge, England.
New York, New York, NY.
New York Theatre Critics' Reviews. New York, NY.
New York Times, New York, NY.
New York Times Book Review, New York, NY.
New Yorker. New York, NY.
Newsweek. New York, NY.
Nexus. Dayton, OH.
Nieman Reports. Cambridge, MA.
Nineteenth Century Theatre. Amherst, MA.
North American Review. Cedar Falls, IA.
Notes on Contemporary Literature. Carollton, GA.
Notes on Mississippi Writers. Hattiesburg, MS.
Ojancano: Revista de Literatura Espanola. Chapel Hill, NC.
Omni. New York, NY.

On the Issues: The Journal of Substance for Progressive Women. Forest Hills, NY.
Opera Monthly. New York, NY.
Opera News. New York, NY.
Opera Quarterly. Durham, NC.
OUT-LOOK: National Lesbian & Gay Quarterly. San Francisco, CA.
Outrage. Australia.
PARABOLA: The Magazine of Myth and Tradition. New York, NY.
Paris Review. New York, NY.
Partisan Review. Boston, MA.
People Weekly. New York, NY.
Performing Arts: The Theatre & Music Magazine. Los Angeles, CA.
Performing Arts & Entertainment in Canada. Toronto, Ontario.
Performing Arts Journal. Baltimore, MD.
Philadelphia Magazine. Philadelphia, PA.
Philological Papers. Morgantown, WV.
Philological Quarterly: Devoted to Scholarly Investigation of the Classical and Modern Languages and Literatures. Iowa City, IA.
Pinter Review: Annual Essays. Tampa, FL.
Playbill: The National Magazine of the Theatre. New York, NY.
Playboy. Chicago, IL.
Plays and Players. Surrey, England.
Plays International. New York, NY.
Ploughshares: A Journal of New Writing. Boston, MA.
Post Script: Essays in Film and the Humanities. Commerce, TX.
Premiere. New York, NY.
Primer acto. Madrid, Spain.
Progressive. Madison, WI.
Prospects: An Annual Journal of American Cultural Studies. Cambridge, England.
Psychoanalysis and Contemporary Thought: A Quarterly of Integrative and Interdisciplinary Studies. Madison, CT.
Publish. São Paulo, Brazil.
Publishers Weekly: The International News Magazine of Book Publishing. New York, NY.
Quarterly Journal of Speech. Annandale, VA.
Quebec Studies. Bowling Green, OH.
Queen's Quarterly: A Canadian Review. Kingston, Ontario.
Raritan: A Quarterly Review. New Brunswick, NJ.
Redneck Review of Literature. Twin Falls, ID.
Rethinking Marxism. New York, NY.
Review of Contemporary Fiction. Elmwood Park, IL.
Rolling Stone. New York, NY.
Runner's World. Emmaus, PA.
Saturday Night: Canada's Leading Magazine of Comment and Opinion. Toronto, Ontario.
Scripsi. Australia.
Seventeen. New York, NY.
Sewanee Review. Sewanee, TN.
Shakespeare Bulletin. Easton, PA.
Shenandoah: The Washington and Lee University Review. Lexington, VA.

Sight Sound. New York, NY.
South African Theatre Journal. Sunnyside, South Africa.
South Atlantic Quarterly. Durham, NC.
South Central Review. College Station, TX.
Southern California Quarterly. Los Angeles, CA.
Southern Literary Journal. Chapel Hill, NC.
Southern Quarterly: A Journal of the Arts in the South. Hattiesburg, MS.
Southern Review: A Literary and Critical Quarterly Magazine. Baton Rouge, LA.
Spectator. London, England.
Steinbeck Quarterly. Muncie, IN.
Studies in American Drama, 1945-Present. Columbus, OH.
Studies in American Fiction. Boston, MA.
Studies in American Jewish Literature. Kent, OH.
Studies in Culture and the Humanities. Indiana, PA.
Studies in the Humanities. Indiana, PA.
Studies in the Literary Imagination. Atlanta, GA.
TCI. New York, NY.
TDR: A Journal of Performance Studies. Cambridge, MA.
T V Guide. Radnor, PA.
Tamkang Review: A Journal Mainly Devoted to Comparative Studies Between Chinese and Foreign Literatures. Taiwan.
Tennessee Williams Literary Journal. Metarie, LA.
Texas Monthly. Austin, TX.
Texas Review. Huntsville, TX.
Texas Studies in Literature and Language: A Journal of the Humanities. Austin, TX.
Text and Performance Quarterly. Taos, NM.
Text & Presentation: The Journal of the Comparative Drama Conference. Gainesville, FL.
Theater. New Haven, CT.
Theater Magazine. Columbus, OH.
TheaterWeek. New York, NY.
Theatre Annual. Akron, OH.
Theatre Crafts. New York, NY.
Theatre History in Canada/ Histoire du Theatre au Canada. Toronto, Ontario.
Theatre History Studies. Grand Forks, ND.
Theatre Insight. Austin, TX.
Theatre Journal. Baltimore, MD.
Theatre Research International. Oxford, England.
Theatre Studies. Columbus, OH.
Theatre Survey. Bloomington, IN.
Theory and Society: Renewal and Critique in Social Theory. Dordrecht, Netherlands.
Time: The Weekly Newsmagazine. New York, NY.
Times Educational Supplement. London, England.
Times Literary Supplement. London, England.
TriQuarterly. Evanston, IL.
Tulsa Studies in Women's Literature. Tulsa, OK.
U S News & World Report. New York, NY.
University of Mississippi Studies in English. Lafayette, MS.

University of Toronto Quarterly: A Canadian Journal of the Humanities. Downs-
  view, Ontario.
Vanity Fair. New York, NY.
Variety. New York, NY.
Visibilities. Olney, MD.
Vogue. New York, NY.
Wall Street Journal. New York, NY.
West Virginia University Philological Papers.
Western American Literature. Logan, UT.
Western European Stages. New York, NY.
Women and Language. Fairfax, VA.
Word & Image: A Journal of Verbal/Visual Enquiry. Nashville, TN.
World Literature Written in English. Guelph, Ontario.
World P Review: News and Views from Around the World. New York, NY.
Writer's Digest. Cincinnati, OH.
Yale Journal of Criticism: Interpretation in the Humanities. Oxford, England.
*Yale Review. New Haven, CT.
Zeitschrift fuer Anglistik und Amerikanistik. Leipzig, Germany.

INDEX OF CRITICS

INDEX OF ADAPTED AUTHORS AND WORKS

INDEX OF TITLES

INDEX OF PLAYWRIGHTS

(dates noted when available)